Teri Pichot, LCSW
Yvonne M. Dolan, MA

Solution-Focused Brief Therapy
Its Effective Use in Agency Settings

Pre-publication
REVIEWS,
COMMENTARIES,
EVALUATIONS . . .

"Pichot and Dolan have successfully demonstrated the skillful application of the art and science of solution-focused therapy in their book, *Solution-Focused Brief Therapy.*

The authors have produced a work that will assist novices and experts of all disciplines. This thought-provoking work challenges traditional treatments and offers fresh ideas on a client-focused model that keeps the locus of control where it truly belongs—with the client. Pichot and Dolan define the role of the therapist as a change expert, and the role of the client as a self expert. This point of clarification emphasizes that it is from the partnership of these two experts that miracles happen.

The authors extend the use of solution-focused therapy outside its traditional confines to the world of supervision and management—an intriguing leadership technique that has the potential to build a strong, dynamic clinician and treatment plan. This book is stimulating, inspiring, and a practical guide to developing and sharpening skills."

Ruby J. Martinez, RN, PhD, CS
Assistant Professor,
University of Colorado School of Nursing; Vice President,
National Latino Behavioral Health Association

More pre-publication
REVIEWS, COMMENTARIES, EVALUATIONS . . .

"In this book, therapists have at their fingertips a road map for navigating agency policy and politics, and utilizing the client's natural inclination to distrust the 'system.' This is a wonderful book for both beginning and seasoned therapists who want to find an effective way to work with externally motivated populations. Pichot and Dolan bring a creative and concise style (like the solution-focused model they elegantly detail) to this book. It will be of interest to any therapist who has ever worked for or with an agency that serves mandated clients. The chapters on the miracle question, working with adolescents, and interagency diplomacy are exceptional. Although these topics have often been written about, the authors' ability to communicate their rationales for using various techniques and interventions make the reading accessible and persuasive."

Jeffrey Goldman, LCSW, BCD
Director, Peaceful Alternatives
in The Home (PATH),
Denver, CO

"This thoughtful and inspiring book provides detailed and practical guidelines for working with drug abusers. A joy to read, it touches the heart of the reader in showing how a courageously respectful attitude helps even the most resistant clients to leave their old habits behind and improve their lives. Pichot and Dolan show how to tackle in a creative and resourceful way the tricky problem of working with mandated clients and their referral sources. They offer detailed treatment plans and protocols on a wide range of topics, from individual and group therapy to team supervision, and show how to release the untapped creative energy of both staff and clients."

Luc Isebaert, MD
Senior Consultant,
Department of Psychiatry
and Psychosomatics,
St. John's Hospital, Bruges, Belgium;
President, Bruges Group;
Head of Teaching Faculty,
Korzybski Institutes of Bruges,
Paris, and Netherlands

"Pichot and Dolan do a wonderful job outlining applications of solution-focused techniques and tackling the extremely difficult undertaking of 'interagency diplomacy.' Communicating with other agencies is necessary. As many solution-focused therapists have experienced, such communication can create alienation. Pichot and Dolan give wonderful insights about co-creating collaborative relationships with those not practicing solution-focused therapy. A must-read for agencies seriously committed to integrating solution-focused principles and techniques beyond a superficial level."

Tracy Todd, PhD
Consultant to the Substance Abuse
Counseling Program, Brief Therapy
Institute of Denver, Inc.

More pre-publication
REVIEWS, COMMENTARIES, EVALUATIONS . . .

"After serving for twenty-five years as professor or chair of the Department of Human Services at MSCD, I am pleased to finally read a text that so effectively addresses the intricacies of implementing a solution-focused approach at an agency level. While numerous publications elaborate on the strategies for using solution-focused therapy, Pichot and Dolan are the first to detail its adoption as an agency-wide model. With a sensitivity that can only come from years of personal experience, Pichot and Dolan describe their struggle to offer a solution-focused approach to a problem-focused world. Their eventual success in this challenge makes this book essential reading for both treatment administrators as well as agency staff hoping to implement a solution-focused approach in their centers."

J. Michael Faragher, PsyD, CACIII
Dean, School of Professional Studies,
Metropolitan State College of Denver

"At a time when many agencies, driven by the influence of managed care and economic rationalism, have adopted more pathologizing and problem-focused approaches to service delivery than ever, these authors break new ground. Providing a fresh and optimistic alternative, they demystify the process of working with a solution focus in an agency serving a substance abuse population.

This book is valuable for anyone working in any agency environment. The authors clearly illustrate specific 'difficult' clients. They expand the model to group work, supervision, work with adolescents, case management, and more. Finally, they offer principles and methods for learning to speak ideologically bilingual, and work effectively with professionals whose dominant discourse is problem focused. This timely book is a must-read for beginning and advanced clinicians, caseworks, supervisors, and managers of agencies. Buy one for yourself, one for the library, and put the ideas into practice!"

Jim Duvall, MEd
Director, Brief Therapy
Training Centres International™,
Toronto, Canada

"*Solution-Focused Brief Therapy* is an enticing exploration that extends solution-focused therapy into new territories. Creative and well-grounded, it should be required reading for the practice of contemporary psychotherapy."

Jeffrey K. Zeig, PhD
Director,
The Milton H. Erickson Foundation,
Phoenix, AZ

The Haworth Clinical Practice Press
An Imprint of The Haworth Press, Inc.
New York • London • Oxford

NOTES FOR PROFESSIONAL LIBRARIANS AND LIBRARY USERS

This is an original book title published by The Haworth Clinical Practice Press, an imprint of The Haworth Press, Inc. Unless otherwise noted in specific chapters with attribution, materials in this book have not been previously published elsewhere in any format or language.

CONSERVATION AND PRESERVATION NOTES

All books published by The Haworth Press, Inc. and its imprints are printed on certified pH neutral, acid free book grade paper. This paper meets the minimum requirements of American National Standard for Information Sciences-Permanence of Paper for Printed Material, ANSI Z39.48-1984.

Solution-Focused Brief Therapy
Its Effective Use in Agency Settings

HAWORTH Marriage and the Family
Terry S. Trepper, PhD
Executive Editor

Chinese Americans and Their Immigrant Parents: Conflict, Identity, and Values by May Paomay Tung

Together Through Thick and Thin: A Multinational Picture of Long-Term Marriages by Shlomo A. Sharlin, Florence W. Kaslow, and Helga Hemmerschmidt

Developmental-Systemic Family Therapy with Adolescents by Ronald Jay Werner-Wilson

The Effect of Children on Parents, Second Edition by Anne-Marie Ambert

Couples Therapy, Second Edition by Linda Berg-Cross

Family Therapy and Mental Health: Innovations in Theory and Practice by Malcolm M. MacFarlane

How to Work with Sex Offenders: A Handbook for Criminal Justice, Human Service, and Mental Health Professionals by Rudy Flora

Marital and Sexual Lifestyles in the United States: Attitudes, Behaviors, and Relationships in Social Context by Linda P. Rouse

Psychotherapy with People in the Arts: Nuturing Creativity by Gerald Schoenwolf

Critical Incidents in Marital and Family Therapy: A Practitoner's Guide by David A. Baptiste Jr.

Family Solutions for Substance Abuse: Clinical and Counseling Approaches by Eric E. McCollum and Terry S. Trepper

Between Father's and Son's: Critical Incident Narratives in the Development of Men's Lives: by Robert J. Pellegrini and Theodore R. Sarbin

Women's Stories of Divorce at Childbirth: When the Baby Rocks the Cradle by Hilary Hoge

The Therapist's Notebook for Families: Solution-Oriented Exercises for Working with Parents, Children, and Adolescents by Bob Bertolino and Gary Schultheis

Treating Marital Stress: Support-Based Approaches by Robert P. Rugel

An Introduction to Marriage and Family Therapy by Lorna L. Hecker and Joseph L. Wetchler

Solution-Focused Brief Therapy: Its Effective Use in Agency Settings by Teri Pichot and Yvonne M. Dolan

Creativity in Psychotherapy: Reaching New Heights with Individuals, Couples, and Families by David K. Carson and Kent W. Becker

Understanding and Treating Schizophrenia: Contemporary Research, Theory, and Practice by Glenn D. Shean

Becoming a Solution Detective: Identifying Your Clients' Strengths in Practical Brief Therapy by John Sharry, Brendan Madden, and Melissa Darmody

Family Involvement in Treating Schizophrenia: Models, Essential Skills, and Process by James A. Marley

Transgender Emergence: Therapeutic Guidelines for Working with Gender-Variant People and Their Families by Istar Lev

Solution-Focused Brief Therapy
Its Effective Use in Agency Settings

Teri Pichot, LCSW
Yvonne M. Dolan, MA

The Haworth Clinical Practice Press
An Imprint of The Haworth Press, Inc.
New York • London • Oxford

Published by

The Haworth Clinical Practice Press, an imprint of The Haworth Press, Inc., 10 Alice Street, Binghamton, NY 13904-1580.

TR: 3.9.04

PUBLISHER'S NOTE
Identities and circumstances of individuals discussed in this book have been changed to protect confidentiality. Any resemblance to actual persons, living or dead, is entirely coincidental.

Cover design by Jennifer M. Gaska.

Library of Congress Cataloging-in-Publication Data

Pichot, Teri.
Solution-focused brief therapy : its effective use in agency settings / Teri Pichot, Yvonne M. Dolan.
p. cm.
Includes bibliographical references and index.
ISBN 0-7890-1553-6 (hard : alk. paper)—ISBN 0-7890-1554-4 (soft : alk. paper)
1. Solution-focused brief therapy. I. Title: Solution-focused brief therapy. II. Dolan, Yvonne M., 1951- III. Title.

RC489.S65 P53 2003
616.89'14—dc21

2002027641

To Irene Ogle, my maternal grandmother
who believed in the inherent goodness of people. YD

To Mark, my best friend and life partner. TP

ABOUT THE AUTHORS

Teri Pichot, LCSW, began her career as a psychotherapist in 1989 and holds the highest level of both state and national certification as an addictions specialist. A widely published author, Ms. Pichot has designed and implemented innovative programs that utilize solution-focused therapy with both adults and adolescents. She is currently the program manager of the Substance Abuse Counseling Program at the Jefferson County Department of Health and Environment in addition to maintaining a private practice in the Denver area.

Yvonne Dolan, MA, has been a psychotherapist since 1977. She conducts training in solution-focused and Ericksonian therapy and maintains a private practice in Denver. Ms. Dolan is the author of *Resolving Sexual Abuse: Solution-Focused Therapy and Ericksonian Hypnosis for Adult Survivors, A Path with a Heart: Ericksonian Utilization with Chronic and Resistant Clients,* and *One Small Step: Moving Beyond Trauma and Therapy to a Life of Joy,* and is co-author of *Tales of Solution.*

CONTENTS

Foreword

This book is an important contribution to the field of substance abuse treatment, and it is particularly important to those programs and their staff that are contemplating the transition from a traditional treatment model to a more efficient, effective, and respectful method of working with clients who have suffered so much.

At times, it is difficult to remember that Teri Pichot manages a publicly funded program that exclusively treats clients with heavy-duty diagnostic categories and some tough, at times life-threatening, problems. Teri Pichot has an amazing ability to see through those problems, along with clients' initial "attitudes" that do not win the hearts of many counselors, and to uncover clients' creativity, goodwill, and resourcefulness that they use to get their lives back on track. Beneath her optimistic, hopeful, and respectful view of clients' abilities lies a very realistic, pragmatic, and tough backbone, which she needs to deal with the reality of funding sources and credentialing bodies' demands for accountability. She has a way of turning every stumbling block into a useful opportunity to rise above the problem and learn from it. I always thought that such mettle, professional intuition, and wisdom required years of life experience to acquire, but Teri proves an exception.

Yvonne Dolan's gentle and lovely storytelling style turns what could potentially be mundane material into a captivating and lively storybook. I had a hard time putting down the book once I began to read.

The book contains not only the familiar solution-focused brief therapy tools such as miracle, scales, coping, exception-finding questions, and others, but also detailed descriptions of how to structure a group therapy session, format supervision, relate to and work collaboratively with referring sources, and even how to write session notes that will satisfy problem-focused credentialing bodies.

Although written for professionals working in substance abuse treatment programs, this book is a useful resource for workers in many other programs, such as community mental health centers, residential treatment programs, day care facilities, schools, halfway houses, and many other human services providers and their agencies. I also recommend this book to program managers and consultants.

Insoo Kim Berg
Milwaukee, Wisconsin

Preface

I (YD) meet many people in our field because I teach training workshops on solution-focused therapy and Ericksonian hypnotherapy. I have been conducting these workshops throughout the United States and abroad since 1989, and over the past decade I had become increasingly concerned by the descriptions of apparent exhaustion, weariness, and burnout I heard about almost routinely from my colleagues.

I assure you, these folks were not what you would call whiners. In fact, many of them were among the most dedicated and hardworking professionals one could ever meet, but they were in many cases contemplating leaving their jobs because, as they told me, "Morale is at an all-time low at the agency where I work. Something has to change, or I just can't go on."

Every time I heard this, I could not help but think of an agency near my hometown of Denver, where the therapists always seemed energized and creative. Staff turnover was at an all-time low, and their clients were consistently evidencing significant and lasting progress in recovery from drug and alcohol abuse. Most of these clients were involuntary, court-mandated clients who initially did not want to come to treatment! I kept thinking of my colleague Teri Pichot and her team. Over and over again I had watched them work effectively with multiproblem, court-mandated clients. The staff always looked vibrant and healthy and the team had a reputation for maintaining an environment characterized by lots of humor and enthusiasm as well as high clinical standards. I kept asking myself, "How does she (TP) do it and how does her team do it?" This book is, among other things, an attempt to answer that question.

We also wanted to provide our colleagues with access to some of the very practical aspects of using the solution-focused approach that Teri and her team learned from working with multiproblem, court-mandated clients day in and day out in a community-based agency setting. Of course, there was also the fact that deep in our hearts Teri and I were both rebels of a sort. We had dared to question some of the clinical advice we had been given early in our careers. We learned a great deal as a result, and we were ready to share what we had learned.

Not surprisingly, the most challenging cases and situations taught us the most, and this book reflects that. Throughout the pages of this book we invite you into our offices, to sit in on team discussions, and even to eavesdrop occasionally on our private midnight ruminations, in which we will share with you the best of what we have learned from our wonderful clients and colleagues.

Acknowledgments

First and foremost, I (TP) would like to thank the clients of the Substance Abuse Counseling Program (SACP) for all that they have taught us during this journey. They have demonstrated the power of change and the importance of setting aside the "expert" role to take the time to hear their wisdom. They are the true teachers to all of us.

Second, a special thanks to my administrators, Elise Lubell and Dr. Mark Johnson. Without them and their acceptance of change, solution-focused therapy could not have been implemented to the degree it has been at this agency. They are unquestionably the most supportive administrators with whom I have ever had the privilege of working. They have welcomed my ideas and have been open to the changes made in the Substance Abuse Counseling Program. They have perfected the art of remaining skeptical enough to ensure that new ideas are sound, while embracing innovation. They have stood beside me through the tears and laughter that accompanied this transition, for which I will always be grateful.

I especially want to thank my treatment team: Marc Coulter, Calyn Crow, Brian Duncan, Jonathan Heitsmith, Karen Nielsen, Darla Oglevie, Megan Shea, Diane Strouse, and Charlene Wilson. Regardless of how long each has been a part of the team, each has had a unique role in our transition to using solution-focused therapy. This tremendously talented and dedicated group of therapists has taught me so much! Their humor, dedication, curiosity, and love of this approach has brought the team through the difficult times. I have spent hours with this wonderful group of people, and I have come to love and appreciate them all. In addition, Megan was there on countless occasions (despite her own heavy workload) to help solve my computer problems and to allow me to bounce ideas off of her. She, Calyn, Jon, Char, and Darla took the time to repeatedly proof the manuscript to ensure it was understandable and to find the many typos that can plague a project such as this.

In addition, I want to thank our administrative support team: Twyla Hassel, Lisa Gray, Jennifer Drago, and Lisa Emanuel. Their support, flexibility, and help with deadlines and countless day-to-day tasks are invaluable to this program's success and were instrumental in maintaining my sanity during this project.

I would like to say a special thank you to Steve de Shazer and Insoo Kim Berg, for without their pervasive influence on my way of thinking and viewing the world, this book would not have been possible. They are probably unaware of how deeply they have impacted my work. In addition, I would like to thank those of you who took me "under your wing" (especially Charlie Johnson) to challenge my thinking and introduce me to a new way of working with clients. I am forever grateful.

Last, I would like to thank the Substance Abuse Counseling Program's advisory board members: Dr. Ruby Martinez, Dr. Tracy Todd, Dr. Michael Faragher, Dr. Connie Beehler, retired Judge Don Abram, Yvonne Dolan, Gene Giron, and Commissioner Rick Sheehan. Their dedication to providing ideas and guidance on behalf of substance-abusing clients in Colorado and to volunteering their time to ensure that the full continuum of alternatives is available to clients is truly appreciated.

As always, I (YD) am grateful to my wonderful colleagues and dear friends, Insoo Kim Berg and Steve de Shazer, for their inspiration, instruction, and support. A big hug to Terry Trepper for giving this book a home and for his generosity of spirit. Many thanks to the Jefferson County SACP team and especially to Teri Pichot for the privilege and pleasure of observing her work. I am grateful for the encouragement and support of Charlie Johnson early on in this project. Thanks to each of you from the bottom of my heart.

Introduction

WHY CHANGE AN ENTIRE AGENCY'S FOCUS TO SOLUTION-FOCUSED THERAPY?

During my (TP) training as a therapist, a professor told me that therapy is an art, and that I was to learn myriad theories so that I could use these concepts as the medium for this art. I was excited! Art implied creativity, a sense of purposeful spontaneity, and enjoyment of the process. The concept of blending the structure of theory with the unpredictability of humanity seemed just what I was hoping for. However, once I began to work in the field of substance abuse treatment, I quickly learned that theory was often not a driving part of the therapy process. Some agencies had a governing theoretical basis, yet the therapists often used what had worked for them in their own lives, and many readily shared their own stories of recovery in an effort to assist the clients in making changes. This was often effective. Other times, it was not. It was difficult to ascertain why a given intervention was chosen and what the desired outcome was. Therapists often seemed puzzled when I asked for the reasoning behind their interventions. I was frequently told, "I don't know why I asked that. Just a gut feeling, I guess." When I asked what theory they were using, they often claimed to be "eclectic."

Somewhat discouraged, I hoped that observing these therapists complete substance abuse evaluations would enlighten me as to how assessments were made and what the desired result was (other than to stop using substances, of course). Unfortunately, this did not provide the insight I desired, for the therapists' evaluations often appeared to be based on therapist assumption rather than on what the clients had reported or on evidence. I often wondered why, when lacking clear information, therapists would assume the worst about client behavior and intentions rather than assume the best.

As I continued to learn from my more experienced peers, I saw clients and therapists engage in power struggles as they disagreed on what the clients' problems were and what the clients' solutions should be. I watched as many therapists complained about client behavior, lost hope that client change was possible, and then left their jobs or the field of substance abuse altogether. High staff turnover and burnout appeared to be expected, and a lack of agency and team stability was part of the norm. The clients' successes were often overlooked or minimized in an effort to ferret out and resolve problems. Recovery was viewed as a lifelong process, and small changes that clients made were seen as tenuous and not predictive of long-term success. Both therapist and client appeared to be disempowered, discouraged, and overcome by a sense of hopelessness. Even the therapists who remained loyal to the field often cautioned, "Get out while you are young." My enthusiasm and belief in the clients' changes were viewed as naive—a common beginner's error.

As the years passed and I gained maturity and experience as a therapist, I came to realize that my early experiences in the field of substance abuse were not the exception. I decided that in order for me to find the art and the fulfillment of being a therapist, I had to actively seek it. I was introduced to solution-focused therapy (de Shazer, 1985) when I attended a controversial workshop about using this approach with couples who were experiencing domestic violence. The workshop leader spoke about the desire of both parties to have a safe home, and how many professionals overlook this mutual goal by focusing on the problem of violence. He stated that clients' problems often resolve themselves when the therapist focuses on how the clients want their lives to be. This approach made sense to me, and I absorbed any information I could find, eager to learn how to work with clients in this respectful way. I was intrigued by the simplicity of the approach and the incredible client results I witnessed in a short period of time. I surrounded myself with mentors who would challenge my thinking and hone my understanding of these concepts. I was hooked! I began to wonder how powerful this approach would be if an entire substance abuse counseling program adopted this practice of working with clients. The impact on staff and clients could be tremendous. When I became a clinical supervisor, I put my ideas to the test—secretly at first, hoping to test the waters with minimal risk to my career. As my confidence grew with each success, I became determined to lead a strong team of substance abuse therapists who were rooted in theory and purpose. Unfortunately, my newly acquired team of therapists did not share this vision.

I saw my new role as a challenge for me to foster curiosity within the team. If these traditionally trained therapists could become curious, they could become respectful of change and purposeful in their interventions. I decided that the only way to change their thinking was to allow the evidence to be their teacher. So, I began to question everything. I asked them to tell me why they chose the interventions they did and where their evidence was that the intervention worked. What would the clients tell me about what worked and how a given intervention applied to them? It was amazing to see the therapists begin to question. Underlying assumptions came to light and were challenged, and the therapists began to be excited. An amazing journey had begun.

I would be remiss to imply that this process was painless or easy. Some staff members left, and many unexpected issues surfaced along the way. The first was how ingrained traditional substance abuse treatment concepts were in the staff. Miller and Berg (1995) state, "The typical alcohol counselor . . . is bombarded with information that is, by and large, limited to the 'three Ds': disease, denial, and dysfunction" (p. 12). The therapists were often unaware when they had slipped into using traditional interventions. Using solution-focused therapy requires much more than a rudimentary understanding and ability to apply the techniques. It requires an integration of the underlying principles. Without this, therapists often fall back on how they were initially trained. The therapists had to become aware of their automatic judgments, assumptions, and agendas. Although the basic tenets of solution-focused therapy are quite simple, this approach requires that therapists become genuinely curious and that they trust the clients to be the experts in their lives. This is extremely difficult to master and quickly became the primary theme of our journey. As the therapists began to challenge their assumptions, to be accountable for their clinical decisions, and to see positive results in the clients, a sense of team ownership and commitment emerged. Staff turnover and burnout decreased, and staff morale markedly increased.

The second issue we discovered was a lack of acceptance of our approach by other therapists and by governing bodies. We often dealt with other professionals who firmly believed that they were solution focused, yet they did not adhere to the underlying principles of this approach. Agencies attempted to mandate solution-focused concepts; however, we often found that these mandates were actually problem focused in nature, and the client's agenda was often overlooked. We also struggled to maintain our solution-focused approach amid mandates to remain problem focused. For example, all licensed agencies in the state of Colorado are required to assess clients from a problem-focused perspective regardless of their theoretical approach. The following is a list of the elements that must be assessed in each client:

> Functional and dysfunctional aspects of psychological patterns and family and social structures including histories of physical, emotional, and sexual abuse; biological systems including current physical and mental health status and client and family health histories; client and family alcohol and other drug use/abuse histories; factors affecting client, family, and community safety; leisure-time activities; education and vocational history; religious or spiritual life; legal status; life skill acquisition; information from previous treatment experiences; cultural factors including racial and ethnic background, age, gender, sexual orientation, and linguistic abilities; physical and mental disabilities; personal strengths; and motivation for treatment. (Colorado Department of Human Services [CDHS], 1999, p. 5)

If the client is a woman, licensed agencies in Colorado are mandated to ensure that therapeutic services and treatment planning specifically address the following issues: alcohol/other drug abuse; emotional, physical, and sexual abuse; relationships; mental health; and parenting (CDHS, 1999). Although the relevance of many of these required elements is not in question, the evaluation and inclusion of these issues are clearly the agenda of the professionals rather than the client. There is no suggestion to assess the client's perception of what issues are of importance or to assess the client's view of the solution. This means that we had to continue to assess the problem in order to maintain our Colorado license and then implement a solution-building approach in addition.

The third issue was a lack of literature to assist in explaining the subtle concepts of solution-focused therapy, specifically in our work with agencies. The approach itself has been described as simple (de Shazer, 1988; Berg and Reuss, 1998; Metcalf, 1998); however, it is very difficult to integrate this approach in the work with clients.

Therapists often read the available literature, tried a described intervention, and then became discouraged at the lack of expected results. They often questioned whether this approach would work with their client population. The literature seemed to be lacking information about the personal struggle that therapists endure during the paradigm shift from problem to solution focused.

We also discovered that available solution-focused literature was often tainted with problem-solving concepts. Solution-focused therapists are often described in the literature as suggesting problem-solving interventions (Metcalf, 1998; Department of Health and Human Services [DHHS], 1999). The focus is often on strengths and exception finding (Metcalf, 1997, 1998; Selekman, 1997; DHHS, 1999) rather than on utilizing the miracle question (de Shazer, 1988, 1994; Berg and Miller, 1992; Berg, 1994; Berg and Reuss, 1998) to reach a place in which the problem does not exist. Much of the literature approaches solution building from the front end of the problem. This results in increased confusion by the therapists about the differences between solution-focused therapy and problem solving.

In order to minimize this confusion, we depended heavily on video training tapes from the Brief Family Therapy Center in Milwaukee, Wisconsin. In addition, we relied on the original works of Steve de Shazer (1985, 1988, 1994), Insoo Berg (1994), and the combined work of Insoo Berg and Scott Miller (1992; Miller and Berg, 1995) and Insoo Berg and Norm Reuss (1998).

The final issue was the awareness that the more we learn about this approach, the more we have to learn. This is not an approach that one can study, apply, and master. We have discovered that the more we try to apply these basic concepts to all areas of our team and the more success we experience, the higher our expectations of ourselves become. We have learned that both the potential and the impact of this approach are endless, and that our understanding of solution-focused therapy would be best viewed as a journey rather than a destination. Although this can be frustrating at times, it fuels our excitement, curiosity, and enthusiasm. As we apply this approach and use the underlying concepts as the structure for our interventions, we are able to be creative and spontaneous—some might call this art. This is what we find energizing and what solidifies our team.

Now, seven years after our journey began, we invite you to read our stories, learn from our frustrations and successes, experiment with the applications we have discovered, and join us on our journey. It is a journey to look beyond client problems, to a place where miracles are a reality. We hope that our curiosity becomes contagious and that our vision touches your life. We wish you the joy of purposeful spontaneity—the art of psychotherapy.

WHAT TO EXPECT FROM THIS BOOK

This book is intended as a practical guide for people (therapists, supervisors, and administrators) who want to implement the solution-focused (SF) approach in individual, group, or agency settings. Although the examples given involve an outpatient treatment setting, this approach can be used in myriad other therapeutic modalities involving multiproblem clients. Our agency's primary population consists of clients that are struggling with substance abuse. However, the concepts and methods described in the following pages are not limited to drug and alcohol abuse, protective service issues, or court-mandated treatment work with reluctant or court-ordered clients. Our hope is that these concepts and ideas can be readily generalized to the agency or setting in which you work and will be beneficial to your work with your population.

The following is an overview of the chapters of this book:

Chapter 1: The Solution-Focused Basics

This chapter provides a "master recipe" for the solution-focused approach and reviews its basic tenets, highlighting points of contrast with major traditional approaches. Special considerations are given to implementation of the approach in agency settings.

Chapter 2: Individual Session Road Map

This chapter provides a step-by-step "map" of how an agency can implement the solution-focused approach individually with substance abusing, court-mandated, and other clients. Also included are special considerations for working with angry and reluctant clients.

Chapter 3: Solution-Focused Groups

This chapter includes a detailed description of how we apply solution-focused therapy in our agency's substance abuse treatment groups, provides a step-by-step group session map, and includes considerations for clients who have experienced unsuccessful treatment in problem-oriented group treatment approaches.

Chapter 4: Many Miracles: Adaptations and Applications of the Miracle Question

Focusing on a "problem that is solved rather than a problem that needs to be solved" is at the core of the solution-focused approach. This chapter examines the principles behind the miracle question and offers additional applications of the future focus.

Chapter 5: Sustaining the Miracle

This chapter shows how to integrate the problem-focused concept of relapse prevention into solution-focused work and includes practical suggestions for helping clients maintain therapeutic gains during times of stress or crisis.

Chapter 6: "This Is Stupid, I Don't Need This, and I Don't Want to Be Here": Working with Adolescents

This chapter shows how the SF approach can be used successfully in an adolescent substance abuse treatment program and explains why this approach is especially well suited to this population. Also included are reflections on the various lessons we learned as we joined our adolescent clients on their journey toward solutions.

Chapter 7: The Art of Speaking "French": Interagency Diplomacy

Solution-focused therapists need to communicate effectively in a problem-focused treatment world. This chapter describes how we found ways to communicate respectfully and collaboratively with colleagues whose philosophies differed from ours, while staying true to our solution-focused model.

Chapter 8: Solution-Focused Supervision: Leading from One Step Behind

This chapter describes the structure and principles of a solution-focused approach to supervision.

Chapter 9: Maintaining the Team's Miracle: Observations from Our Solution-Focused Team

Developing and maintaining an effective team environment can be a challenging process. Many agencies claim that their management supports a team environment, but they are nevertheless vulnerable to pitfalls that can damage working relationships. This chapter describes how to create an effective team environment and offers strategies for avoiding the pitfalls.

Chapter 10: Case Examples of Clients Who Changed Their Lives and Our Way of Working

Our clients have shown us that they have the resources to make their miracles a reality. This chapter is composed of a selection of the cases that taught us about using the solution-focused approach with beleaguered, angry, and court-ordered clients.

Chapter 1

The Solution-Focused Basics

We do not see things the way they are, we see them as we are.

Anais Nin

SOLUTION-FOCUSED THERAPY BASICS

This chapter reviews the basic tenets of the SF approach and provides a "master recipe" for implementing it. In order to clarify why and how this approach is dramatically different from other therapy models, we highlight points of contrast with more traditional approaches. We then describe the basic solution-focused questions that are the foundation of our program with special consideration given to implementation in agency settings.

"Like Good Soup"

Many years ago, when I (YD) was first learning to cook, I read a book that provided a "master recipe" for good soup, which included a basic recipe and a series of variations designed to utilize seasonal ingredients. After preparing the basic recipe, I set about carefully trying all the variations. After repeated successes and some memorable failures, one day I realized that I had been making decent and reliable soup for some time using whatever happened to be on hand, even oc-

---

We would like to credit the following authors for their significant influence on the content of this chapter: Berg, 1994; Berg and Dolan, 2001; Berg and Miller, 1992; Berg and Reuss, 1998; DeJong and Berg, 1998; de Shazer, 1985, 1988, 1991, 1994; Miller, 1997.

casionally incorporating new ingredients while remaining faithful to the basic pattern of the recipe.

Learning SF "basics" is similar to learning the master recipe for good soup. Once you know the basic principles of making a soup base, preparing and adding seasonings and other ingredients, you can use the same general recipe with a wide variety of ingredients depending on what is available on any given day. As long as you follow the basic principles of the recipe, you can cook in a flexible and creative manner and manage to avoid culinary disasters. The kind of soup prepared is likely to be influenced by the cook's individual style and the range of available ingredients, but the result is clearly recognizable as soup. Likewise, the SF approach can look different in various settings depending on the personalities of the therapist and client and the general ambiance of the treatment setting, but the method is consistent with the overall pattern and principles of solution building. By the time you finish reading this chapter you will be familiar with the "basic recipe" for solution-focused therapy, which can then be tailored to fit your clients, goals, and environment.

What Does "Doing" the Solution-Focused Approach Really Entail?

Over the years, we have encountered many people who initially told us they practice solution-focused therapy when in fact they are simply incorporating a solution-focused technique or two into an otherwise traditional, problem-focused treatment approach. For example, recently I (YD) was chatting with a group of colleagues from out of town. They told me that they used solution-focused therapy in their treatment groups and it did not seem to them to be much different from what they had already done in the history of their very traditional, medically oriented treatment program. I was puzzled because the solution-focused approach differs greatly from traditional approaches. So, I asked them to describe their work, and they described a decidedly problem-focused approach. I asked them to help me understand how they were using a solution-focused approach in their program. They answered impatiently, "We ask a solution-focused question (scaling) in every session along with providing psycho-education, cognitive, and behavioral therapies."

Perhaps after reading their response, you are asking, "What's wrong with that?" The answer is absolutely nothing is wrong with it, except that it is rather limiting. Certainly, incorporating a solution-focused technique into a problem-oriented approach can result in new therapeutic possibilities; however, its impact is probably going to be limited. Like a weak vaccine, it is only a "watered down" version of the real thing—and although it is probably better than nothing, it is not going to be as effective as the full dose. Furthermore, people who do not know that the vaccine was administered incorrectly, because a weakened version was used instead of the original, may mistakenly assume that "vaccine-focused" therapy does not work very well!

As therapists learn about the possibilities that solution-focused therapy can offer (when used "full strength"), they are challenged to explore the degree to which they will incorporate it into their work. Over the course of our journey to becoming solution focused, we discovered three distinct stages for both the therapists as well as the agency:

1. Incorporating solution-focused interventions into a problem-focused philosophy (Therapists at this stage often incorporate interventions from a wide variety of theories, with the SF approach being just one of many)
2. Incorporating both the SF interventions and philosophy in the work with clients while remaining problem focused in interactions with co-workers, day-to-day tasks, politics, and other functions of the agency
3. Incorporating both the SF interventions and philosophy in both the work with clients as well as the day-to-day personal and professional tasks

Although incorporating a technique associated with solution-focused therapy into an existing program (stage one) can be part of a transition into that approach, as our team learned, truly becoming solution focused to the extent that one reaps the full therapeutic benefits of the approach (stage three) involves a major paradigm shift.

Over and over again in my (YD) consulting work with other agencies I have heard, "We did not fully comprehend how different this method of working was until we began to implement it in our own program." In order to convey the immensity of the change we made in shifting our agency from a traditional problem-focused substance abuse treatment model to a solution-focused one, we will examine the SF approach alongside the more traditional model. By doing so you will see how using it required us to radically shift our pattern of thinking and working with our clients.

Problem Solving versus Solution Building

According to DeJong and Berg (1998), the activities and process of thinking necessary for solution building are very different from those associated with the traditional problem-solving approach, also known as the "scientific" or "medical" model. For example, problem solving typically takes place as follows: The helping professional gathers information in order to identify the problem. Most often, this includes finding out when, where, and how the problem first occurred and making a detailed list of all the symptoms and effects associated with the problem. Then, the helping professional takes some time to speculate about the underlying cause(s) of the problem. Sometimes additional helping professionals are called in at this point to contribute their observations and speculations. Finally, based on what is determined to be the "real" cause of the problem, a course of treatment is prescribed with the intention of either resolving the problem or reducing the severity of the associated symptoms.

In sharp contrast to problem solving, the first step of solution building (as practiced in the SF model) begins with asking clients to describe how they want their lives to be different as a result of coming to therapy. Solution building starts with the end of the story of the clients' future success as opposed to the beginning of their problems. Because most of us have been trained to eliminate problems rather than develop and implement solutions, the SF method of working usually feels quite unfamiliar in the beginning. It is not surprising, therefore, that clinicians as well as clients often find the task of developing proactive, sustainable goals to be more difficult than they initially expected. As our team learned, solution building, as with other activities requiring discipline and practice, is an acquired skill.

In the second step of solution building, the helping professional and the client remain vigilant to instances in which the client has already experienced or is currently experiencing any aspects of the solution identified in step one, even in the smallest way. This process of noticing current aspects of the solution continues throughout all of the steps of solution building.

The third step of the SF approach departs even further from the traditional models by focusing intensely on empowering the client to develop an extremely detailed and vivid description of the exact desired outcome. If this is done well, the client has an immediate, firsthand "virtual" experience of how life will be after the desired outcome (solution) is achieved.

Several advantages to this approach previews the client's desired positive outcome. Because the goals are described in such vivid detail, the result begins to feel more "real," and therefore more possible, so the clients begin to feel more hopeful about their abilities to achieve the desired change. Also, because describing the goal in great detail provides a foretaste of the rewards associated with it, the clients feel more motivated. Advantages exist for the caregivers as well as for the clients. We learned to do it by beginning with the solution-focused basics. These principles are as follows:

Solution-Focused Principles

1. If it's not broken, don't fix it.
2. If something is working, do more of it.
3. If it is not working, do something different.
4. Small steps can lead to large changes.
5. The solution is not necessarily directly related to the problem.
6. The language requirements for solution development are different from those needed to describe a problem.
7. No problem happens all the time. There are always exceptions that can be utilized.
8. The future is both created and negotiable.

Although we could devote this entire book to the nuances of these principles, the remainder of this chapter will place special emphasis on the last one, which we believe is most central to the SF approach: *The future is both created and negotiable.*

Future Focus

Focusing on a future *in which the problem is solved* is both central to the SF approach and contributive to the power and effectiveness of all other solution-focused techniques. SF therapists empower their clients to envision and construct a highly personalized and unique version of a desirable future in which, among other things, they are free from the problem that brought them to therapy. This is typically accomplished by asking the SF miracle question.

THE MIRACLE QUESTION

Peter DeJong and Insoo Kim Berg (1998) word the miracle question as follows:

> Now, I want to ask you a strange question. Suppose that while you are sleeping tonight and the entire house is quiet, a miracle happens. The miracle is that the problem which brought you here is solved. However, because you are sleeping, you don't know that the miracle has happened. So, when you wake up tomorrow morning, what will be different that will tell you a miracle has happened and the problem which brought you here is solved? (pp. 77-78)

Invented by Insoo Kim Berg and Steve de Shazer at the Brief Family Therapy Center in Milwaukee in the mid-1980s (Berg and Dolan, 2001), the miracle question gives clients permission and invites them to imagine a version of the future that may currently appear unattainable. Not surprisingly, asking the miracle question often evokes a major shift away from the clients' (and the therapists'!) customary thought process. The therapist must ask the question very gently and thoughtfully, and follow with a comfortable pause so that the client feels free to think for a moment or two before answering.

Inviting the client to answer the miracle question not only strengthens the hope that change is possible, it also provides the client with a preview of the benefit of the change, while providing a vehicle for defining the goal of treatment in terms upon which both therapist and client can agree.

Listening carefully to the client's response to the miracle question allows the therapist to momentarily view the solution through the client's eyes, which ensures that the treatment goal is culturally sensitive and more likely to be embraced by the client (for it is the client's goal). Furthermore, using this technique lessens the therapist's likelihood of falling into problem-solving or expert-based interventions that are probably not going to be helpful with court-mandated or otherwise reluctant clients. As Cade and O'Hanlon (1993) point out,

- Clients are more likely to be persuaded by therapists when they feel that the therapists understand and respect their concerns and experiences.
- Persuasive therapists' suggestions and directives are usually congruent with clients' perspectives, experiences, and desires.
- Clients are most likely to implement ideas for change that they generate or that they believe to be their own.

EXCEPTION QUESTIONS

Exception questions empower the client to identify those times when the problem does not exist or is less severe. They often uncover skills or resources that the client has not noticed or has forgotten. Exceptions are seen as "precursors to goals . . . and solutions" (de Shazer, 1991, p. 90). Exception questions are especially powerful when combined with the future focus, which is the hallmark of solution-focused therapy. When used in this manner, the therapist magnifies or accentuates exceptions that the client has already mentioned.

Once an exception is identified, the therapist can explore the impact of the exception or the client's underlying wisdom that resulted in the different behavior. The therapist's role when using this technique is to listen for exceptions that lead toward the client's solution. Well-meaning therapists who are new to this approach commonly use exception finding as a means to gently convince the client that someone else's (e.g., the referral source's) solution is correct. Unfortunately, this is often ineffective. The challenge is to discover exceptions that lead the clients closer to what is truly important to them. These discovered client-driven exceptions guide the direction of the therapist's questions. The following example demonstrates how this is done:

A client was referred for services after his children were removed from the home due to severe neglect. Empty liquor bottles were found in the home at the time the children were removed.

CLIENT: I don't need to come to treatment. I know that my caseworker believes that I have a problem with alcohol, yet I quit using two years ago. I don't know why she thinks that my drinking is a problem. I guess she is suspicious of everyone.

THERAPIST: Did I hear you right? You quit two years ago?

CLIENT: Yeah, it was no big deal.

THERAPIST: Why did you decide to quit?

CLIENT: Well, my drinking was getting out of hand. I would come home drunk, and I was afraid I would get a DUI or worse if I didn't do something.

THERAPIST: So you quit? Wow! I'm so impressed! How did you do that?

CLIENT: I changed who I was hanging around with, and that made a big difference. I hooked up with my old friend, Bob. He's always been a good friend, yet I didn't spend much time with him when I was drinking.

THERAPIST: What made you remember him?

CLIENT: I drive by his house every day on the way to work, and one day I noticed his car. I got to thinking that I should look him up.

THERAPIST: Was that different for you to pick up the phone and call?

CLIENT: Sure was! He was shocked!

THERAPIST: Yet you did it anyway! How did you know that would be the right thing for you to do?

CLIENT: I was so tired of how life was going, and I think I was ready to take the chance.

THERAPIST: What other things did you learn during that difficult time?

This client interaction demonstrates the multiple verbal paths from which the therapist must choose during every clinical interaction. The therapist could have asked why the client's caseworker thought he has a problem with alcohol, how much he currently drinks, what was happening to let him know his drinking was out of control, or why he started drinking again. However, these paths would have explored the problem rather than built upon the solution. By choosing the path to explore the exception (the time that he quit drinking), the therapist empowered the client to discover the tools used and lessons learned from his past experience. Of course, by carefully listening to the client's words, the therapist was able to recognize and use this path to an exception. This listening resulted in the path being client driven rather than therapist driven.

Exceptions are scattered throughout client conversation, and it takes a well-trained ear to recognize them and to appreciate the opportunities they offer. Therapists are trained to evaluate the problem, which desensitizes our hearing to the small changes about which the clients speak. Once therapists understand the value of exploring these exceptions, their way of listening changes. It is very important to magnify the exceptions that clients mention and to question how the clients brought these changes to be, for clients often interpret exceptions to be random or unpredictable. Once they understand that these exceptions are under their control, they are able to re-create them in the future. Steve de Shazer (1991) spoke of this when he stated, "It seems best to assume that these 'random' exceptions are not random and are indeed embedded in certain, as yet undescribed, contexts or patterns which, if described, would allow for their being predicted and thus prescribed" (p. 88).

The change process often appears arduous, and exceptions often offer a glimmer of hope that change is underfoot and can be a reality. As exceptions come to light, clients gain hope, for they begin to see that part of their miracle is happening today. Therapists must not step in front of the clients and try to convince them that uncovered exceptions contain more meaning and potential than the clients ascribe to them.

By listening to the client and questioning what difference these exceptions make we learn the true meaning of these exceptions. Therapists must trust that the clients will see potential solutions in these exceptions when the right solution exists, and that it was not the correct solution if the client decides to walk away from it. Sometimes clients abandon previously successful solutions because they are no longer effective. Through careful listening the therapist can understand how the clients know when these exceptions will lead toward their miracle.

Clients do not always readily volunteer obvious paths that lead to exploration of exceptions. This brings us naturally to scaling questions, which provide another opportunity to identify times in which the problem is less severe or nonexistent.

A BRIEF HISTORY OF SCALING

Although scaling is uniquely emphasized in solution-focused therapy, it has been used widely over the years in a variety of approaches. For example, behaviorists such as Wolpe (1969, 1973) used what is called a self-anchored scale to assist clients in evaluating their anxiety level on a scale from 0 to 100 (100 equaled the worst anxiety that the client had ever experienced or could imagine, and 0 equaled absolute calm). These scales are "anchored" with concrete examples that clearly define specific points on the scale (Coulton and Solomon, 1977). At a minimum, the start and end points on the scales are defined. The client must understand and recognize an equal difference among the points on the scale. Since these scales are often individualized for each client depending on the clinical need, reliability data is not available. However, these scales do have high face validity when used correctly and are able to evaluate information that cannot be assessed by other means (Bloom and Fischer, 1982).

Scales have been used with varying numbers of points (up to 100); however, the majority of clinical scales use ten or fewer points due to the difficulty differentiating among numbers on a larger scale. Four- or five-point scales are commonly used due to therapists' ability to easily anchor each point on the scale. These types of scales may omit the numbers and rely directly upon the point definitions. The therapist asks the clients to identify where they are on the scale. These types of scales are termed Likert scales (Smith, 1990) and are commonly used to evaluate a group of items such as mood. For example, Burns (1999) uses this type of scaling to assist clients in evaluating themselves through questions such as the following:

> I think of myself as "lazy" or as a procrastinator:
>
> ____ not at all; ____ somewhat; ____ moderately; ____ a lot. (p. 701)

Regardless of the number of points on the scale, the client's progress can be measured and documented by using the same scale on several occasions and noting the change in client identification on the scale. Although Likert scales resemble some of the ways scaling can be used in SF therapy, SF therapists most typically use scaling in the form of questions.

SCALING QUESTIONS

As most typically used by solution-focused therapists, scaling questions ask clients to rank aspects of their life on ten-point scales (Miller, 1997). These questions provide valuable information about where the clients are in relationship to their "miracle" or goal. Scaling presents wonderful opportunities to empower clients to explore exceptions and how they created them. The following example demonstrates how scaling can open opportunities to emphasize exception:

This is an excerpt from a family session. The family recently began having weekend visits with their son after he had been removed from the home for violent and aggressive behavior. This exchange occurred between the therapist and the son.

THERAPIST: So, on a scale of one to ten (ten being that you have the relationship you want with your parents, and one being that it is the worst it has ever been) where would you put it?

CLIENT: About a four.

THERAPIST: What lets you know that it is a four?

CLIENT: Well, we aren't yelling as much. We actually sat down and had dinner together last night. We didn't really talk or anything, but we had dinner.

THERAPIST: Wow! You had dinner together and have cut back on the yelling. How did you do that?

CLIENT: I got to thinking about what we talked about last time. You know, when you asked about my miracle? We used to have dinner together every night. So I thought it might make my mom happy.

THERAPIST: Did it?

CLIENT: Yeah. I think she was surprised I was there. She seemed happy.

Scaling is used in many approaches due to its ability to assist the therapist in evaluating otherwise difficult concepts. For example, scales are often used to quantify internal thoughts and feelings and the intensity of these thoughts and feelings. When used in traditional problem-focused approaches, the highest point on the scale is linked to the most problematic state. This is where SF scaling differs significantly. Because solution-focused therapists focus on the client's relationship to the desired goal rather than to the problem, the highest point on the scale is always anchored to the client's desired outcome. This results in clients measuring their current progress rather than measuring the degree of their symptoms. In addition, solution-focused scales typically have ten points. This allows a large enough number of points that the client can recognize small changes, and a small enough number that the client can easily differentiate among the points on the scale. The therapist purposefully defines the start and end points of the scale according to the aspect being measured to allow the scale to maintain high face validity.

In addition, scaling is valuable in assisting therapists when they must evaluate traditionally problem-focused areas such as suicide risk or other active mental health symptoms. Traditional methods of evaluating these issues often result in the client becoming more focused on the problem, making it increasingly difficult to begin effective solution-focused work. Scaling is extremely helpful in assessing these traditionally problem-focused areas while allowing the clients to maintain their future focus. When using scaling in this manner, it is important to define the scale in a way that will provide the needed information. For example, when assessing suicide risk, the therapist is most concerned about any imminent plan the client has for self-harm. Clients who are experiencing a depressive episode often report that they feel like harming themselves, but these feelings do not indicate imminent risk or necessitate protective action from the therapist. Therefore, the scale's start point will indicate whether protective action is needed, and its end point will be the client's desired goal. This allows the scale to be used as a therapeutic intervention in addition to an evaluative tool. The following example demonstrates how scaling can be used to assess current client safety:

This is a client who had been diagnosed by her mental health therapist as having borderline personality disorder and major depressive disorder. She has a history of suicidal ideation and multiple hospitalizations.

THERAPIST: I am very impressed that you kept your appointment even though you have been feeling so poorly. I can tell that you really want your life to be different.

CLIENT: Yeah, I do; but I don't think it will ever happen. I don't think it is worth going on. My family deserves so much more.

THERAPIST: Let me ask you an important question. Remember when you told me how your miracle day would be? You mentioned that your mood would no longer be an issue, you would be happy, you would be able to handle the normal ups and downs in life, and you would enjoy the day-to-day things like watching the sunset. Is that right?

CLIENT: Yes.

THERAPIST: So, on a scale of one to ten (ten is that this miracle you described has come true, and one is that you are going to kill yourself today) where would you put yourself on that scale?

CLIENT: About a five. I'm not going to hurt myself. I know that would only make everything worse for my family.

THERAPIST: Where is the lowest point you have been on that scale?

CLIENT: About a one and a half. I have thought about it, but I didn't follow through.

THERAPIST: What did you do to get from a one and a half up to a five?

CLIENT: Well, it was about five years ago. I didn't have my son yet, and killing myself seemed like a way out. My son has changed my life. I could never put him through that.

This interaction has provided the therapist with the necessary information to assess the client's current level of safety. The therapist knows from this interaction that the client does not have a history of suicide attempts, yet had at least one episode of suicidal ideation five years ago. The therapist also knows that the client is not currently experiencing suicidal ideation and that the client is aware of the negative impact that suicide would have on her family members. The therapist now knows that the client's son is an important person in her life for whom the client wants to make positive changes. All of this information was obtained while remaining future focused and asking questions about where the client is in relation to the miracle and what is different now. This results in the client volunteering assessment information for the purpose of comparison of where she wants to be. Although the therapist is carefully gathering evaluative data that is needed to ensure client safety and is often required by problem-focused regulatory agencies, the client remains focused on how she wants her life to be and what she has done to implement changes. The therapist obtains needed information and the solution focus is not compromised.

Scaling provides special flexibility when working with clients who are shy, taciturn, or understandably cautious about how much they tell the therapist. It is not necessary for the therapist to know the specific meaning of the scale's starting point; only the client needs to know that. Solution-focused therapists accentuate and magnify the details of upward movement between points on the scale.

DIFFERENCE QUESTIONS

Difference questions identify and accentuate the effects of the clients' changes or potential changes, thereby providing an "ecology check" to ensure that proposed changes are realistic, feasible, and worthwhile. Difference questions also can enhance awareness or deepen the meaning clients ascribe to proposed goals, thereby increasing motivation to make additional changes. They often result in increased hope that change is both possible and worthwhile. The following case excerpt, occurring between the therapist and the son from the previously mentioned family session, illustrates this:

THERAPIST: I'm just curious. When you used to have dinner together every night, what difference did that make for your relationship with your parents?

CLIENT: Well, we seemed closer. I think it was because we had a chance to be together during times that I wasn't in trouble. My parents have never liked talking about stuff I do wrong over dinner, so that makes it a safer place to hang out. We never yell during dinner.

THERAPIST: So, when you had that time together with no yelling, what difference did that make on the rest of the time with your parents?

CLIENT: The rest of the time seems to go better too. I guess I never realized how much it means to my mom when she is able to know the day-to-day stuff. It seems like she gives me more space when she hears about my day and what I'm up to.

Difference questions provide the magnification needed to light a fire within the client. Typically they are asked after clients have identified a specific current, past, or potential change. The therapist can then explore the impact of this new behavior, which will assist the client in determining its long-term impact.

Difference questions that explore the impact of past changes are often useful in assisting clients in determining whether similar change would be useful in the current situation. This type of questioning often results in recognition of previously forgotten skills and successes. Questions that explore current change are useful in assisting clients in determining if the new behavior is one that will lead them to the desired goal. Questions that explore potential change (e.g., changes that occur on the miracle day or once the problem is resolved) are helpful in determining how the clients' miracles will result in long-term, lasting benefit for all involved. The following case excerpt illustrates the use of difference questions with current and potential change. The therapist is speaking with a single, unemployed mother who has been struggling with cocaine addiction and major depressive disorder.

THERAPIST: You have been talking about all of the changes you have made this past week. You mentioned that you have looked into getting your GED, spoken to your mother about her watching your child, and started to look in the newspapers for potential jobs. That is a lot! I'm curious about what difference all these changes have made for you.

CLIENT: Well, it seems real for the first time. I'm actually excited that I might be able to get my GED and get a good job!

THERAPIST: What difference does that excitement make?

CLIENT: I have energy. I can hardly wait for the paper to come each morning so I can look through it to see what is available. I've been starting to think about what I need to do to organize my day better so I will have time to study for my GED and have a job. It's going to take some work, yet I have the energy for the first time. I want to make this work.

THERAPIST: What difference do these changes make for your son?

CLIENT: I don't think he knows what is going on, but he does know that I am up off the couch and more attentive to him. He doesn't fuss so much now. I think getting my GED and working is going to make a big difference for him in the future.

THERAPIST: How so?

CLIENT: I will be setting a good example for him. I want him to finish school and support his family when he gets older. I also want him to learn that you can always turn your life around and make a fresh start.

THERAPIST: How will it help him to know that?

CLIENT: It will help him be hopeful, even when things look pretty dark. It will make sure that he never gives up.

RELATIONSHIP QUESTIONS

Through the use of relationship questions, the fifth type of intervention, the therapist assists the client in viewing the desired solution from a variety of perspectives. Relationship questions require the clients to respond from the imagined viewpoint of another person in their lives, thereby eliciting details from the clients' real life, which are both very vivid and rich in personal meaning for the clients. As the following excerpt demonstrates, relationship questions also increase the clients' understanding of and empathy for the people around them. This is a woman who was referred for services by her probation officer due to repeated alcohol-related legal charges. In addition, her alcohol use and resulting legal problems were causing marital strain.

THERAPIST: How might your husband know that a miracle has occurred overnight and your drinking problem is resolved?

CLIENT: He wouldn't see me acting all hungover and grumpy in the morning.

THERAPIST: How would he notice you acting instead?

CLIENT: I would be talkative, in a good mood, ready to start the day. . . .

THERAPIST: How would he react?

CLIENT: He would be really happy. He might even kiss me! Poor guy, he must be so tired of me waking up in a bad mood.

Relationship questions help clients assess the impact achieving their goals will have on the important people in their life. This typically increases the clients' motivation to continue working toward their miracle, as the following interaction demonstrates.

This is a mother who was charged with child endangerment after her son suffered severe brain damage from physical abuse. The mother was under the influence of methamphetamine at the time that the abuse occurred and had left her son alone with a stranger.

THERAPIST: I'm curious what your son would tell me if he were old enough to talk. What is going to be different for him once you have reached your miracle?

CLIENT: He will feel secure and safe. He will know that nothing like this will ever happen again.

THERAPIST: How will he know that?

CLIENT: Because I will be much more aware of what is happening in his world. I won't allow strangers to care for him, and I will be around a lot more.

THERAPIST: When you are more aware and he feels more safe and secure, what difference will that make for him both now and in the long term?

CLIENT: He won't cry as much, he will be happier and laugh more, and he will have the confidence that he needs later on in life.

THERAPIST: So, on a scale from one to ten (ten being that this miracle has come true and one is the worst it has ever been), where would he say he is?

CLIENT: About a six. He's still in foster care, so I'm not able to be there all the time, yet I know he can tell that I'm paying more attention when I can be there. He cries less when I'm around, and he smiles more. I can tell that he misses me because he cries now when I leave. He didn't use to do that.

The client's increased awareness of her child's perspective gives a deeper and more poignant meaning to the changes she is making. She is able to use her child's behavior as a meaningful barometer of her own changes. And by seeing the long-term benefit in her child's life, she is motivated to make better parental choices. Seeing the impact of her behavior through the eyes of her child is a meaningful and useful skill that can continue even after therapy has concluded.

This interpersonal impact from one person's change within the family system is the result of the systemic nature of solution-focused therapy. Although the client's change may initially be the result of his or her personal quest for change, this change cannot help but impact others within the family system. This concept is fundamental in Steve de Shazer's statement, "A small change in one person's behavior can make profound and far-reaching differences in the behavior of all persons involved" (1985, p. 16).

COMPLIMENTS AS INTERVENTIONS

Although positive reinforcement and validation characterizes many approaches to therapy, they are such an integral part of SF therapy sessions that we would be remiss not to include them in this chapter. SF compliments are uniquely used in solution-focused therapy in that the therapist reinforces or validates only behaviors that the clients identify as useful in working toward their goals, thereby remaining client driven. They are used to highlight what the client is doing that works that might otherwise be overshadowed by the immensity of the client's problems. We believe that validating and acknowledging what clients are doing that works and how difficult their problems are gives them permission to change and allows them to chart new courses of action. It also seems to allow them to think about how to make their lives more satisfying for themselves and others (Berg and Dolan, 2001).

The key to a successful compliment is genuineness on the part of the therapist. It is not necessary to be wildly enthusiastic when complimenting clients; in fact, this may make some people uncomfortable depending on their cultural background and personality style. A more subtle, and often more effective, method of complimenting is the two-step "process compliment" I (YD) learned many years ago from Insoo Kim Berg. It goes as follows:

1. Express positive surprise in reaction to one of the client's accomplishments.
2. Ask the client how she or he did it.

Typically, in the process of explaining how they did it, the clients inadvertently compliment themselves and the therapist can then simply validate what the clients said as a further compliment. This form of complimenting usually feels more natural for both therapist and client and since the details actually come from the client, it is also more likely to be perceived as both accurate and respectful.

The following example illustrates how complimenting can be used to identify resources and strengthen a client's sense of hope:

CLIENT: I've known for a long time I would have to give up smoking and drinking if I wanted to live past my fifties. I knew it even before I lost my driver's license because of the DUIs. [The client was arrested because of repeated "driving under the influence" charges.] My liver is bad, and I gave up smoking last year when I had a cancer scare.

THERAPIST: You already gave up smoking?

CLIENT: Yes. It's been thirteen months and eleven days since I quit.

THERAPIST: That's great—already over a year! How did you do it?

CLIENT: Well, I just set my mind to it. It was real hard the first couple of days but, you know, I just decided.

THERAPIST: You made up your mind and just like that you did it even though, like you said, it must have been really hard, especially at first. How did you get yourself to do it?

CLIENT: Oh, yeah, it was hard, all right. But when I make up my mind, I make up my mind. I'm a pretty strong lady, way down deep.

THERAPIST: I can see that.

THE REWARDS OF BECOMING SOLUTION FOCUSED

Our agency's transition to becoming solution focused was characterized at various times by excitement, resentment, impatience, frustration, and, eventually, wonder and enthusiasm. We do not want to paint an overly rosy picture of this transition. If it was simple for an agency to change, this book would not be necessary, nor would we have learned all the valuable lessons that were essential in order to make the changes, both personally and systemically. The rewards we eventually reaped from this dramatic shift were preceded by and often intermingled with moments of angst, exhaustion, and much hard work.

So what were the benefits that made the angst and exhaustion worthwhile? As we (our team of therapists and supervisor, TP) intentionally shifted our emphasis away from the traditional pathology-focused orientation with which we had been originally trained to view our clients and moved toward a more positive, solution-focused view, two things happened:

1. We began to see our clients differently; we began to perceive them as more likable, and our work became more enjoyable.
2. We were amazed at the changes we observed in *them*. Bit by bit, many of our most "resistant," "undermotivated," "recalcitrant," and "angry" clients began to respond in a decidedly more cooperative and oftentimes fully collaborative manner.

SUMMARY

Although SF therapy is well known for its use of the miracle question and scaling, the SF therapists' adherence to and valuing of the future focus (focusing on a problem that is solved) makes these and other interventions most effective and unique.

The "basics" of the approach can initially appear deceptively simple, but effectively mastering them often requires extensive practice, discipline, and concentration. The therapists (and agencies) who do so, however, are richly rewarded with the experience of repeatedly watching their clients' (and referral sources') cherished hopes and miracles become reality.

Chapter 2 will explain how we developed our own application of the SF approach to address the legal requirements of our agency and to meet the real-life needs of our reluctant and dispirited court-mandated clients.

Chapter 2

Individual Session Road Map

Keep the needle in sight despite the haystack.

Teri Pichot

This chapter will provide a step-by-step "map" of how our agency works individually with our substance abusing clients (many of whom are court mandated), as well as considerations for working with angry and reluctant clients.

CHIPS ON THEIR SHOULDERS

Many of the clients who are referred to us come through the door with the proverbial "chips on their shoulders." They are angry that they have been ordered by an external source (e.g., the courts, parents) to come. They do not want to be there. Furthermore, the majority of clients who come to our agency do not believe they have a problem with substances despite the fact that a referral source is mandating their attendance.

New clients are likely to sit in their first session with their arms crossed in a you-can't-make-me-say-anything pose. Other clients openly attack the "system" and make it clear that they were unjustly accused. They are what problem-focused models would call "resistive clients" (Rosenthal, 1987; Miller and Rollnick, 1991). These clients may have previously experienced severe criticism from law enforcement or social service personnel and, in addition, suffered a series of losses as a consequence of their substance abuse. For example, many of the clients referred to our agency have lost custody of a child or risk losing custody; many have lost jobs, marriages, or friendships. They may have had their driver's licenses revoked for driving while chemically impaired. Many have engaged in prior treatment at other agencies. The fact that they are mandated to come to our agency in itself implies that they have lost some of their personal freedom.

Looking Beyond the Anger

Early on we realized that if we looked past the angry expressions on our clients' faces and listened to the meaning rather than the content of their hostile words, we saw despair. More often than not, our clients were people who had been beaten up by life and were close to the point of giving up on their situations ever getting better.

We knew we needed to find some way to empower our clients to take charge of their lives again in a productive way, and although we knew that identifying strengths and exceptions would be helpful in counteracting despair, we also knew that it would probably not be enough.

We agreed with the authors who stated that these elements of solution-focused therapy are important (Metcalf, 1998), but we firmly believed that more was needed if we were actually going to make a difference in the lives of our clients. In order for our program to be successful, our clients would need to be able to live rewarding, healthy, satisfying lives after they left. In almost all cases, this meant empowering them to rediscover their motivation to take charge of their destiny, that is, finding out what really mattered to them so that somehow they could find the strength to turn their lives around.

This was no easy task. Our therapists clearly needed a basic map for individual sessions that would serve as an outline of this model and a guide when they did not know what to do next. Following is that map and what we have learned through its use.

INDIVIDUAL SESSION MAP

1. Find out what needs to happen (client's goal) in order for treatment to be useful for the client.

To a therapist new to solution-focused therapy, this can be a daunting task. Our mandated clients often initially say that nothing needs to be different, for they do not believe they need treatment. We have learned the importance of persistence and trusting that the client does want something to be different, otherwise they would not have made the effort to comply with the mandate for treatment. It is often helpful to gently push through these initial client statements in order to discover what is meaningful to the client. The following excerpt illustrates this.

The excerpts in this chapter are from a session with a father whose son was removed from his custody due to his continued cocaine use, his multiple cocaine-related legal charges, and the resultant child neglect and unsafe living environment. His caseworker is recommending that his parental rights be terminated due to continued concerns for the welfare of the child and lack of compliance with social services' requirements.

THERAPIST: So, what are you hoping is going to be different as a result of coming to treatment here?

CLIENT: Nothing. I don't need anything to be different. I don't have a problem.

THERAPIST: Hmm [said with a genuinely puzzled tone]. So what brings you here?

CLIENT: My caseworker said that I have to complete these classes.

THERAPIST: What is it that your caseworker will see in you once you complete the classes that will let her know that these classes have been worth your time?

CLIENT: That I completed them.

THERAPIST: How will that be helpful?

CLIENT: Well, I started some before, but I didn't finish. I think she is worried that I didn't follow through.

THERAPIST: And what difference will it make for your caseworker to see that you completed them and followed through?

CLIENT: I think she will feel more comfortable that I'll do what I say and that I won't go back to using cocaine.

THERAPIST: And what difference will it make for you when your caseworker knows this about you?

CLIENT: She will see that I really am a good parent and that drugs won't stop me from raising my son!

Proving to his caseworker that he is a "good parent" is truly important to this client. Although the client believes that he is already a good parent, the caseworker's apparent lack of confidence in the client due to his past history of cocaine use is the client's problem. By trusting that the client is a customer for change (de Shazer, 1988) despite his initial statements, the therapist is able to uncover what is important to the client.

2. Verify that the therapist's understanding of the goal is accurate by asking difference questions or scaling questions. If the goal is unclear, repeat step one.

Taking the time to verify that what the therapist discovered through this initial conversation is really what is most important to the client is an often overlooked step. Well-intentioned therapists can become relieved that they have discovered something that the client appears to want to be different and then rush ahead without ensuring that they are still walking beside their client in the journey of change. The following example demonstrates this step:

THERAPIST: So, I'm curious what difference it will make for you when your caseworker really gets what a good parent you are and that drugs aren't a part of your life anymore?

CLIENT: It will change everything! I will get my son back and we can live our lives without all this crap!

THERAPIST: OK. That sounds pretty important. So, on a scale of one to ten (ten being that working on this while you are here would make your time worthwhile, and one being the opposite) where would you put yourself?

CLIENT: A ten! If we could make that happen, it would be great!

A high number on this scale indicates that the therapist has succeeded in hearing what the client wants to be different. A low number would indicate that the therapist has left the main route, gone down a "bunny trail," and has not yet discovered what the client is hoping to gain from treatment. The therapist would then return to step one and continue to explore what the client would like to be different as a result of treatment.

3. Ask the miracle question and get as many details of the miracle as possible.

An example of how the therapist might ask the miracle question in the previous example is as follows:

> Imagine that while you are asleep tonight a miracle happens. The miracle is that somehow your caseworker is now convinced that you are a good parent and that drugs are only in your past. However, because you and the caseworker were both asleep, neither of you knows that this miracle happened. What is the first thing your caseworker will notice about you that lets her know that this miracle happened?

Therapists commonly see physical changes in the clients as they describe life without the problem and explore the details of this problem-resolved place. Clients often smile, become more animated or relaxed, increase eye contact, or show other nonverbal clues that the discussion is meaningful. Without the vivid exploration of the details of the miracle the concept of change can lose its power, become just another conversation, and therefore lack the emotional attraction and resulting belief that change is meaningful and possible.

In our example, the client does not initially see anything that he needs to do differently. His goal is for the caseworker to notice what he currently does, for which he does not believe he is receiving credit. Because of this, the wording of the miracle in this example includes the caseworker (thus demonstrating the enormous flexibility of the question to be tailored to the client's needs). Beginning therapists have expressed concern when they have heard the miracle question worded in this way, and they have told me (TP) that they worry the client will not understand what he needs to do differently. They worry that the client will see the solution as the caseworker being different rather than the client "taking responsibility" for his behavior.

Solution-focused therapy is a systemic approach rooted in the belief that a small change by one person will result in changes throughout the system. Therefore, by beginning with a perceived change in the caseworker, the therapist can skillfully explore the changes that result in the client. The following excerpt demonstrates this:

CLIENT: Wow! That would be a miracle! . . . I guess she would receive a phone call from you saying that I was attending my classes and participating. She would probably also get a message from me letting her know about my plans to get housing and do all of the things she has been after me about.

THERAPIST: And how would these phone calls make a difference in convincing her?

CLIENT: Well, I've been rather angry, so I haven't let her see all that I have been doing.

THERAPIST: How will this be different on this miracle day?

CLIENT: She will be hearing all about everything I'm doing. I guess on this day, I would want her to know.

THERAPIST: What would she be seeing to know that everything she was hearing was for real?

CLIENT: Probably my attitude would be gone.

THERAPIST: How would she know that?

CLIENT: Oh, she would know [laughing]!

THERAPIST: How?

CLIENT: Well, I would volunteer stuff. I would do all of the things that I know I need to do anyway and not put them off just because I was being told to do them.

The therapist can increase the meaning of the potential change by asking difference questions. Recall from Chapter 1 that these are questions which encourage the clients to explore the difference the noticed changes make as they explore their miracle day. This is often very motivating to clients who previously felt overwhelmed by the magnitude of the problem. Steve de Shazer (1988) states, "Once something different is noticed, then the excitement builds again as the observers look for similar events and patterns" (pp. 2-3). For example:

THERAPIST: What difference will this miracle make for you and your son?

CLIENT: It would make a big difference! I would be putting my energy into taking care of business and getting him back rather than fighting my caseworker. I probably would feel more relaxed and less stressed.

4. Listen for exceptions and follow up on them by getting as many details as possible. If no exceptions are identified, move on to step five.

In the fourth step the discussion moves to times when the miracle is happening *even a little bit*. It is often through this discussion that clients begin to discover small, positive steps that they are currently taking or that would not be that difficult to resume. They begin to discover that these are the same behaviors they will be doing when the problem does not exist and these are signs that part of the miracle is occurring in the present.

THERAPIST: In your miracle it sounds as if you are doing what you have to do to get your son back. You will be going to these groups and working on stuff.

CLIENT: Yeah. I'm doing that now too, but with an attitude.

THERAPIST: So your attitude will be different on this miracle day.

CLIENT: Yeah! You probably don't see that attitude because I don't have it here anymore. Remember how I was when I first came in? [Both laugh while remembering.]

THERAPIST: So how did you ever set that aside?

CLIENT: You know, I don't know. I think these questions have just made me focus on what is important, and that attitude doesn't help me get what I want.

THERAPIST: So how do you remember to let that go since getting your son back is so much more important?

5. Ask a scaling question to determine clients' current levels of progress toward their goals.

Once the clients have a clear concept of what life will be like without the problem and have a sense of the positive impact that this new life will have on them and those around, it is time to move to the fifth part of the map: scaling. The therapist's role during this portion of the map is to determine where the client is in relationship to the client's miracle (or accomplished goal). This is done through scaling. The following example demonstrates how scaling is used to accomplish this task with our client:

> So, on a scale of one to ten (ten is that your miracle has come true, and one is that your caseworker has absolutely no confidence in you at all), where are you right now?

This places the client in context with the miracle and challenges him to determine how much of the miracle is currently part of his reality. This initiates a search for times in which the problem does not currently exist (exceptions), or times in which he is able to triumph over the problem, even "just a little." It takes the client out of the all-or-none mind-set that the problem is either all consuming or resolved. This creates an environment in which small steps are an expected and integral part of the journey toward the desired miracle. Clients often express a sense of hope as they realize that they have already done part of the work. They often recognize for the first time that they have been making meaningful changes. This serves to increase hope and provide renewed energy to continue working toward the miracle. At times it is helpful for the therapist to solidify the client's number on this scale. This is done primarily when the client appears to be disappointed in a lower number or vacillating between two numbers. The following example demonstrates how the therapist accomplishes this task of solidifying a client's number:

CLIENT: I guess I would say only a four. Sometimes I would say it's a five, but I think it's a four right now.

THERAPIST: What is it that lets you know that it is definitely a four and not a three?

CLIENT: Well, I am able to call when I have to. I guess there are times when I could avoid calling her, but I still do call and do what has to be done.

By solidifying the client's position on the scale, the therapist has assisted the client in clarifying what he is able to do that keeps him from being even lower on this scale. This empowers the client by clarifying that he does indeed know where he is on the scale and what he is doing that makes a difference.

6. Referring to the previous scaling question, find out what the client has done to reach and maintain the current level of progress.

Clients sometimes succumb to believing that positive change has occurred by happenstance. This belief can lead to inactivity, for the clients do not recognize the role they played in creating the success. This part of the map serves to assist the clients in discovering how much control they actually have over the changes they have made and, therefore, how much control they have to maintain the changes in the future. It creates a sense of mastery in the clients, which is crucial for long-term success. This task is often referred to in more traditional approaches as assisting a client to transition from external to internal locus of control (Greene and Ephross, 1991). The following illustrates how this is done:

THERAPIST: A four is pretty high. It's almost halfway there. I hear that you have been calling when you could have decided not to follow through. What else have you been doing that has resulted in your caseworker having so much confidence in you?

CLIENT: Well, I guess I have been signing up for classes, such as these and my parenting classes.

THERAPIST: Even though you still have an attitude sometimes, you have been able to sign up?

CLIENT: Yeah! I know it's important, even though I hate it, so I have been doing it anyway.

THERAPIST: How have you been able to push through even though you hate it?

CLIENT: By remembering that it is for my son.

THERAPIST: So that motivates you and gets you through the tough times.

CLIENT: Yeah. That helps a lot. I keep a picture of him with me to remind me of why I'm doing all this. It doesn't seem as hard that way.

7. Find out where on the previously mentioned scale (step five) the clients think others (probation officer, caseworker,

children, spouse or partner, pets, employer, etc.) in their lives would rate them.

Relational questions are also helpful during this process. These questions help clients to assess how much confidence important people have in them, how much confidence they would like these important people to have, and what they will be doing differently in the future that will result in others' increased confidence. We include pets in this section because relational questions about pets often evoke subtle observations from clients that might be missed otherwise.

Sometimes clients begin the process at this stage (such as the client in our illustration). They come to treatment stating that they have already made the needed changes and that their referral source is still requiring that they have treatment. We have found it very useful to begin the work at this point and assist the client in determining what the referral source will be seeing when the referral source is a ten on this confidence scale. This allows the clients to identify a purpose for the required treatment, and the clients quickly begin to work to increase the referral source's confidence. These same clients often report a personal benefit as they make the changes that will increase other people's confidence in them. The following excerpt illustrates how the therapist would use relational questions:

THERAPIST: Where would your caseworker say you are on this scale of gaining her confidence?

CLIENT: She'd say I was a three.

THERAPIST: What is it that you know about your parenting skills that she doesn't see yet?

CLIENT: She doesn't see that I used to read to my son every night and that I am there when he is scared. I love my son!

THERAPIST: What difference would it make if your caseworker was able to see that side of you?

CLIENT: It would probably make a big difference. I guess my attitude is keeping her from seeing the softer side of me.

At this point combining difference questions with relational questions can be useful in order to assist the client in identifying what difference the changes (either current or potential) would have on others in the client's life. For example:

THERAPIST: So what difference would it make for your caseworker if she was able to see that softer side of you?

CLIENT: She would see that I do love my son and that I can put his needs before anything else.

THERAPIST: What difference would that make?

CLIENT: It would surprise her. I think she thinks that I'm a hothead and that probably worries her.

8. Find out what the client thinks the significant people identified in step seven would say that the client is doing which caused them to rate the client at the level described in step seven.

This step is important in assisting the client to identify specific behaviors from the point of view of other significant people. This prompts clients to recognize the small things that they are currently doing to make a positive difference. Often clients overlook these efforts due to the magnitude of the problem and the resulting feeling of hopelessness. This step helps put the problem in perspective and gives the clients recognition for what they are currently doing. The following dialogue exemplifies this:

THERAPIST: If your caseworker were here, what do you think she would tell me that she currently sees in you that would make her rate you a three rather than a two?

CLIENT: I think she would say that my urine screens have been clean. She doesn't have any signs that I have been using drugs, and that I have been doing what she said.

THERAPIST: So those things give her some confidence in you.

CLIENT: Yeah. I think they are making a difference.

9. Ask the clients what difference they think significant others would say the behaviors identified in step eight are making.

THERAPIST: What difference would you say those behaviors are having?

CLIENT: I'm sure that she has other clients who don't even do those basic things. She has probably seen much worse cases than mine.

THERAPIST: So those things let her know that your case is not as bad as some of her other cases.

CLIENT: Yeah! It has to give her some hope since I'm hanging in there even though I've made it very clear I don't want to do this.

THERAPIST: What else does it tell her to see you hanging in there?

CLIENT: That my son is important to me. It would be a lot easier just to quit, but I don't because my son is too important.

10. Ask the clients where on the scale (in step five) they hope to be by the next session. Continue to ask questions about how the clients will know they are at this specific place on the scale, what will be different then, etc.

This part of the map helps the clients to identify what will be different when they progress even further on the scale. This is where inexperienced solution-focused therapists often slip into problem solving. It is important to remember that this part of the map is not about troubleshooting. Instead, the therapist must continue to ask questions from a place in which the problem does not exist. This invites the client to imagine a place just slightly further up the scale and to then again look backward from this place to discover the wisdom there. The following example demonstrates this:

THERAPIST: So, where do you hope to be on your miracle scale next time we meet?

CLIENT: About a five.

THERAPIST: You mentioned previously that you have been a five before. What did you notice that was different during those times?

CLIENT: There were periods of time when I almost forgot that my caseworker was making me do this stuff. I would get into it and see how it could benefit me and my son.

THERAPIST: What else did you notice during these times?

By continuing this line of conversation, the client gradually formulates what is associated with the desired number and identifies what difference the associated behaviors will make for both him and those around him. Clients are often more able to determine what they "did" (as they imagine from a future state) rather than trying to figure out what they "need to do" to solve a problem. Through this type of questioning from session to session, the client will move up the scale to the desired point. The client will decide the pace and will report the observed impact of the changes. By asking relational questions, the clients are able to make changes that are inclusive of those realities that are in their lives.

11. Use scaling questions for the clients to rate their confidence in their ability to sustain the changes (or to scale the referral source's confidence that the clients can sustain the changes). Although we list scaling confidence questions at this stage, we also use this question as needed at any stage throughout the therapy process.

Once the clients have moved up the scale in step five toward their "miracle" and have high numbers on this scale, it is time to move to this part of the map. This stage is used when the clients have a sense that treatment has been helpful and their goals are complete. (This step in the map may or may not occur at step eleven, for the therapist would skip this step and proceed with step twelve if the client had not completed the identified goal and was not high on the scale described in step five.) The therapist's task during this part of the map is to assist the clients in evaluating their confidence in their ability to maintain the changes made. (This stage is referred to as relapse prevention in traditional substance abuse treatment settings.) Scaling is also helpful in accomplishing this task. The following example demonstrates how scaling is used:

> On a scale of one to ten (ten is that you have complete confidence that you can maintain the changes you have made, and one is that you have no confidence at all), where would you put yourself on that scale?

When working with a client whose goal is to gain the referral source's confidence, the scaling question would be worded this way:

> On a scale of one to ten (ten is that your caseworker has complete confidence that you will maintain the changes he or she has seen, and one is that he or she has no confidence at all), where do you think he or she would put you on that scale?

The therapist would then use the procedures described in steps ten and eleven to work with the client until the numbers on this scale are high.

12. Based on responses to questions one through eleven, invite the client to assign self homework.

It is often tempting to tell clients what they should do that will make a significant difference in their lives. As therapists, this is often viewed as part of our role. Unfortunately, despite our best intentions, clients do not always agree with our well-thought-out homework assignments. Sometimes our homework assignments are too ambitious. Other times, the assignments are limited by our own understanding of the client's solution and by what we would find helpful if we were the client.

Through the process of identifying what works, how they want life to be, and how they will know that they are higher on their miracle scale, clients most often discover something that would make a significant difference in their lives. Sometimes the step is small; other times it is quite large, but always the size of the step is the perfect fit for them. We have been amazed by the wisdom of our clients as we have listened to them identify what they want to do between sessions. Sometimes the homework is exactly what we would have assigned, while other times we are surprised at the creativity that our clients demonstrate. Regardless of what the clients assign themselves for homework, two guidelines should be followed:

1. The clients are asked to explain what difference the homework will make in assisting them to get closer to their goal.
2. If at any point the homework is not working, the clients are to stop and do something different.

These guidelines allow the clients flexibility and creativity while holding them accountable to ensure that the homework is meaningful. In addition, the second guideline gives the unspoken message that the client is to pay attention to what is working and to make small adjustments as necessary to create positive change. One of my (TP) clients once told me that this way of giving homework was the factor that made the most difference in treatment. She stated, "You believing in my ability to know what was best for me was the very thing I needed from coming to therapy. It taught me to trust myself and to find my own answers."

Occasionally we have come across clients that are not comfortable assigning themselves homework (this is typically only in the first session). In that case the therapist would then ask the clients to notice what they do between sessions that either makes a positive change or keeps the situation from getting worse. By using this kind of "noticing" homework, the clients are able to readily identify what would be helpful to assign themselves for the following session. The following excerpt demonstrates how the therapist assists the client in assigning homework:

THERAPIST: We have talked about a lot of stuff today. I'm wondering: as you think about being that five on your scale, what is the most important thing that you did in between sessions that helped you to get there?

CLIENT: I think putting my son's picture out where I can see it every day and staying focused on why I am doing this.

THERAPIST: If it was next week and you were telling me how you accomplished this, what would you tell me that you did to help you stay so focused?

CLIENT: I would have found three things in every class that I am forced to go to that are really helpful to me and my son. That way I will remember that I can learn something from them even though I'm being forced to go. Yeah, that's what I'm going to do.

SUMMARY

The majority of our clients come to us due to the requirements of others, but even these clients comply with these mandates because they want something. They too want their lives to be different. In order for treatment to be successful, the therapist must discover what is important to the clients and walk beside them in the journey to discover a place in which the problem does not exist. By using this basic outline, the therapist can remain focused on what is important and skillfully guide the client on the journey while not becoming lost with the many distractions along the way.

Chapter 3 explains how we expand this individual map and apply solution-focused therapy in a group session to hear and utilize the multiple voices that the group session brings.

Chapter 3

Solution-Focused Groups

The simplest questions are the most profound.

Richard Bach

This chapter includes considerations for clients who have experienced problem-oriented group treatment approaches, a detailed description of how we apply solution-focused therapy in our agency's substance abuse treatment groups, a step-by-step group session map, and an explanation of our decision to use cotherapy teams.

THE EFFECTS OF CLIENTS' PAST PROBLEM-ORIENTED GROUP EXPERIENCES

Clients frequently enter therapy with the preconceived idea that they will be asked to identify and express emotions because this was done in previous groups they attended. Some may have embraced this concept; others became determined to withhold their feelings. Unfortunately, when clients are repeatedly encouraged to "vent" in a group, a negative culture often becomes the norm. Clients frequently find commonality in their complaining and negative emotions. By allowing this, therapists "risk creating a tragic life story," thereby confirming the "victim status" of the clients (Miller and de Shazer, 1998, p. 370).

Contrary to mainstream thought, many clients do make significant changes without this cathartic process. DeJong and Berg (1998) state that they "have not found that our clients regularly need to focus on and own their feelings (especially so-called repressed feelings) in order to feel understood or to make progress" (p. 34). Many of our clients who report pretreatment change observe that they made changes when they were tired of their current reality. Once they became tired they spontaneously turned their focus to how they wanted their lives to be. The problem was not resolved, yet they changed their focus. This future focus was the turning point of change.

Solution-focused therapy assists clients in obtaining this future focus, thereby creating the opportunity for change. Once clients are able to imagine life without the problem, they are able to see the solutions by which they can resolve their currently unresolved emotions. Although many times these solutions are similar to the ones suggested by problem-solving approaches (e.g., rituals, assertive conversation, self-nurturing activities), they are client driven and situation specific. Our clients often report that long-standing anger or pain is resolved once they begin to focus on how they want their lives to be. This future focus allows them to put these powerful emotions into perspective rather than allowing the emotions to have a disproportionate place in their lives. In short, this is why we do not encourage venting in our groups.

As our therapists learned the solution-focused approach, they sometimes mistakenly assumed that feelings are not addressed by this method. I (TP) have even heard solution-focused therapists erroneously described as "feeling-phobic." As with all therapeutic approaches, solution-focused therapists are faced with multiple verbal paths during every client conversation. The underlying principles of the approach dictate which path the therapist will choose to explore with the client. Solution-focused therapy focuses on identifying paths that lead to the solved problem. For this reason, solution-focused therapists do not explore a client's current emotions unless they are identified by the client as part of the desired solution. DeJong and Berg (1998) encourage therapists to "avoid amplifying negative feelings" (p. 37). They further state that they "have found that such statements tend to drive clients further into those aspects of their lives that are least useful for generating positive change" (p. 37). Solution-focused therapists avoid exploring current, painful emotions not because they are leery of these emotions but because such exploration is not useful to their purpose.

During our journey to integrate solution-focused therapy into our group work, our therapists wanted to know how to work with clients who were experiencing very painful emotions and who cried uncontrollably during the session. The therapists did not want to amplify the client's negative emotion, nor did they want to appear insensitive to the client's pain. They often struggled with old teachings, and they were sometimes overheard saying, "The client just needs to get it out." We soon discovered that when they allowed clients to vent, it was because they did not know what else to do. The clients' pain had a paralyzing effect on them.

During these times, we found it helpful to remember that clients come to therapy because they want something to be different. Typically, they come to treatment not because they lack a place to express their emotions but rather because they are not sure how to get to a place in which the pain is resolved. Once the therapists understood the importance and resulting compassion of assisting the clients to imagine a place in which their pain was resolved, the therapists could then remain focused on their helping role. They learned to gently validate the client's emotion while respectfully maintaining focus on what the client came to therapy to obtain. They soon learned to view pain as an opportunity to explore client coping skills and resources. By assisting the clients in looking past their emotion to a place in which these emotions were successfully integrated into who they are, the clients discovered the solution to their unresolved emotion.

Clients often come to therapy expecting to have to talk about "the problem" and to be pressured to identify as having a problem. This scenario is portrayed in the media, and is often what clients have experienced in past treatment episodes (including those using strength-based models). Although strength-based group models, for example, traditionally build upon client strengths and successes in order to solve the client problems, they rely heavily upon basic problem-solving principles (defining the problem and troubleshooting solutions to solve the problem). Clients who have attended these and other problem-focused groups are often pleasantly surprised at the difference that addressing problems from a future-focused stance makes. They are often baffled that the problem identification stage is omitted altogether.

Clients frequently admit, "I thought I was going to have to say, 'my name is Sam, and I'm an alcoholic.' " Others note that they are surprised we do not try to convince them that using substances is "bad." Because of these internal expectations, many clients come to group angry and defensive. Nonetheless, group therapy has traditionally been used in substance abuse treatment, and there is no doubt that this can be a powerful modality through which clients can benefit from clinical interventions as well as from needed peer support. Our challenge is to provide our clients with a group that empowers them to make positive change in their lives, without unnecessarily eliciting resentment and resistance from them.

Our primary treatment modality is group treatment. Although we do offer individual sessions for clients, these are used primarily for crisis work, for establishing the initial treatment goal, or for other case management purposes. When we first began to apply solution-focused therapy to group sessions, the team therapists became rather overwhelmed. Their familiar, traditional methods of providing group structure (e.g., using group topics and confrontation, providing interpretation, soliciting feedback from group members, exploring feelings) are not part of solution-focused therapy.

Instead, they were challenged to listen to their clients and to respond in a purposeful way to the needs of each client in the group sessions. They could not fall back onto a curriculum of predetermined topics that the experts had determined all clients in similar situations need to discuss and understand. Each client was viewed as having meaningful and unique goals, desires, and needs. Nor could the therapists rely on the feedback of other group members, for we now rejected the concept that the group was a microcosm of the world in which the clients were to work through life issues. We further rejected the common notion that treatment groups need to center around an identified problem, to increase insight, or to target unconscious factors (Corey and Corey, 1987; Brown, 1991).

We postulated that the most important work is the work that clients do outside of the sessions, and that the role of the group is to provide a safe environment in which the group members can explore how they want their lives to be. We decided that the therapist's primary tasks would be to maintain the safe environment, to ask questions that assist the clients in identifying what life will be like without the problem and what steps they took to get there, and then to empower the clients to take the necessary steps to make reaching this imagined life a reality. We set out to design a practical group format map to address this, which resulted in the following.

GROUP SESSION MAP

1. Ask an introduction question. Invite group members to say their names and answer the introduction question.

2. Group leader silently identifies common themes from group answers and finds a broader theme that includes all the common themes. This is done through silently asking self questions that assist the therapist in hearing what is important to all of the clients.
3. Group leader reflects (aloud) similarities among group members' responses, summarizing common themes until all are included, and then suggests one broad, inclusive theme.
4. Group leader asks the group's permission for the group to address the theme identified in step three unless there is another (emergency) issue that needs to be addressed.
5. Ask the miracle question (or similar future-oriented question) based on the theme identified in step three.
6. Get as many details as possible about the miracle question (or similar question asked in step five.)
7. Listen for exceptions, and follow up by getting as many details as possible. If no exceptions are identified, move on to next step.
8. Ask a scaling question to determine clients' current level of progress toward their goals.
9. Referring to the previous scaling question, find out what the clients have done to reach and maintain current level of progress.
10. Find out where on the scale (step eight) the clients think others (probation officer, caseworker, children, spouse or partner, pets, employer, etc.) in their lives would rate them and what the clients are doing that would cause this rating.
11. Ask group members what role this conversation (steps one through ten) regarding the group theme plays in working toward their miracles. (How was this conversation helpful in getting closer to the miracle?)
12. Based on their responses to questions one through eleven, invite the clients to assign themselves homework.
13. Give group members feedback.

Following is a description of each of these steps in detail.

1. **Ask an introduction question. Invite group members to say their names and answer the introduction question.**

The first part of the group map is to ask an introduction question, which serves to direct the clients' thinking toward a future focus, to demonstrate that the focus of group is on something other than a "problem," and to create a sense of comfort and familiarity among the clients. The therapist can either ask the clients to say their names and to answer the question using a round-robin technique or can allow the clients to answer as they feel comfortable until all have answered the question and introduced themselves. Sample introduction questions are as follows:

- "What is one thing that you have done between now and last time you were here that has helped you get closer to your goal?"
- "What would your family members tell me is the most important quality you have?"
- "Who is the most important person in your life and why?"
- "Who do you admire the most and why?"
- "If you could have one quality that you currently don't have, what would it be?"
- "What has been the most important accomplishment in your life?"
- "What is one thing that you are proud of that no one else knows about you?"

These types of introduction questions provide a window into what is important to the group members. The therapist's role is to carefully listen to each group member's answer and to make a mental list of what each person says is most important that day, while recognizing individual or group issues that need to be revisited. We have been amazed at the clients' ability to ensure that any important personal issues are mentioned during this brief check-in period. Clients often make direct statements that inform the therapist of any crisis or personal issue that needs to be addressed during group sessions. When clients do mention these pressing issues, the therapist acknowledges the importance of the issue while continuing to focus on the brief introduction format. The following illustrates this point:

Sara sought treatment services at social services' insistence due to her extensive use of methamphetamine, cocaine, and marijuana. Her drug use was resulting in child neglect and concerns about the safety of the child's environment. She had received services on several occasions, yet had always returned to using substances when life problems occurred.

THERAPIST: Sara, how about you? What is one thing that you have done since last time you were here to help you get closer to where you want to be?

SARA: Well, it's hard to say. My grandmother died last Sunday, and that made it hard to follow through with my plans.

THERAPIST: I'm so sorry to hear that. What did you do to cope with that loss?

SARA: I hung around my family and tried to stay busy. That seemed to help a lot. I have a really good family. It's been a very hard week.

THERAPIST: It sounds like you did exactly what you needed to do in order to get through this. Let's come back to this once we are finished with check-in. Would that be OK with you?

SARA: Yeah. That would be fine.

In this example, the therapist made a mental note that what was most important to Sara was getting through this crisis of losing her grandmother. In addition, the therapist noted that this loss should be revisited (either individually or during the group session) to ensure that Sara had the services and support she needs. Once the therapist completed that mental task, the therapist asked a follow-up question to demonstrate to the group and to Sara that the group focus is on something other than the "problem" despite the introduction of problems by group members during the group session. This follow-up question further invited Sara to look beyond the crisis to explore her current coping skills that she may have otherwise overlooked. The therapist's ability to demonstrate empathy and genuine concern while gently maintaining a future focus is crucial to the group's success. Without this skill, group members may feel discounted and believe that their problems are not an acceptable topic. This would result in a superficial group with dissatisfied group members.

By listening for what is important to each group member, and by asking only those follow-up questions that are needed for clarification or to provide needed group structure, the check-in period can be kept brief yet meaningful. The therapist is able to focus on each person's response and can then revisit individual client issues and can identify the themes that the clients mention. This process becomes much more difficult if the therapist allows tangential conversations or begins to address personal issues during this initial phase of group.

We also find that groups have less norm-related issues (Brown, 1991) if the therapist closely adheres to the group structure and directs clients to save personal issues until the working phase of the group session. However, this is effective only as long as the therapist remembers these issues and follows up by revisiting them as agreed. Solution-focused therapists do not abandon basic group skills such as setting and enforcing group norms. The groups are open-ended, and the group dynamics fluctuate accordingly. However, once clients see that the therapist is truly interested in listening to them and in knowing what is important to them, many of the traditional group-related problems cease to exist.

2. Group leader silently identifies common themes from group answers and finds a broader theme that includes all the common themes. This is done through silently asking self questions that assist the therapist in hearing what is important to all of the clients.

As the clients answer the introduction question, the therapist is listening carefully to hear what is important to each client that day. Through this process of hearing what is important to the individuals the group theme emerges. The "theme" can best be understood as a very broad content area that all of the clients in the group are saying is important to them. The theme will always be unique to each group due to the uniqueness of each client and their lives each day. The following questions are useful for therapists to ask themselves while listening to each group member:

- What is the client telling me is most important today?
- Do I really understand how this answer touches on what is really important to the client? (If not, clarification questions are needed.)
- Am I assuming that I understand what is really important based on previous conversations with this or other clients, or did the client really tell me? (If you are assuming, check it out with the client.)
- What similarities exist between what is most important to this client and what previous clients have mentioned is most important to them?

- What does this tell me about what this client wants to be different?
- What is the meaning behind the words? (Do the adjectives that the client is using give clues to the emotion or meaning behind the words?)

The following excerpt illustrates this process:

Joe was referred for services after a methamphetamine lab was discovered in his home and his children were removed from his care due to the inherent danger. Joe also has an extensive history of cocaine use.

THERAPIST: Joe, what is one thing you have done since last time you were here to help you get closer to where you want to be?

JOE: I have been attending classes and doing what my caseworker is requiring of me. I applied for a job.

THERAPIST: And how do these things help get you closer to where you want to be?

JOE: Then my kids can come home and we can put this whole mess behind us.

THERAPIST: (Mentally: While Joe is doing what he needs to do, what is most important to Joe is getting through this crisis with social services to have his kids home.)

THERAPIST: Sara, how about you? What is one thing that you have done since last time you were here to help you get closer to where you want to be?

SARA: Well, it's hard to say. My grandmother died last Sunday, and that made it hard to follow through with my plans.

THERAPIST: I'm so sorry to hear that. What did you do to cope with that loss?

SARA: I hung around my family and tried to stay busy. That seemed to help a lot. I have a really good family. It's been a very hard week.

THERAPIST: It sounds like you did exactly what you needed to do in order to get through this. Let's come back to this once we are finished with check-in. Would that be OK with you?

SARA: Yeah. That would be fine.

THERAPIST: (Mentally: While the support of family and structure seems to be helpful, what is most important to Sara is getting through this crisis of her grandmother dying.)

THERAPIST: Vickie, how about you?

Vickie was referred for services by the mental health center. She has been diagnosed with bipolar disorder, and her marijuana and methamphetamine use is interfering with her psychotropic medication.

VICKIE: Well, my house flooded. It's been a real mess!

THERAPIST: Wow! That doesn't sound fun. So, how did you get through that?

VICKIE: I called my brother, and he helped me clean up.

THERAPIST: And how did cleaning up all the water help you get closer to what's important to you?

VICKIE: I have always gotten overwhelmed with stuff like that before. I want to be able to deal with problems as they come.

THERAPIST: (Mentally: What is most important to Vickie is her ability to get through the unexpected. Although the support of Vickie's brother was important, the most meaningful factor was her ability to get through the situation.)

THERAPIST: Max?

Max was referred for services by his probation officer. Max was arrested for growing marijuana in his backyard. Cocaine was also discovered in his home by the police, and Max provided several urine samples to his probation officer that tested positive for cocaine.

MAX: Nothing really. I'm just here because the court is making me come.

THERAPIST: What specifically have you done that has been helpful?

MAX: I have court on Thursday, so I called my attorney to get a plan together. I'm tired of all this legal stuff, and I just want it to be over.

THERAPIST: (Mentally: While Max is also doing just what he needs to do, important to him is getting through a pending court date and through his legal problems.)

THERAPIST: I don't think I've met you yet. And you are?

SUSAN: I'm Susan. I'm here because social services is making me come. I guess what I've done is I have been looking into getting a divorce. I've been going back and forth on this thing, but I know it needs to happen.

Susan was referred by social services after a domestic violence incident in which alcohol was involved. Although she and her husband separated, she maintained contact with him. Her caseworker had expressed concern about the safety of the home environment due to the continued relationship and resulting violence when they are together.

THERAPIST: So you have made the decision and now are looking to make it final?

SUSAN: Yeah. It's been doomed for a while. We have been separated for three years. I need to move on, make it legal and all.

THERAPIST: (Mentally: What is most important to Susan is getting through the formality of divorce. She has made the decision, yet implementing it seems to be a hurdle.)

Accurately hearing what is most important to each client and then skillfully developing a group theme are essential in order to assist the group to move to the working phase. Focusing on a theme ensures that the conversation will be meaningful and will promote change for each client due to the theme's balance of individuality and inclusiveness.

It is important to highlight the distinction between a topic and a theme. Topics often lead to problem talk. Themes are instrumental in setting the stage for solution talk. Clients often mention topics when they are asked what they would like to discuss in the group. The therapist should broaden the topic(s) into a theme. Topics are narrow and tend to limit conversation; themes are broad and more inclusive. Topics are similar to the small, colored pieces of tile in a mosaic. They are necessary to create the larger picture. Each unique combination of tiles creates a different picture or theme.

When one focuses on the individual colored tiles, one misses the beauty of the work of art. When topics become the focus of group conversation, some clients will feel excluded because they cannot directly relate to the conversation. This often results in the therapist trying to fit these outlying clients into the topic, rather than suggesting a theme that encompasses all the group members. Other times clients readily participate and relate to the topic being discussed, although this may not translate into any meaningful change if the topic is not part of the clients' specific goals.

Therapists often struggle with the concept of identifying themes since we have been trained to focus much more narrowly. For example, the group members in our excerpt mentioned many potential topics:

- Grief and loss (Sara, Joe, Susan)
- Support (Sara and Vickie)
- Family (Sara, Vickie, Joe)
- Legal issues (Joe, Max, Susan)
- Change (Susan, Sara)
- Loss of control (Max and Vickie)

Focusing on any of these topics would miss the broader concept (theme) that each of them was implicitly saying was most important: mastering the "bumps in the road." This broader theme is inclusive of the more narrow concepts, such as death/dying, change, disappointment, coping, traumatic events, while remaining respectful that some of the group members' "bumps" are much larger than others. This theme is inclusive of every group member and allows all of the clients in the room to personally relate this theme to their own current journeys.

3. Group leader reflects (aloud) similarities among group members' responses, summarizing common themes until all are included, and then suggests one broad, inclusive theme.

The third part of the map is to reflect back the theme and tabled issues that the therapist heard during the check-in period. Following is an example of how the therapist reflects group themes back to the group:

> I heard so much as all of you spoke. Several of you mentioned dealing with loss (Sara with the death of her grandmother, Joe with his kids being placed in foster care, and Susan with a potential divorce). I also heard people dealing with how to cope

with issues that are out of your control (Max with his pending court date and Vickie with her house flooding). Those are all really big issues. What comes to mind is that all of you are on your own journey, yet you have encountered these bumps in the road. Some of the bumps are just annoying; others are very large and very difficult to get around.

This theme provides the necessary bridge to help the clients as a group get to the other side of the problem. Without this, the group work will become individualized, slow paced, and at times even lethargic. The therapist can use verbal "connectors" throughout this process to remind the clients how their initial statements are part of the theme, therefore connecting them personally to the solution talk during the working phase of the group.

The connectors are easily seen in our example when the therapist verbally linked Sara, Joe, and Susan as having the similarity of dealing with loss, and again through linking Max and Vickie as coping with events that are out of their control. An important element in the use of connectors is reminding the group what the individual clients said that resulted in the therapist's logic in linking the clients' stories together. Without this, clients may become resistant and believe that the therapist is making assumptions about them. By watching for nonverbal clues (e.g., head nods, smiles) the therapist is assured that the linkages are correct and client based. If these clues are not present, the therapist may be venturing ahead of the clients and the clients may not understand how they personally fit into the theme. Slowing down and using the client's language in the verbal connections usually remedies this problem and ensures that the clients and therapist are working concurrently.

The development of a clear group theme in combination with the skillful use of connectors allows the therapist to assist group members in creating a productive environment in which they can work toward their individual miracles while maintaining a cohesive group setting. The process could be compared to that of threading a needle with multistrand yarn in order to begin creating the desired pattern. Imagine each client conversation as a strand of the yarn. The therapist must skillfully combine these conversations in a meaningful fashion and then take them (as one) to the other side of the problem.

The threading of the needle is completed relatively quickly in order to move on to the important work of sewing. In order to ensure that all of the strands of yarn are threaded through the needle, the seamstress may gently twist the end to make it one piece so that it can easily pass through the eye of the needle to the other side.

Without this, the yarn would fray and only part of it would pass through the eye of the needle, negatively impacting the quality of the work. Once the yarn is on the other side of the needle, the work of sewing can begin. Similarly, all of the clients must see strong connections among what is important to them as individuals in order to move as one to a place where they can explore a life in which their presenting problems are resolved.

The ability to identify themes takes time, for the therapist must perfect the skill of turning off the internal "chatter" that is commonly occurring in a novice solution-focused therapist's head. Therapists have told me (TP) that as they were learning this approach, they worked so hard to remember the basic map that they had difficulty hearing the clients' responses. They often stated that they were so intent on trying to remember the next part of the map or determining how to interrupt problem talk without appearing rude that they missed what the clients stated was most important to them.

Many times therapists have processed what happened in a group session and expressed frustration regarding the lack of an identified theme. The therapists were unable to assist the clients to get to the other side of the problem and so the time felt wasted. As I listened to them talk, however, the theme was clear. The therapists reported all of the elements that were present during the group that are necessary to discover the theme.

When I reflected the theme back to the therapists, they expressed disappointment in themselves that the theme was in front of them the entire time and yet remained undetected. They had become so lost in their own internal chatter (e.g., "What do I do now? How do I make that solution focused? I'm sure that is not relevant. How do I interrupt? Is that a topic or a theme?") that they became distracted by the individual tiles of the mosaic, keeping the larger image from appearing to them.

The fourth part of the map is to invite the clients to participate in deciding what would be most helpful to address in the group setting, thereby ensuring that the therapist has included what is most important to each group member.

4. Group leader asks group's permission for the group to address the theme identified in step three unless there is another (emergency) issue that needs to be addressed.

Although the therapist has already skillfully woven any individual crisis into the group theme, it is important to ask permission from the group members before proceeding. Without this important step, the clients may not clearly understand how an issue that is very important to them is a distinct part in the journey upon which the group is about to embark. The answer to this question lets the therapist know if stronger connectors need to be made between individual issues and the identified theme to ensure that everyone is clearly included. The following dialogue demonstrates how this is done:

THERAPIST: Given what everyone mentioned, what would be most helpful for us to talk about today?

VICKIE: I think we should talk about Sara's grandmother dying. That is something that we have all gone through or will at some time.

THERAPIST: All right. That is a very important topic. Sara is going through a very painful type of loss, the kind caused by death. As I listened to all of you, I was struck that each of you mentioned that you are struggling with some type of loss. Death is the most obvious type, yet Joe has lost his kids for a while, Max has lost his freedom, and Susan has lost her marriage. Vickie, even you lost the comfort of a dry, predictable home for a while there.

In this example, Vickie was voicing a need to make a stronger connection to Sara. Although the therapist had already mentioned how Sara connected into the theme of "bumps in the road," Vickie was voicing a need to strengthen the concept of "loss" as a connector to more solidly connect Sara. The theme does not change, yet the therapist will now remember the importance of using more clear connectors to demonstrate how Sara's significant loss connects with the work at hand.

In our example, the group ensured that the therapist could directly address Sara's recent loss in the group setting through the use of strong connectors. On occasion, the group will not make such a direct offer of this kind. Even in these circumstances, the client's issue will still be incorporated into the group theme, thereby addressing the issue during the group setting. However, should the therapist determine that the personal issue was not adequately addressed in the group setting, it is important to directly address the issue in an individual setting immediately following the group session. Group members typically address personal issues that they have heard other members mention, but it is important to respect that not all individual issues are best addressed directly in the group setting.

By allowing the group members to decide what the group conversation should address, the therapist avoids many of the power struggles and problems that are inherent in more traditional groups. Although groups that follow this structure typically address the same issues that more traditional groups address, the clients are more invested. For example, the clients made the decision to talk about grief and loss instead of having it forced upon them by a preset group agenda. If individual clients' issues are not directly addressed in the group, the clients are assured that the therapist will address them individually prior to leaving.

Regardless of what the group members decide would be helpful for them to discuss during the group time, the therapist's role is to get the group to the other side of the problem. This process differentiates a solution-focused group from that of a problem-solving group. Any topic and any issue that a client mentions can be easily incorporated into the group theme, allowing it to be discussed from a place in which the problem does not exist. This is the fifth part of the group session map.

5. Ask the miracle question (or similar future-oriented question) based on the theme identified in step three.

In this step we return to the all-important concept of "future focus." The therapist's ultimate goal is to lead the clients to a place in the future from where they can look back to gain the wisdom that this future place holds. We term this place where the problem no longer exists the "other side." Since the theme stems from what is important to the clients today, there is always a strong connection to each client's personal miracle or long-term goals. We have found that the group theme is most often closely related to an ability, trait, or quality that the clients desire to obtain or improve. By addressing the theme in the group setting, each client is actually working on a part of his or her personal miracle; however, we do not make that direct connection until step eleven. The working phase of the group begins once all of the clients are in this future place looking back and discussing the group theme. The following excerpt illustrates how this is done:

THERAPIST: Let me ask you all this: Imagine that we are all meeting as a group for a reunion. It is one year from today, and each of you has somehow gotten to a place in which your loss (your grandmother, your freedom, or whatever bump in the road you are going through right now) has become a part of who you are. You have been changed forever, yet you have been able to become a better person because of your loss. What would you be telling us about how you are different now, one year later?

The therapist has broadened the topic of Sara's grandmother's death (the topic that Vickie wanted to discuss) back into the theme (bumps in the road) that includes everyone, and then invited each client to explore life one year later. The therapist has used connectors (verbal statements that remind the clients of their previous statement and how they connect to the larger theme) to ensure that individual clients see themselves personally in the discussion—"your grandmother, your freedom, or whatever bump in the road you are going through right now . . ." The question provides a bridge to the future and acknowledges the depth of the bumps in the road that the clients have mentioned, and connects them to the topic that they stated would be helpful to discuss. At the same time, the therapist has implied that these losses and bumps will be explored from a future focus—a focus from which the grief is resolved.

This future focus is maintained through persistent, gentle interruption when clients stray into the more familiar problem-focused world. Clients do not return to problem-focused talk because they find it more helpful but because it is their primary language. These gentle interruptions by the therapist create a tight verbal structure that keeps the clients focused on the future place. As clients become familiar with this type of conversation, they seldom return to address the problem from a problem-solving stance. Clients find that addressing issues from this future-focused stance is empowering, rejuvenating, and extremely effective. The following illustrates how the therapist gently maintains the future focus:

SARA: It's just so hard! I really loved my grandmother [bursting into tears]!

THERAPIST: Hold on a minute [said gently, yet interrupting the client's verbal direction]. I can see how important your grandmother was in your life and how much she has impacted you. What I'm curious about is as we are looking back, from this reunion, what piece of your grandmother lives on in your heart?

This gentle interaction demonstrates the therapist's empathy for the client's loss while inviting her to hold on to a cherished part of her grandmother. This reminds the client that her grandmother can be with her in this future place, thereby encouraging the client to think differently, to see both the pain and the possibility as part of her reality.

It is powerful to watch clients smile and laugh through their tears as they talk about the amazing lessons that they have learned from a deceased relative or other traumatic loss. Once the working phase is shifted to the place in which the problem no longer exists, the clients have the energy and excitement to move forward even when addressing heavy and painful issues. Clients gain hope that change is possible and gain a vision of where they hope to go. Even the most skeptical client is often moved by this process and begins to participate.

6. Get as many details as possible about the miracle question (or similar question asked in step five).

As the therapist works to clarify what will be different for each client once the presenting problems are resolved, there is a risk of the work becoming individualized. Although there are some positive aspects of this, the negative aspects often outweigh them. The pacing often slows as clients politely wait their turn. Others become bored, not understanding the relevance of the conversation to them. In order to prevent this, we have found it most helpful to ask our questions to specific subgroups (the subgroups are based upon the linkages discussed in step three). This results in increased energy and encourages clients to be attentive during conversations that may not directly apply to them. The following illustrates how this is accomplished:

THERAPIST: Max and Vickie, you both mentioned having to deal with situations that are out of your control. I'm wondering what you will be telling us at the one-year reunion about how you are different?

MAX: Well . . .

VICKIE: I think . . . [both accidentally interrupting each other in eagerness to answer the question]

MAX: Go ahead [obviously still thinking about how the question applies to him].

VICKIE: OK. Thanks. I think I would be saying that I've learned how to go with the flow.

MAX: Maybe not take stuff for granted anymore.

VICKIE: Yeah! That's it [looking at Max and nodding enthusiastically]! I think I would be more easygoing and more accepting when problems do come up.

THERAPIST: Susan, you are nodding. What are you thinking?

SUSAN: Yeah! I agree with Max and Vickie. I will also be more easygoing, and I really can relate to not taking things for granted. I think that was part of my problem.

THERAPIST: I saw other people nodding as Susan was talking about not taking things for granted. What will you be telling me at this reunion about this?

JOE: [Quickly jumping in] I will be saying how much I am enjoying my kids and savoring every minute I have with them. I will be taking them to the park and enjoying playing and laughing together.

THERAPIST: How about those of you who have been dealing with a pretty significant loss. Sara? Susan? Joe? What will be different there?

SARA: I will be telling you that I am more patient. My grandmother was a very patient woman. I always admired that. I notice that I am much happier when I can go with the flow.

THERAPIST: That sounds very similar to what Max and Vickie were saying about being easygoing.

SARA: Exactly [Max and Vickie nodding simultaneously]!

This demonstrates the energy that is generated as the therapist notices similarities and nonverbal clues, and invites clients to simultaneously think about and discuss how life will be in this future place. By listening to other group members, ideas are sparked. There is a sense of camaraderie as the clients explore their individual futures.

7. Listen for exceptions, and follow up by getting as many details as possible. If no exceptions are identified, move on to next step.

As the clients explore how life will be, they often drop clues that some of these aspects are already part of their reality. The therapist should be attentive to this and assist the clients in exploring how they were able to make those positive changes. The following dialogue illustrates this:

THERAPIST: Sara, you mentioned that you are much happier when you are able to go with the flow. What are those times like?

SARA: I am just more relaxed. When something does go wrong, I am able to say, "Oh well" and just move on. It doesn't seem like that big of a deal even when I'm really disappointed that it went wrong.

THERAPIST: How are you able to do that?

SARA: Well, I don't know. Sometimes it just happens.

THERAPIST: Hmm. I can't help but wonder what's different about those times.

MAX: I think I'm able to be more easygoing when I have done what I can, and when I can trust that if something goes wrong there wasn't anything I could have done to prevent it.

VICKIE: Yeah, I've noticed that too. Like when my house flooded. It wasn't my fault. It had rained really hard, and several houses got flooded. I was able to just call my brother and feel confident that I had done my best.

THERAPIST: Wow! So several of you have discovered times when you are able to be more easygoing.

By exploring Susan's statement about times in which she was able to go with the flow, two other clients were able to identify something that they have done in the past that made it easier for them to be easygoing. This results in a synergistic effect within the group, as individual members explore exceptions while others listen to the wisdom they discover.

8. Ask scaling question to determine clients' current level of progress toward their goals.

Once clients have identified how their lives will be different in this future place, it is important to assist them in determining how much of this desired ability, trait, or quality they currently have. In our example, the therapist would want to explore the clients' current ability to successfully navigate the bumps in the road. The question might be asked as follows:

> On a scale of one to ten (ten is that you are handling life's difficulties just how you would want to handle them, and one is the opposite), where would you put yourself today?

This allows clients to explore times in which their ability to handle life's difficulties is just a little better and to discover the small adjustments that have made a difference. By doing this in a group setting, clients are able to learn from one another and generate excitement and hope in the possibility of change. Clients who are higher on the scale frequently provide hope to group members who are struggling.

9. Referring to previous scaling question, find out what the clients have done to reach and maintain current level of progress.

Solution-focused therapy stresses the importance of exploring how clients have achieved their successes. Without this important step, clients run the risk of believing that change was circumstantial and, therefore, not able to be re-created. The therapist's role is to empower the clients to take responsibility for the changes. This brings the behaviors and positive consequences under their control. The following conversation illustrates this point:

THERAPIST: Sara, you mentioned that you are a three on our scale. What have you been doing that has resulted in you being so high even though you have had such a difficult week?

SARA: Well, I didn't use drugs, and I have just been doing what I have to do.

THERAPIST: How did you do that despite all the stress?

SARA: Well, I just can't go back to using drugs. I've come too far.

THERAPIST: Many people aren't as strong as that. How did you remember how important staying clean was during this difficult time?

SARA: Well, I stayed busy, and I hung around my family. They don't use drugs or alcohol, so I think that really helped since it wasn't there to tempt me.

THERAPIST: It sounds like you made some really helpful decisions.

SARA: Yeah. I guess I did.

10. Find out where on the scale (step eight) the clients think others (probation officer, caseworker, children, spouse or partner, pets, employer, etc.) in their lives would rate them and what the clients are doing that would cause this rating.

Due to the systemic underpinnings of this approach, the perspective of others in the clients' lives is important to consider. Solution-focused therapy can initially mistakenly appear to be superficial and unrealistic to the untrained eye due to its talk of miracles and encouragement of clients to explore how they would like life to be. Critics of this approach have said that drug addicts will always want to have a perfect life and still use drugs. Although we have encountered occasional clients who have said that they would like this to be possible, when we ask these clients what their referral source would say, they are quick to say that this is not possible or not worth exploring. We find that although clients may playfully express a desire for the unrealistic (similar to the concept of wanting to have your cake and eat it too), they are eager to explore a realistic life without the problem. By using relational questions to explore how important people (and even family pets or infants, imagining they could speak) in the clients' lives would rate their progress, the therapeutic conversation becomes rich and vivid as clients bring up subject matter that they would not have otherwise explored. The following excerpt illustrates this:

THERAPIST: Max, you mentioned that you are an eight in your ability to deal with the bumps in the road. I'm curious where your probation officer would say you are on that same scale.

MAX: Well, I doubt he would say I was that high. I think he would say I was about a five.

THERAPIST: Really. What is it that you know about yourself that he hasn't learned about you yet?

MAX: I know that I have changed, and that I won't go back to using cocaine when things get tough. I don't think he believes me on that yet.

THERAPIST: What lets you know that the drugs are behind you and that you are no longer at risk of going back during the difficult times?

MAX: It's just not worth it. I don't hang out with the friends I used to, and I have other things to do, like play basketball.

THERAPIST: What difference will it make for your probation officer when he sees these things about you?

MAX: He will probably back off and give me a little more freedom.

This case is typical of what we see. Clients often mention that significant others in their lives are lower on the scale, and exploring what the client knows that these other people do not yet know is helpful in seeing a broader perspective. The next step ties the work that was done in the group setting directly to the client's individual goals or miracle.

11. Ask group members what role this conversation (steps one through ten) regarding the group theme plays in working toward their miracles. (How was this conversation helpful in getting closer to the miracle?)

During the group conversation, clients frequently make reference to their miracle or larger goal. Clients are often able to make a clear connection as to how their progress on the identified theme (navigating the bumps in the road in this example) will make a significantly positive impact on their larger goal. Sometimes the therapist needs to solidify the connection to ensure that all group members see the group conversation as beneficial to them personally. The following dialogue demonstrates how this can be done:

THERAPIST: Joe, you have been talking about how your priorities will have shifted one year from now and how you will have learned the importance of enjoying your children when they are around rather than being annoyed by them. You have even mentioned that you are a five on our scale on achieving this. I remember that you said earlier that your goal is to learn to control your cravings for cocaine. I am curious how your newfound enjoyment of your children and changed priorities will help you accomplish this goal.

JOE: Well, keeping my kids will be the most important thing to me. I can't imagine life without them. I didn't feel that way when I was using. When I am enjoying my children and remembering how important they really are to me, I just don't have cravings. I guess I never realized that I never had cravings when my kids and I were having a good time together.

THERAPIST: So, one year from now, how are you remembering how important your children are to you and that you never want to jeopardize your time together?

JOE: By putting family time first, and not spending time with people who I know aren't good for me. The cravings don't come up as much when I do that, and when they do I don't have the drugs around like when I'm around my using buddies. I'm already noticing that I don't like spending time with those people. It's more fun to be with my kids. Things are changing already!

In addition to ensuring that clients make a clear connection between the group conversation and their personal miracles, we find it useful to ask the group members how the group was helpful for them. This also helps to solidify the work that the clients have done by challenging them to articulate the benefits of the group conversation. Last, it helps to give objective feedback to the therapist about what he or she did that was beneficial and to identify any unresolved issues that need to be addressed prior to ending group or on an individual basis after the group session has ended.

12. Based on their responses to questions one through eleven, invite the clients to assign themselves homework.

In order to encourage clients to actively work toward their goals between sessions, we ask the group members to identify one task that they will commit to doing before the next time they are scheduled to return to the agency which will help them to achieve their goal. This also helps them to break up their larger goal into small, manageable steps. Many times the clients' self-assigned homework follows directly from the group discussion, and other times the connection is not as apparent. The clients then write a brief summary of how the group has been helpful and what they have assigned as homework (see Figure 3.1 for a sample form). This gives the client some time to reflect upon the session and the next step, as well as gives a written record in the client's own writing of his or her progress. The therapist keeps these as documentation of the process to allow for future tracking of client information for referral sources or external auditors (see Chapter 7 for further discussion of integrating with problem-focused agencies). The group leader then asks all of the clients to share with the group what has been helpful about the group and what they have given themselves for homework.

THERAPIST: Sara, let's start with you. How has this been helpful today?

SARA: It made me realize that I really did a lot and did continue to work on what I needed to even though my grandmother died. I hadn't realized that before.

THERAPIST: Great! What did you write down for your homework?

SARA: I put that I would call my sister for support and that I would go to my parenting class.

Giving clients compliments and therapeutic messages are common interventions in solution-focused therapy. This is the final part of the skeleton.

13. Give group members feedback.

While the clients are writing down their session summaries and homework, the therapist leaves the room to develop the feedback. Steve de Shazer (1985) stresses the importance of leaving the room to develop the feedback since the therapist's absence results in the clients' wonderment of what the therapist will say upon return; it fosters the "building of a 'response attentiveness'" (p. 91). Compliments are frequently used as the beginning of an end-of-session message. Steve de Shazer (1985) describes their purpose in this context as to "build a

JEFFERSON COUNTY DEPARTMENT OF HEALTH AND ENVIRONMENT
SACP GROUP NOTES

DATE: ____________ **CLIENT SIGNATURE:** ________________________

CLIENT NOTES:

1. What did you do between now and last time you came here to work on what is important to you?____

____

2. What will you need to do to reach your goal and to get what you want from coming to SACP?____

____

3. What are you willing to do between now and next time you come to SACP to work toward getting what you want?______________________________

____

____

COUNSELOR NOTES:

____

____

____

____

____

____

GROUP: ________________________ DATE & TIME: ______________

CLIENT NAME: ____________________ CLIENT #: __________________

Progress Toward Treatment Plan: 1 2 3 4 5 6 7 8 9 10

Does a new treatment plan need to be created? Y N

COUNSELOR SIGNATURE: ______________________________________

FIGURE 3.1. Sample Group Note Form

'yes set' that helps to get the client into a frame of mind to accept something new—the therapeutic task or directive" (p. 91).[1]

Compliments are often associated with praise (e.g., "You did a good job speaking up in group today") and as such risk being misused as a behavioral technique to reinforce group behaviors that are desired by the therapist. They can also be confused with strength based interventions in which the therapist uses compliments to shape the client's behavior by emphasizing those behaviors that the therapist has identified as useful for the client. We try to refrain from both of these uses.

Some clients associate "compliments" with "criticism." This connection results in some clients believing that the therapist withheld the negative comments, thereby invalidating the compliments. Because of this, we find it helpful to refer to the compliments as "feedback" when presenting them to the clients. This assures the clients that the therapists have given all of their thoughts and opinions about the clients' work and not just the positive ones. Last, we find this to be more inclusive and accurate, for this step also includes any therapeutic messages that the therapist finds appropriate.

The most effective compliments focus on what the clients are doing outside of group that is useful in working toward their miracle, and should reflect a direct statement about a strength or skill that the client has identified as useful. Compliments can be directed to the group as a whole or to individual clients. Some examples follow:

- "I'm so impressed by your awareness of how your daughter feels."
- "I'm struck by how hard you have worked to make sure your home is safe for your children."
- "I'm very impressed by your ability to hear your mom's concerns and let her know how much you care."
- "I'm impressed by your wisdom in knowing what you needed to do when your son ran away."
- "I'm struck by your wisdom in knowing when you need to ask for help and whom you can trust."
- "I'm very impressed by how much all of you love your children."

Therapeutic messages or suggestions leave the client pondering new possibilities. The most effective therapeutic messages often integrate wisdom, ideas, or answers that the clients themselves stated, which they may not have heard themselves say. The message should stem from the clients' statements and not be an expert-driven intervention. It is easy for the therapist to view this time as an opportunity to slip in a quick word of advice, particularly if a client states that advice would be helpful; however, solution-focused therapists typically refrain from giving advice. Instead, these situations are wonderful opportunities to gently remind the clients of the advice that they gave themselves during the group time or to highlight sources of wisdom the clients have identified in their own lives. Some examples of this are as follows:

- "I'm curious about what advice you will give others about problems such as these when you are all older and wiser."
- "Pay attention to those moments when you are a three on this scale. I am very curious about how you got there."
- "I wonder what your children will notice when you are one step higher on the scale."
- "Pay attention to what others notice when you are a six on that scale."

A well-crafted therapeutic compliment integrates this therapeutic message into the compliment itself. Of course this requires that the therapist listen to what the client has already described as being essential to the client's miracle. (The clients typically do not consistently recognize the connection of specific strengths or skills to their miracle, even though they were the ones who made the original connection.)

Some examples of therapeutic compliments follow:

- "Sam, I'm struck by your wisdom when you stated that life is a journey. I wonder what path you will choose to get where you are hoping to go and how you will know you made the right decision."
- "I'm very impressed by your awareness of how important you are to your children and how much you impact their lives. I wonder what they will learn from how you get through this tough time."

In our example, the therapeutic message might be as follows:

> I'm really struck by your wisdom in knowing that loss is often a part of the journey of life and, as you have all discovered, bumps in the road often litter the path. I'm impressed that you have all already discovered that an important part of success is learning to skillfully navigate these bumps and to become wiser from the process.

This message gently compliments the clients as a group for their wisdom and skills that they discovered during the group process. In addition, it suggests that problems are to be expected, yet clients have the choice to learn from these problems and to grow as a result of them.

When a therapeutic compliment is accurate, the clients will indicate this through body language (e.g., nodding, smiling, relaxing into the chair) and often express relief that the therapist has heard how hard they have worked or what was most important. Clients often report during future sessions that they continued to think about the statement that the therapist made and that it continued to hold deep meaning for them.

THE IMPORTANCE OF COTHERAPY IN GROUPS

We have found that utilizing the time and resources to have each group led by two therapists is a worthwhile investment, as it allows an extra set of ears to hear the clients, and it provides more perspective when discussing the process after group to learn from the experience. When clinical or norm-related problems do arise in the group setting, they can be resolved more quickly, for the group therapist is not alone in understanding and applying these concepts.

Other agency supervisors have often asked how we can afford the luxury of cotherapists. I have often wondered how we could afford not to invest the time and resources. Solution-focused group work is extremely energizing, and it often provides the needed reminder to the therapists of why they work so hard. The field of substance abuse treatment can be draining and unrewarding due to high client relapse, low pay, problem-focused external regulations, and the daunting amount of required paperwork. Using cotherapists not only provides more objectivity for the clients and ensures better quality of care, but it decreases therapist burnout and turnover and reminds us all that clinical work is the heart of the agency.

SUMMARY

Solution-focused therapy has traditionally been applied in individual and family settings, yet the majority of substance abuse treatment is done in a group setting. Groups provide support and a sense of not being alone that is often lacking in individual settings. This allows the group therapist to skillfully assist the group members, as a whole, to get to a place where the problem is resolved. Relational and scaling questions are instrumental in ensuring that the clients are including the opinions of those who are influential in their lives. The individual and group skeletons share many essential elements, and they provide session road maps for the therapist to ensure purposefulness in the interventions, and to provide direction when needed. This allows the therapists to listen and hear the clients' desired destinations. Through this purposeful listening the therapist becomes the tour guide on this incredible journey to a place in which the problem is resolved. Learning the subtleties of applying solution-focused therapy in the group setting can be compared to learning to drive a manual transmission automobile. There are many things to remember: when to shift, when to press the accelerator, when to press the clutch, which gear is which. Although the learning process can be arduous, ability improves with time and practice.

Chapter 4

Many Miracles: Adaptations and Applications of the Miracle Question

All change is a miracle to contemplate; but it is a miracle which is taking place every instant.

Henry David Thoreau

As we discussed in the first chapter of this book ("The Solution-Focused Basics"), focusing on a "problem that is solved rather than a problem that needs to be solved" (Berg, 1994, p. 98) is at the core of the solution-focused approach. The miracle question is key to empowering the client to envision the problem from this perspective. This chapter will explore the principles behind the miracle question and offer additional applications of the future focus.

BEWARE OF THE PERILS OF PROBLEM SOLVING

Many times during the transition to becoming solution focused it was (and continues to be) tempting for our team to revert to the comfort and familiarity of our old problem-focused model. We soon discovered that the therapists inevitably became stuck whenever they or the client began to problem solve in an attempt to find solutions. When the problem solving was initiated by the therapist, power struggles and therapist frustration often resulted.

When initiated by the client, the therapist or other group members often joined in the problem solving, resulting once again in power struggles and mutual frustration. In addition there were other disadvantages to the problem-solving approach. Problem solving seldom invites creativity, and it is often dependent on the client's current view of the unsolved problem. In fact, it typically results in the client offering explanations of all of the past attempts to problem solve that have failed, thereby further demoralizing the client.

How Frustration Led to Creativity

In the process of learning solution-focused therapy, the therapists on our team frequently became stuck. They struggled when clients did not respond to the miracle question in the expected way, or when clients stated that they wanted the therapist to help them obtain seemingly unobtainable goals (e.g., win the lottery, become taller, or keep custody of their children despite pending parental rights termination). Sometimes the clients did not want to participate in the group discussion despite an external mandate. Other times clients would give sarcastic answers to the therapists' queries.

Over time, a norm was established for the therapists to ask for guidance during the group break period whenever this was needed. This became a time for quick consultation and a time in which many spontaneous interventions were created.

Some were effective and some were not; yet, despite the outcome, staff members gained a greater understanding of the basic elements of the miracle question and the underlying principles that formed the foundation of the interventions that they tried. The therapists began to see their apparent failures and frustrations as opportunities to deepen their knowledge and skills. This was the therapists' first experimentation with the artistic qualities of this approach.

In an attempt to prevent these problems, the interventions that I suggested to the therapists were based on the basic elements of the miracle question. This resulted in the group conversation spontaneously shifting away from problem solving to the other side of the problem where the group members and therapists could mutually explore a solved problem. The therapists were initially amazed at the results of the interventions. However, similar to apprentice magicians, they had to understand the underpinnings of the interventions before they could effectively replicate them or create their own.

PRINCIPLES BEHIND THE MIRACLE QUESTION

Before describing some of the interventions that were created during this time period, a review of the basic elements of the miracle question might be useful. The miracle question came into being by happenstance. Insoo Kim Berg first experimented with this intervention at the suggestion of her client, who stated, "Maybe only a miracle will help" (DeJong and Berg, 1998, p. 77). Berg and her colleagues quickly discovered the power of using this concept to invite clients to imagine how life will be once the problem is solved. Steve de Shazer (1988) originally worded the miracle questions as follows:

> Suppose that one night, while you were asleep, there was a miracle and this problem was solved. How would you know? What would be different? How will your husband know without your saying a word to him about it? (p. 5)

Other authors describe this intervention using similar wording. As mentioned in Chapter 1, Peter DeJong and Insoo Kim Berg (1998) recommend the following:

> Now, I want to ask you a strange question. Suppose that while you are sleeping tonight and the entire house is quiet, a miracle happens. The miracle is that the problem which brought you here is solved. However, because you are sleeping, you don't know that the miracle has happened. So, when you wake up tomorrow morning, what will be different that will tell you a miracle has happened and the problem which brought you here is solved? (pp. 77-78)

Five crucial elements compose the miracle question. If one of these elements is missing, the question loses some of its effectiveness. The first element is the concept of a change occurring that is of some significance to the client and that would not occur naturally. This element is captured in the wording, "a miracle happens." This invites the notion that a previously unattainable change is possible, and that the change will be meaningful to the client in some way. People rarely describe an event as a "miracle" unless it was originally perceived as possessing value and is otherwise unattainable. *The*

American Heritage College Dictionary (1993) defines the word miracle as "one that excites admiring awe" (p. 870).

The second element is a basic understanding of what the miracle is. The miracle is most often defined in the literature as "the problem that brought you here is solved." This wording is very effective for clients who are clear as to why they are seeking services. These clients are often seeking some trait or skills that they currently view themselves as lacking (e.g., ability to parent effectively, ability to be happy in a relationship, ability to remain substance free when faced with temptations). Working with clients who are initially externally motivated for services is more challenging. These clients often state that they do not need anything to change and that they are here only because they must be in order to satisfy the referral source. Additional questioning in order to uncover the client's desired miracle is often effective in these circumstances. Without this questioning, the client may be confused by the miracle question, and the therapist may become frustrated at the apparent failure of the intervention. Following is an example of the kind of questioning found to be effective in defining a client's miracle:

The client in this case was referred for services by her caseworker after the children were removed from her custody for neglect. The client's two-year-old child was found wandering alone in the neighborhood, and the client was later found to be intoxicated and unaware that her child was missing.

THERAPIST: So, what brought you here today?

CLIENT: I don't know. My caseworker just said I had to come. I guess she sends everyone for alcohol classes when their kids are taken away.

THERAPIST: What do you think she is hoping to see as a result of your coming here?

CLIENT: Nothing. There is nothing to see because I don't have a problem. She just needs to know that I showed up.

THERAPIST: What will be different for you once she learns that you showed up?

CLIENT: Nothing. I just have to complete all this stuff, so I can get my kids back.

THERAPIST: Please forgive me if this sounds like a stupid question, but I am wondering why you are working so hard to get your children back. Many parents wouldn't do this, especially when they don't have a problem.

CLIENT: [Surprised look] I love my kids! I would do anything for them! I can't imagine going on without them in my life! Not doing all this stuff is not an option!

THERAPIST: Does your caseworker know how much you love your children and how committed you are to being a good parent?

CLIENT: No. I get so angry when I talk to her. She just doesn't understand!

THERAPIST: What difference would it make if she knew this about you?

CLIENT: I guess that she might lighten up a little. Then we might be able to talk. It is so hard to calm down and stay focused on what is important when I'm around her.

THERAPIST: Would that be a miracle if you were able to do that and she was able to see how you really feel about your kids?

CLIENT: It sure would!

This interaction demonstrates how a therapist can assist a client in going from an event that is determined by an external force (regaining custody of her children) to a trait that is desired by the client (the ability to control her emotions while dealing with her caseworker). The therapist can now assist the client in focusing on what shape the miracle would take for her:

> Imagine that while you are asleep tonight, a miracle happens. The miracle is that you suddenly have the ability to stay focused on your children and on what is important to you when you interact with your caseworker. However, because you are asleep, you don't know that the miracle has happened. So, when you wake up tomorrow morning, what will be different that will let you know that a miracle has happened and that you have this new ability? What would your caseworker notice about you?

The third element of the miracle question is immediacy. The miracle is described as happening tonight and in a setting that will normally occur. This ensures that there will be naturally occurring environmental cues that the client can later associate with the possibility of immediate change. The client may wake up tomorrow morning and playfully wonder, "Hmm, I wonder if a miracle happened last night?" This powerfully suggests that change can and does happen all of the time, and that the client would be wise to look for small changes in order to detect evidence of possible miracles. This increases the client's vigilance of change. Without the feeling of immediacy, the environmental cues will not be present until a later date. The client may forget to look for differences until the environmental cue is present, thereby missing the smaller day-to-day changes.

The fourth element is that the client is unaware that the miracle has occurred. It is crucial to stress to the clients that they are unaware of the occurrence of the miracle because they were asleep. Without this detail, there is nothing for the client to discover.

This leads directly to the fifth element, which is the importance of encouraging the client to methodically discover the small telltale signs which indicate that the miracle has occurred. This element is often illuminated through therapist questioning such as, "How will you know that a miracle occurred?" or "What will be different that will let you know that this miracle has taken place?" Relational questions are also used to determine the changes that others will notice in the client. Such questions might be, "So what will your wife see that lets her know something is different this morning?" or "What will your cat notice that will let him know something is different with you today?" (Asking relational questions that involve family pets is a very effective way to elicit small changes that other family members would not notice. This is as effective with adults as it is with children.)

The miracle question and the elements contained in it are the foundation of solution-focused therapy. Without these elements, therapists are unlikely to be able to assist their clients in getting to the other side of the problem and are not capturing the essence and power of solution-focused therapy. The result of having a solid understanding of the miracle question and its elements is that the therapist is then able to assist the client in creating a destination that is enticing to the client. The client is then able to work backward to determine what "first steps he needs to take to find solutions and [the miracle] will show him how his life *will* change, thus giving him hope that his life *can* change" (Berg, 1994, p. 100). Steve de Shazer (1994) states, "The 'miracle question' is a way to begin constructing a bridge between therapist and client built around the (future) success of the therapy" (p. 95).

Clients are able to see how seemingly small changes can have tremendous impact on them and those around them. They become energized and excited during this process. Hope is discovered and change is perceived as possible, often for the first time. Clients who initially appeared to be motivated only externally start striving for a miracle that is meaningful and obtainable.

APPLYING THE MIRACLE QUESTION ELEMENTS

There are few substitutes for the miracle question in its original form. In fact, it is often most effective to simply ask the miracle question directly rather than to create alternative interventions. However, there have been occasions when becoming creative has been very helpful. In order to be effective with this type of creativity, therapists must solidly understand the importance and purpose of each element. This is the essence of purposeful spontaneity. Following are just a few of the interventions we have created.

Magic Door

The magic door question is asked as follows:

> Imagine that it is time to leave here today, and you go through the door to go home. However, that door is a magic door, and as you go through it you are given a gift. The gift is that the problem that brought you here is gone [or an alternatively defined miracle as previously discussed]. You are unaware that the door is magic, so you are unaware that this gift was given to you. As you get in your car, or get on the bus to go home, what changes do you notice that let you know that something is different?

This intervention contains all of the elements of the miracle question. It contains the concept of a meaningful change that is perceived as unlikely to occur naturally, a clearly defined gift, the element of immediacy, the lack of knowledge that the gift was given, and the challenge to discover the small changes that will signal that a gift was received. However, this intervention is weaker than the miracle question because the environmental cue is linked to the agency rather than to the client's natural environment. Although a natural reminder is provided each time the client passes through the identified door, the goal of therapy is to get the clients out of therapy and back into their lives.

This intervention can be useful when the miracle question has already been asked and the client or the group perceives the miracle question as being redundant. Sometimes this occurs when the clients are unsure what changes they want and the therapist proceeds with the miracle question prior to exploring what the clients truly desire. The following interaction describes how this might occur:

THERAPIST: So, what brings you here today?

CLIENT: Nothing. My caseworker just said that I need to come. I guess she sends everyone here when their children are taken away.

THERAPIST: I want to ask you a strange question. I want you to imagine that when you are sleeping tonight, a miracle happens. The miracle is that the problem that brought you here is resolved. Yet, since you are asleep, you are not aware that the miracle happened. When you wake up tomorrow morning, what will let you know that the miracle happened and this problem is resolved?

CLIENT: My kids will be home.

THERAPIST: How would you know that?

CLIENT: I would hear them fighting in the next room.

THERAPIST: What difference would that make for you and your kids for them to be home?

CLIENT: We would just go on as normal. We would be a family again.

THERAPIST: What difference would it make for you to be a family again?

CLIENT: I don't know. It would just be normal.

This train of conversation leads to a superficial miracle contingent on the caseworker and the judge returning the children to the parent's custody. Furthermore, it is unlikely that the children will be home tomorrow morning and therefore the miracle is unlikely to occur regardless of what changes the parent makes overnight. It is externally grounded and has lost the element of immediacy. Although a highly skilled therapist would probably be able to continue this conversation meaningfully and would most likely be able to assist the client in identifying a desired trait or skill, a beginning or intermediate level therapist might become frustrated and give up at this point. One approach to avoid this dilemma would be to utilize a line of questioning that is designed to uncover a desired trait or skill (e.g., being a good parent, increasing family trust) prior to asking this client the miracle question. However, once the miracle question has been asked without success, the magic door question can be effectively used if the therapist has determined what specific trait the client is hoping to obtain.

Possessed Time Machine

The possessed time machine intervention is asked as follows:

> Imagine that you are stepping into a time machine. This time machine takes you into the future, exactly one year from today [or any other future point in time]. However, this time machine is "possessed." It likes to give everyone who travels in it a trait or skill that will make all the difference in the world for that person in the future. As you get out of the time machine, what lets you know that it gave you this trait?

This intervention contains many of the elements of the miracle question. It contains the concept of a meaningful change that is perceived as unlikely to occur naturally, the lack of knowledge that the gift was given, and the challenge to discover the small changes that will signal that a gift was received. However, it does not have a clearly defined change and it lacks the concept of immediacy. This intervention's lack of a clearly defined change encourages clients to be creative and to expand their thinking to determine what trait or skill they would pick if they could have anything they wanted. It may be useful for clients who state that they have everything they currently want and struggle with identifying anything that therapy can do for them. It takes the conversation out of the typical realm and into an imaginative sci-fi world. Due to its playful nature, this intervention is especially useful with adolescents. Clients typically smile when this question is asked. However, this intervention lacks the implication of immediacy because the change is not scheduled to take place until the designated point in the future, thereby eliminating the benefit of an immediate environmental cue. However, once the trait is identified and the difference that obtaining this trait has been discussed, the miracle question can be used as a follow-up to secure the missing elements.

Therapist Casting a Spell/Giving a Gift

The intervention is asked as follows:

> Imagine that sometime during this session, I magically give you a gift [or cast a spell]. The gift is that the problem which brought you here is gone [or an alternatively defined miracle as previously discussed]. However, you are unaware that this gift was given to you. As you get in your car or get on the bus to go home, what changes do you notice that let you know that something is different?

Although this intervention contains all of the elements of the miracle question, it lacks some of the miracle question's strength. It contains the concept of a meaningful change that is perceived as unlikely to occur naturally, a clearly defined gift, the element of immediacy, the lack of knowledge that the gift was given, and the challenge to discover the small changes that will signal that a gift was received. However, like the magic door intervention, it shares the disadvantage of the environmental cue being linked to the therapist rather than to the client's natural environment. This intervention can be useful when a client has placed the therapist in the expert role and expects the therapist to "fix" the problem. Although a therapist in this position is wise to make every effort to empower the clients to view themselves as the change agents, this is not always possible. This intervention can be a useful exercise to honor the place in which the client has placed the therapist while assisting the client to take credit for the changes that occur as a result of the intervention. This combination of interventions can be quite effective in changing this therapist/client dynamic.

Fast Forward to the End of the Session

This intervention is asked as follows:

> Imagine that it is the end of this session, and you are walking out of the building. As you get into your car or go to catch the bus,

> you suddenly realize that you have gotten just what you needed out of group today, that group was not a waste of your time. What lets you know that you have gotten something useful? What do others around you (spouse, family) notice when you get home that lets them know that going to group today was useful?

This intervention contains some of the elements of the miracle question. It contains the concept of a meaningful change that may or may not be perceived as unlikely to occur naturally, the element of immediacy, the lack of knowledge that the gift was given, and the challenge to discover the small changes that will signal that a gift was received. Since the change was defined only vaguely as "group was not a waste of time," the clients can apply this as they find appropriate. For some, this may mean that they received something that they have been searching for; for others, it might be that they received needed support. It is a useful intervention for a group or individual setting in which the therapist is questioning what the client was hoping to obtain from the therapy interaction.

Therapists can become frustrated when clients behave in ways that are different from what the therapist would expect (e.g., minimal verbal participation). This intervention encourages the clients to question what they need and what would make the time useful, and it challenges the therapists to set aside their own assumptions of how the clients would behave if they were getting what they needed from the therapeutic process. Often therapists are surprised to learn that clients are getting what they want from the session and that the clients may not share the therapists' view that the session has been unproductive. However, this intervention is limited to what will be different for clients at the end of group rather than on what will be different for them once the problems that brought them to treatment are solved. It is not effectively used in place of the miracle question due to this constraint.

Magic Wand

The magic wand intervention, commonly used as a group check-in question, is asked as follows:

> If you could change one thing about yourself, what would it be?

This question does not contain any of the elements of the miracle question, and it cannot be used as an alternative for that intervention. It is used as a general means to discover what traits or skills the clients are interested in obtaining. This question is helpful to set the stage to ask the miracle question in a group or individual setting. In order for this question to be effective, the therapist must be posed to handle any answer that might be given. For example, the following interaction might occur:

THERAPIST: If you could change one thing about yourself, what would it be?

CLIENT: I would be taller.

THERAPIST: What difference would it make for you if you were taller?

CLIENT: Other people would respect me more and wouldn't look down on me.

A common beginning therapist mistake would be to narrow or restrict the client's answer. A therapist in this situation might restrict this client's answer by saying, "It must be something that you are able to control." Therapists using solution-focused questioning should always accept the client's answers and invite creativity. Any attempt to restrict or limit a client's answers may result in the loss of a possible path to a solution. By accepting the client's answer that he or she would be taller, the therapist was able to discover the trait (feeling respected by others) that was of value to this client. The therapist can then ask the miracle question in the following way:

> Imagine that while you are asleep tonight, a miracle happens. The miracle is that you suddenly feel respected by others. However, because you are asleep, you don't know that the miracle has happened. So, when you wake up tomorrow morning, what will be different that will let you know that a miracle has happened and that you are respected?

Therapists have encountered clients who respond that they would change nothing with the magic wand. In this case, it may be helpful to rephrase this intervention as follows:

> Imagine that this magic wand had the power to take away all of your traits, yet it would leave the one that was most important to you. Which one would you keep?

This is a respectful way to honor the clients' statement that they would not add any additional traits. However, it retains this intervention's original ability to assist the clients in determining what traits they currently value and what difference these traits make to them and those around them.

Trait Shopping

This intervention is asked as follows:

> Imagine that you are in a shopping mall. However, this mall sells only traits and skills. You aren't planning to purchase anything, yet as you go from store to store you find something that you just can't live without. What do you buy? What do your family members (or others) notice that is different about you when you return home that lets them know that you have made this purchase?

This intervention contains some of the elements of the miracle question. It contains the concept of a meaningful change that may or may not be perceived as unlikely to occur naturally. However, this intervention lacks a clearly defined change. Because of this, it is a useful tool to assist the clients in discovering what skills or traits are desirable to them. The clients are aware that the change occurred since the clients purchased the traits in this scenario. This precludes the element of discovery for the clients. However, by adding the element of asking what family members notice when the clients return home, this element is reintroduced. The concept of immediacy is not present since the proposed event may or may not occur immediately; however, it does contain a natural environmental cue (the mall) that will be present after the therapy is complete.

This intervention can be followed with the magic door intervention in order to secure most of the missing elements once the desired traits are discovered. This could be worded as follows:

> Now imagine that it is time to leave the mall, and you walk through the front entrance with your trait in your shopping bag. However, unbeknownst to you, that door is a magic door. As you go through it, the trait in your bag becomes integrated into who you are. As you get in your car or get on the bus to go home, what changes do you notice that let you know that something is different?

By combining these interventions, the only element that remains absent is the element of immediacy.

Call from the Future

This intervention is asked to parents of dependent children as follows:

> Imagine that it is your child's thirtieth birthday. Your telephone rings and it is your adult child, calling to tell you that you were the best parent that he or she could have imagined. What does he or she say that was learned from you that made such a difference in his or her life?

This intervention is commonly used in a group setting with parents or in an individual setting when clients have expressed a desire to make a positive impact on their children's lives. This intervention contains some of the elements of the miracle question. It may contain the concept of a meaningful change if the clients currently perceive themselves as not being the parent that they want to be. In this case, this intervention does contain a clearly defined change, the lack of knowledge that the change was made, and the challenge to discover the small changes which signal that a change was made. However, this intervention lacks the assurance of the concept of immediacy, for the exact time in which the change took place is unknown. The clients will receive the feedback when their children turn thirty years old. The change may happen today or it may happen at a future point in time. This element of the unknown may actually encourage the clients to become more attentive to the possibility of change as the parents begin to view the world from their children's eyes. This intervention has the potential to deepen the impact and perceived importance of the desired change. This intervention will not assist a client to get to the other side of the problem if it is used in a group setting and the parent does not perceive a need to be a better parent.

SUMMARY

The miracle question is an amazingly powerful tool to assist the client in getting to a place where the problem is solved. Once there, clients are able to gain hope that change is possible and to glean ideas of what changes are needed in order to bridge the future to the present. By understanding the fundamental elements of the miracle question, therapists are able to exercise their creativity to design unique interventions that can specifically address client issues. This results in a greater ability for therapists to deal with the unexpected and to think on their feet. The possibilities of the miracle question are endless and are limited only by therapists' understanding of the basic elements and by their own creativity.

Chapter 5

Sustaining the Miracle

The dream is not the destination, but the journey.

Unknown

This chapter describes how we integrated the problem-focused concept of relapse prevention into our solution-focused work.

Open the majority of books about the treatment of substance abuse and you find a grim description of the client's chances for long-term success. "Relapse" is easily found in most indexes with multiple references to the perceived chronicity of addiction and the importance of relapse prevention. Many writers emphasize the need for lifelong treatment or support (Alcoholics Anonymous, 1975; Forrest, 1984, 1997; Wegscheider, 1981). Due to the seriousness of relapse, authors have devoted entire books to its prevention (Gorski and Miller, 1982; Marlatt and Gordon, 1980, 1985).

Despite the seriousness of the consequences of a client's return to substance abuse (or the recurrence of any other problem), the term *relapse* is rarely found in the index of a book about solution-focused therapy. When it is present, it most often points to passages that describe the contrast between the problem-focused and solution-focused languages and their approach to client setbacks (Berg and Miller, 1992; Berg and Reuss, 1998). What is so central to one language (the problem or the return to the problem) is once again found to be intentionally absent or scantly addressed in this contrasting language.

It is missing not out of negligence, but due to the lack of necessity when the focus is the desired future. Unfortunately, this can pose a challenge for solution-focused therapists and agencies that are operating in a problem-focused environment, for referral sources frequently refer clients for the sole purpose of relapse prevention and governing bodies often monitor to ensure that clients are receiving adequate relapse prevention skill training. Therefore, once again, the solution-focused therapist must be skilled at hearing what these other agencies or referral sources are needing and in effectively communicating to them that these needs have been met by the solution-focused work with clients.

CHANGING THE FOCUS

The concept of relapse prevention is commonplace in working with any perceived chronic condition. Relapse is believed to be the direct result of clients lacking skills to adequately cope with high-risk situations (Marlatt and Gordon, 1985). Without these necessary coping skills, a return to the problematic behavior is thought to be imminent.

A common intervention in relapse prevention is to predict possible high-risk situations that might trigger a return to the problematic behavior and then to assist the client in developing coping strategies to prevent the recurrence of the negative behavior. This results in the focus of treatment being on the prediction and preparation for high-risk situations due to the ever-present potential return of problematic behavior. The primary goal of the client then becomes to avoid a return to the problematic behavior.

Clients describe a type of hypervigilance that results from this type of problem focus, for it is necessary to guard against the perceived "enemy" that will return when least expected. Furthermore, they can never fully achieve this goal of avoidance because that would mean discarding their hypervigilance and risking the return of the unwanted behavior. This inability to reach an end point can itself become problematic and all consuming; according to *Alcoholics Anonymous* (1976), when people "focus on the problem, the problem increases" (p. 451). It goes on to say that solutions work in a similar fashion, thereby suggesting a need to change the focus in order to ensure long-term success.

Solution-focused therapy builds on this basic principle, which was discovered and passed along by members of Alcoholics Anonymous. It simply states that when people "focus on the answer, the answer increases" (*Alcoholics Anonymous,* 1976, p. 451). This simple change in focus (a shift to a future focus) can have a dramatic impact on sustaining change.

Although it is not common for people to focus on the desired future rather than on preparing for potential disaster, many who cope successfully with a crisis testify to this lifestyle. Clients with terminal illness have told me (TP), for instance, that their illness has taught them the importance of enjoying their life and that they have a newfound appreciation for what is important. Their focus turned to living rather than fearing death. Their problems were placed in perspective and were no longer all consuming.

This focus on the future does not negate the day-to-day maintenance that clients may engage in while they plan for their future and enjoy their journey, yet this approach takes away the need for hypervigilance and fear (which can be draining and render one ineffective) and allows clients to respond to life problems thoughtfully and purposefully. Once clients have a taste of change and the power that their miracle can offer, they are typically highly motivated to sustain this change. By asking future-oriented questions that help them identify their resources, they are able to purposefully cope with future problems. This change in focus is the result of the therapists' skillful questions that assist the clients in uncovering their existing resources to manage future life problems ("bumps in the road") and ensure that their miracles become and stay their reality.

EMERGENCY ROADSIDE REPAIR KIT

The "emergency roadside repair kit" (Charlie Johnson, personal communication, 1993; Johnson and Webster, 2002) is an analogy we use to assist clients in discovering the tools they currently have to cope with potential problems. We have found it most effective when used in an interactive style as follows:

THERAPIST: I know this may sound strange, but I'm going to ask you anyway, OK?

CLIENT: OK.

THERAPIST: What do you have in your car trunk?

CLIENT: My trunk?

THERAPIST: Yes. What is in there?

CLIENT: Well, I have my workout bag and a box of stuff I need to take to my sister's house.

THERAPIST: What else?

CLIENT: Hmm. There is a gas can, a blanket, a spare tire, a jack. I think there is also a first-aid kit and a flashlight.

THERAPIST: You sound pretty prepared. Why do you have that stuff in there?

CLIENT: It's just stuff everyone carries.

THERAPIST: Are you planning to have an emergency?

CLIENT: No [laughing]. You would just be pretty stupid to live in Colorado without that stuff.

THERAPIST: Do you think a lot about the possibility of having a problem?

CLIENT: No. I guess I don't need to since I know I have what I need in case something was to happen. I don't even think about that stuff except when I run into it when I'm putting something in the trunk.

THERAPIST: Hmm. You have been working really hard toward getting to your miracle, and I'm wondering what type of "emergency stuff" you have in case you hit a bump in the road. What's going to give you that type of confidence to know that you can quickly solve your problem and get back on your way?

CLIENT: Wow, I hadn't even thought of that. If I'm prepared for a car problem it would make sense to prepare for life, since that is so much more important.

THERAPIST: So, what do you think?

CLIENT: Well, I have my friends and family. They are very supportive of the changes that I have made and would be the first to be there and get me going again. I have been reading books and taking time for myself. That always helps me to be focused and relaxed. I also have church. They are really good people, and going helps me to remember what is important. And I think taking the time each week for special time with my kids will help me to stay grounded on my miracle and how I want our family to be. I really enjoy that time together.

THERAPIST: That is quite a list! I'm wondering how confident you are that you will remember you have these tools and how to use them if you do hit a bump in the road. Where would you put yourself on a scale of one to ten (ten being one hundred percent confident, and one being no confidence at all)?

CLIENT: Oh, I'm really high. I would say about a nine. These are things that I do all the time and have become part of my life. So, I guess you could say they are not only there for an emergency, but they also protect me from potential problems as well.

Key Elements of the Emergency Roadside Repair Kit

There are many therapeutic elements of the emergency roadside repair kit intervention. It provides a way to metaphorically normalize potential problems without trivializing the need for preparation. Clients readily identify that they have put some thought into what they would need in case of a roadside emergency. However, this preparation is rarely seen as overwhelming or time consuming. It is most often seen as a commonsense practice that has benefited them or someone they care about.

The second therapeutic benefit is to highlight the clients' coping abilities and confidence in their resources despite problems. I have yet to have clients tell me that they are actually riddled with fear about the possibility of having a roadside emergency. Clients frequently describe the possibility as an inconvenience or potential source of frustration, yet these issues are clearly within their power to manage and overcome should they arise.

Even clients who describe themselves as "automotive illiterate" state that they are fairly confident in their ability to handle an emergency, even if it means they would need to call someone for assistance. Regardless of their planned method of solving the problem, they are prepared. Most important, the clients convey that they will survive the problem with minimal lasting effects even if their planned method fails.

Clients have wisely observed that they could never prepare for every roadside emergency that might arise, yet they still have the confidence in their ability to use their resources to resolve the problem. This might entail asking someone for help or guidance, which is a tool that is available to them. This is an important lesson for clients to remember in life as well. This approach results in future problems remaining in perspective (i.e., as an inconvenience or a temporary impediment to their goal, but not as an overwhelming crisis or a sign that their goal should be abandoned).

The third therapeutic benefit of the emergency roadside repair kit is its implicit focus on future empowerment through preparation. The analogy provides clients with a concrete example of how a small amount of thoughtful preparation can result in a sense of confidence in their ability to handle a potential problem that in turn allows them to focus their attention on their destination.

This is invaluable when assisting clients in addressing potential life problems. It demonstrates that they do not have to be fearfully focused on preventing a problem in order to be adequately prepared to face a potential challenge. This allows them freedom to enjoy the journey knowing that they have the ability to purposefully respond to the situation at hand. This assists clients in understanding that their lack of worry or hypervigilance does not necessarily signal that they are woefully unprepared. In fact, it may signify the opposite—that they have the necessary skills and confidence in their ability to handle normal bumps in the road.

The fourth therapeutic benefit of the emergency roadside repair kit is the comparison to emergency supplies that are often forgotten in the trunk, yet are later remembered by happenstance. Identifying skills and resources the client has that can effectively address future life problems is a goal which can be completed (unlike the goal of avoiding a problematic behavior). Similar to preparing emergency equipment and supplies in case of a roadside emergency, this task has an end. This allows the clients to focus their energy on obtaining and enjoying their miracles.

In the course of everyday life, our clients will periodically encounter these resources and, like a wise traveler, will remember to periodically check the condition of these supplies for their readiness in case they are needed. This normalizes the "forgetting," yet emphasizes the "checking" when the resources are remembered. Clients have often told us that they think about their life skills when they "bump into" their roadside emergency equipment in the trunk of the vehicle. This provides a real-life reminder of the skills that are not as tangible.

RELAPSE PREVENTION WITH RELUCTANT CLIENTS

Some clients come to us eagerly seeking any tool that will assist them in preventing the return of the presenting problem, but this is not the case with all clients. Many of our clients do not agree with their referral sources about the definition of the initial problem that resulted in the requirement of treatment. As a result, these other professionals are frequently concerned that these clients will return to the problematic behavior that initially resulted in their involvement in the clients' lives. Although the clients may not agree with the referral sources' definition of the problem, they do agree that they would like their lives to be very different in the future. By exploring how the clients want their lives to be different, the common ground between the clients and other professionals can often be found. However, the traditional concept of relapse prevention relies on a solid and well-defined definition of the problem. Herein lies a potential source of conflict when using a problem-focused model of treatment and relapse prevention.

Conversely, by using the emergency roadside repair kit intervention, the focus is on what the client wants to maintain (as opposed to on the prevention of the recurrence of a predefined problem), thereby maintaining the focus on the agreed-upon goal of both the client and the referral source. This emergency roadside repair kit analogy assists clients in understanding that in preparing for potential bumps in the road they do not have to agree that a problem ever existed. This allows them to readily identify the wisdom in planning to ensure that their desired miracle can be achieved and sustained despite life's normal ups and downs.

This future focus results in the referral source getting the assurance that the clients have effectively addressed and possess the skills needed to prevent future relapse while respecting the clients' definition of the changes they want to maintain. This allows the intervention to be used effectively with clients who clearly identify a presenting problem as well as with those who are "making the most" out of mandated treatment they do not believe they need. The following excerpt illustrates how this intervention can be used effectively with mandated clients. It is from a session with a father who was referred for services by social services after his children were removed from his care when he was charged with attempted murder. His history of violence and marijuana use was of grave concern to his caseworker.

CLIENT: I don't know why I have to come to these groups. My caseworker said I need "relapse treatment," but I don't have a problem. I only used pot again that one time, and it won't happen again.

THERAPIST: So you already stopped the pot use, even before you came?

CLIENT: Yeah! I can't believe she made me come anyway.

THERAPIST: How did you stop?

CLIENT: It was easy since I'm not addicted or anything.

THERAPIST: What is it that you know that allows you to stop so easily that maybe I could pass on to my clients who are addicted?

CLIENT: That it's just not worth it, man. That stuff can mess you up.

THERAPIST: Is this something that you just learned, or did you believe that before?

CLIENT: I guess I always had heard it. Seeing how much trouble I got in for just one joint has really let me know how bad it is. It's just not worth it!

THERAPIST: So you're pretty convinced you're done for good.

CLIENT: Yeah!

THERAPIST: Where would you put that on our scale? Ten equals no doubt at all?

CLIENT: Definitely at a ten.

THERAPIST: Where would you say your caseworker is on that same scale?

CLIENT: About a four. I think she is worried that I will light up again when problems happen, but that's all behind me.

THERAPIST: Let me ask you a question, OK?

CLIENT: OK.

THERAPIST: What do you have in your car trunk?

CLIENT: My trunk?

THERAPIST: Yeah.

CLIENT: A jack, a tire. You know . . . the normal stuff.

THERAPIST: Why do you have that stuff even though your tires are fine?

CLIENT: In case something happens. You never know.

THERAPIST: It sounds like you know that you have these tools to cope with life problems just like you have these tools to cope with car problems so that you know you don't have to use pot. Your caseworker, however, doesn't know that you are so prepared.

CLIENT: Yeah! I know I'm prepared!

THERAPIST: So, when your caseworker is higher on that scale—maybe an eight or nine—what tools will she have discovered that you have which will convince her you are really prepared?

CLIENT: She would see how well I handle the smaller problems, like when my kids are late for their visit, or when I don't get my way. I'll hold my temper. She will see me being prepared for visits with my kids, maybe bringing them a snack.

This example demonstrates how effective this intervention can be in assisting clients in identifying relapse prevention skills and in finding ways that they can take action to work toward what is important to them even when they do not believe that a problem exists. Through this dialogue, the client became a customer for change. In addition, he was able to understand his caseworker's point of view and discover how he could make positive changes. The client and caseworker still would not agree on the definition of the problem, but the client is now actively working toward a solution.

WHEN TO USE THE EMERGENCY ROADSIDE REPAIR KIT

As with many of the solution-focused interventions, our therapists initially struggled with identifying the most effective time to use this tool. The therapists understood the solution-focused interventions (including the emergency roadside repair kit), yet they were unsure how these interventions worked together to assist the client in obtaining and maintaining the desired changes. For example, the therapists stated that they frequently felt "stuck" when working with clients who continued to attend treatment even though it appeared that they had completed their treatment goals. They could identify the clients' progress, yet were unsure why the client continued to come to treatment (when not mandated by a referral source) or what intervention would be most appropriate to use next. At this point the therapists began to see the importance of understanding the stages of solution-focused treatment through which clients progress and how the skillful use of the interventions (such as the emergency roadside repair kit) guide the clients in obtaining and sustaining their miracles. We divided the process into the following six distinct stages:

1. Defining the miracle
2. Scaling progress working toward the miracle

3. Scaling confidence in maintaining the progress working toward the miracle
4. Scaling important people's confidence in the client's ability to maintain the progress
5. Emergency roadside repair kit
6. Scaling confidence in using the tools in the emergency roadside repair kit

The purpose of defining these stages was for therapist training and to assist the therapists in identifying which intervention would be most useful at a given stage of client work. They were not designed to predict the client's personal process, only to provide a basic outline of the therapeutic process for the therapists to use as a guide. These stages are not time specific; one client may complete several of these stages over a short period of time and another client may spend more time completing a specific stage. The stages can be repeated as necessary as clients identify and work toward additional goals.

The first stage is probably the best known and is unmistakably the foundation of solution-focused therapy. Miller and de Shazer (1998) describe the miracle question as the "centerpiece of this approach" (p. 366). During this initial stage the client and therapist work to develop a clear goal that will define when treatment is complete. I cannot emphasize sufficiently that this goal is based upon a desired future rather than the elimination of an identified problem. (Paradoxically, by achieving the desired future, by definition, the problem will be eliminated.) This stage is usually the focus of the first session (either in a group or individual setting).

During the second stage clients actively work toward the identified goal and notice the small changes or differences that occur during various points during the journey toward obtaining their miracle. Scaling is the intervention that is most commonly used to assist the client and therapist in noticing small changes and in making these changes measurable (see Chapter 1 for a full explanation of scaling and how this intervention is used). The stage is most often begun during the first session and continues throughout treatment.

Once the client has made significant progress toward achieving the identified goal (as evidenced by a high number on the previously mentioned scale), it is time to move to the third stage. At this point the clients are typically feeling excited and hopeful about the changes, and other important people in their lives are frequently noticing the changes as well. Some clients are proud of their accomplishments; others express a "too-good-to-be-true" sentiment and are fearful that the changes might be fleeting. This is when therapists should scale the clients' level of confidence in their ability to sustain the changes, for it is crucial that clients view the changes as being within their control rather than being a random act of fate, which they cannot recreate. Once clients have identified where they are on the ten-point confidence scale, the therapist would then assist them in identifying how they would know when they are higher on the scale. The following illustrates how this is done:

This client was referred for services by her caseworker. Her daughter had tested positive for alcohol at birth, and the client had received multiple past treatment episodes. In addition, the client herself had been raised in foster care.

THERAPIST: We have been talking for some time about all the wonderful changes you have been noticing, and I can't help but wonder how confident you are that you are able to maintain these. So, on a scale of one to ten (ten being that you are one hundred percent confident that you can keep these changes going, and one being the opposite), where would you say you are?

CLIENT: About a five. I think I can keep up some of it, but I have done this before and I slipped back into old habits. That worries me.

THERAPIST: It sounds as though your experience has taught you that it is wise to be cautious and make sure change is lasting. How confident do you need to be to know you can do the rest on your own without treatment and that you will not slip back into those old habits?

CLIENT: At least an eight. I don't want to get cocky, and an eight would mean that I'm realistic yet comfortable.

THERAPIST: Where do you hope to be on this scale next time we meet?

CLIENT: I hope to be a six.

THERAPIST: What will be different when you are at a six that lets you know that you are just a little more confident in your ability to maintain these changes?

CLIENT: Well, I think that the changes will be more natural. I probably won't have to think about what I want to do all the time and will find myself on occasion just doing it automatically.

This conversation assists the client in identifying the small changes that will signify that she is gaining the desired level of confidence. Once the client reaches this desired level of confidence, it is time to move to the next stage.

The fourth stage is to scale the level of confidence that other important people in the client's life (such as the referral source, partner, or parents) have in the client's changes. We have frequently found that clients have lost trust from other important people due to past behaviors. Clients who are involved in the legal system, social services, or another external referral source typically tell us that their referral source is initially skeptical of their changes and needs to see consistency. Because of this, regaining trust and establishing consistency in the eyes of others is most often an important part of the client's miracle. By using a method similar to that described previously, the clients are able to identify where they would rate the level of confidence of other important people in the clients' ability to sustain the changes they have made. We then ask the clients where on this ten-point confidence scale they would want these other people to be prior to their discharge from treatment. This assists the clients in viewing themselves through the eyes of other important people and assists them in making choices.

Once the clients rate their own confidence and the confidence of other important people as high on the ten-point scale, it is time to utilize the emergency roadside repair kit intervention. This frequently signals that the client is near the end of treatment. At this point clients have the necessary confidence to move forward in life without treatment, and one last check on the "emergency supplies" is useful before traveling on. This frequently serves to further boost the clients' confidence level as they discover that they are prepared for the normal bumps in the road that they might encounter.

The final stage is to scale the clients' confidence and other important people's confidence in the clients' ability to remember and effectively use the emergency roadside repair kit when needed. Clients most often place themselves very high on this scale, which serves to further reinforce that they are well on their way. In addition, it assists them in understanding that other people may not be as confident as they are in their ability to sustain the journey. This highlights the importance of remaining patient as other people discover that the clients truly have the necessary skills to deal with life problems.

Some of our clients are referred to us when they are in need of this final stage of work. They have already made the necessary changes on their own, yet someone in their lives (most often the referral source) lacks confidence in the clients' abilities to sustain the necessary changes. When this occurs, the clients' miracle is typically for the referral source to have the necessary confidence in their ability to maintain the changes. Therefore, the clients' work is to identify what the referral source will be seeing in them when the referral source is higher on this final confidence scale. The therapists then skillfully ask questions that assist the clients in discovering what they know about their skills and abilities that the referral source has not yet learned. This line of questioning assists the clients in discovering the clues to achieving their miracle.

SUMMARY

Although the concept of relapse prevention initially comes from problem-focused language, solution-focused therapists are often asked to ensure that clients have the necessary relapse prevention skills to prevent the recurrence of the presenting problem. The term *relapse prevention* comes from the problem-focused approach; however, the goal of sustaining client changes is common to both problem-focused and solution-focused therapists.

This common goal (ensuring that clients have the ability and skills to maintain a life in which the problem does not exist) is one upon which all therapists, regardless of their philosophical approach, can agree. Therefore, it is especially useful for solution-focused therapists to hone their skills to effectively hear what these referral sources are needing and translate the solution-focused work in a way that professionals who work in a traditional model can understand. Although obtaining the miracle is a wonderful achievement, the ultimate goal of both the client and therapist is to ensure that the client has the ability to sustain the miracle in everyday life.

Chapter 6

"This Is Stupid, I Don't Need This, and I Don't Want to Be Here": Working with Adolescents

Never give up. This may be your moment for a miracle.

Albert Einstein

I (YD) remember my hair turning prematurely gray during the first year (nearly twenty years ago) that I worked full time with adolescents. I was a counselor at a program for runaway and homeless teenagers, many of whom were heavily abusing drugs and alcohol and had been repeatedly abused physically, emotionally, and sexually. Our program only had enough money to house each teen for three weeks, and some of the cases were heartbreaking. Both the staff and the clients were working hard to find reasons to have hope about the clients' future. I was desperate to find a way to help these kids, so I began to use the SF approach experimentally since nothing else seemed to be helping. That was when I first experienced the hope-kindling effects of using solution-focused therapy with adolescents.

This chapter describes how we use the SF approach with this fascinating, challenging, sometimes hair-raising (or hair-graying!) population, and explains why we think this approach is especially well suited to this population. We have also included vivid descriptions of mistakes that we made during the transition to using an SF approach with our adolescent clients; we hope these may prevent you from replicating a similar "trial-and-error" process. Through the chapter we highlight the lessons we learned as we joined our adolescent clients on their journey toward solutions.

Our adolescent clients come to us from a variety of concerned sources: parents, social services, legal sources, schools, etc. Only occasionally do we find that the adolescent client agrees with the referral source that services are a "good idea." More often, our adolescents are not in agreement and are complying with services in an attempt to regain their lost freedom or family harmony. Some are openly pro-drug, as they voice their strongly held beliefs that marijuana and other mind-expanding drugs are not only safe but should be legalized and embraced by society. Others are more subdued, offering the minimal answers that often characterize adolescents (e.g., "yeah" or "I don't know").

Our agency offers adolescents all of the same traditional outpatient substance abuse treatment services that we offer to adults: groups, individual sessions, family sessions, abstinence monitoring (e.g., urine screens), case management, etc. However, the use of education groups or topic-driven groups, so common in most traditional outpatient settings for adolescents, are not offered. In addition, our agency is unique in that we have no minimum age limit for adolescent services, which results in younger children also being referred to us for services. These younger children are most often seen individually or in family settings due to the small number that are referred. Our agency offers free services to the children (adolescents as well as younger children) of our adult clients, for we have found that our adult clients often worry about the impact that their substance use has had on their children and seek services for their children to address this.

THE PARADOXICAL POPULATION

Among other things, adolescents can be "simultaneously and paradoxically" (Werner-Wilson, 2000, p. 2)

- wary and sarcastic,
- vulnerable,
- egocentric,
- impressionable,
- stubborn, and
- supremely confident.

As most parents will tell you, the fact that every adult was once a teenager does little to enhance one's credibility with an adolescent. Furthermore, most adolescents are quick to point out that having lived through a similar experience does not mean knowing the best solution to a given problem. True to their developmental task (Werner-Wilson, 2000), adolescents place a high value on finding their own answers, often to the chagrin of adults. Although an adolescent may ultimately come to embrace an idea previously offered by a wise adult, this rarely happens without a period of initial rejection and extensive questioning. Questioning and sometimes outright rejection of traditional ideas and social mores can be understood as necessary for an adolescent to develop critical thinking.

Although not all adolescents take this road of outward resistance, therapists are perhaps more likely to encounter the ones who do. Not surprisingly, therapists sometimes share parents' sense of frustration and bewilderment about how to help adolescents comprehend the potential outcome of their choices. A sense of urgency builds when parents, therapists, and other caregivers witness adolescents' behaviors that risk painful consequences.

Concern over potentially self-destructive behaviors, such as driving while under the influence or dropping out of school, typically results in unsolicited advice, information, and words of wisdom from caring adults. Adolescents, however, are typically bent on discovering their own solutions, and they often reject the adult's offerings out of hand.

Why the SF Approach Fits Well with Natural Adolescent Development

As we mentioned earlier, adolescents are quick to point out they need to do it "their own" way. The developmental task of adolescence involves experimenting with possible future roles while differentiating from one's family of origin (Werner-Wilson, 2000). For adolescents this is, in effect, an exploration of who they are, what they like, what they believe, and what type of future they would like to create.

In an effort to access their creativity and explore the limits of their reality they suspend externally imposed limitations and look within themselves or at their peers for answers. The SF approach fits especially well with this development stage because it implicitly challenges clients to explore and articulate what they want, and evaluate potential decisions and behaviors by identifying which ones will best lead to their desired future. In essence, by using the SF approach, we are inviting our adolescent clients to do what they are developmentally scripted to do but in a productive and focused manner.

CHALLENGING OUR OLD ASSUMPTIONS ABOUT ADOLESCENTS

During the transition to using solution-focused therapy with our adolescent clients we encountered times in which our adolescent treatment groups became very difficult. Some of the problems were due to our unexamined assumption that adolescents' unique problems necessitated an expert-based approach. This caused us to integrate the SF approach into our adolescent program only superficially at first. The therapists initially held firm to the belief that the therapist must initiate important topics and conversations and must confront clients' "unrealistic" thinking. One of the therapists once said, "They are just kids! They don't have any life history to draw from. This [solution-focused therapy] works with adults, but adolescents have to be taught." This type of thinking resulted in topic-driven sessions, with SF interventions only intermingled within a problem-focused philosophy.

However, after we witnessed the therapeutic results of using the SF approach with our adult clients, we became determined to apply it to our adolescent groups, and we began to adapt the approach wholeheartedly. Eventually we decided to revamp the adolescent program to fully integrate the solution-focused approach. This required us to address the staff's lingering problem-focused assumptions in our work with this population.

Because adolescents deal with problems specific to their age group (such as those related to peers, school, and family) and because they traditionally lack significant life experience, it is assumed they require a highly structured, authoritarian, and hierarchical, expert-based form of treatment. Unfortunately, this often fails because adolescents typically hate to be told what to do, no matter how tactful the adults' efforts.

During the period of transition into using the SF model, the adolescent therapists were challenging their own approach and view of their clients. This was a very demanding task because it called into question everything they had previously been taught. Not all of the therapists agreed that this transition was needed, and some staff left during this process as cherished beliefs were challenged. Those who stayed struggled to balance applying the concepts and interventions of this approach with remembering to apply basic limit setting to ensure positive group norms.

Another old assumption we had to correct was the notion that adolescents lack the ability to think about their futures or apply a goal-directed approach. We have found our adolescent clients willing and eager to tell us what they want. Although they rarely identify all of the necessary elements for achieving their desired future, most often they already have some vision of what they want. We utilize this vision to help adolescent clients to develop and carry out realistic, appropriate, readily achievable therapeutic goals.

Over and over again we have been impressed with the remarkable understanding and practicality our adolescents exhibit regarding setting goals for their future.

The following excerpt is from a session with an adolescent male who was referred by the school system for selling drugs on school grounds. He was known for being a "troublemaker" and not attending his classes.

THERAPIST: So imagine with me that it is five years from now, and your life has turned out just how you had hoped. What is it like?

CLIENT: Well, I'd be rich.

THERAPIST: Wow! In five years? I'm impressed.

CLIENT: No, not really, but I wish.

THERAPIST: Me too. So, what is it like?

CLIENT: Well, I will have my own place . . . probably an apartment. I'll have a job. You know, a normal life. Friends.

THERAPIST: What difference will it make once you have your own place and a job?

CLIENT: I will be able to make my own decisions and have my own space.

THERAPIST: As you look back from that place in the future, what decisions did you make that made the most difference in helping you get where you wanted to be?

CLIENT: Probably finishing school. I don't want to be working in fast food, so I have to get my diploma in order to have choices.

THERAPIST: What did you do to make sure you could get through school?

CLIENT: I stayed focused on what was important and stayed away from those kids that always get me in trouble.

THERAPIST: Remind me again what you mean about "what was important."

CLIENT: You know, getting out of school, having fun—but not the kind that leads to trouble.

THERAPIST: How did you do that? How did you stay focused and get through?

CLIENT: By spending time with my "good" friends. I do have some great friends who know how to have fun and stay out of trouble. I really like hanging with them, but I haven't been doing that lately.

This example illustrates the playful spirit that adolescents frequently exhibit (e.g., being rich). Although one could interpret such humor as evidence that adolescents are not knowledgeable about what is required in life, we have observed over the years that adolescents are most often quite aware of the limitations of reality. They (similar to most adults) are not immune from wanting things that they know are unrealistic. However, adolescents are often more forthright than adults are in expressing their desires despite known limitations.

Furthermore, adolescents also sometimes use this type of humor as a sort of test to see if the adult is truly interested in what they are going to say or if the listener will resort to expert thinking or problem solving. When the therapist trusts the client's wisdom (regardless of age), the client quickly moves on to a realistic future. The therapist then formulates questions from a perspective in which the clients have already obtained their desired future, which further elicits the clients' wisdom and successful choices. The adolescent clients become increasingly eager to share their thoughts and decisions, unconcerned of adult criticism. The therapist's questions then serve to assist the clients in further exploration and refinement of the details that created this future.

Another assumption about adolescents that our team needed to revise was the notion that adolescents must have formal structure (such as activities or exercises) in group settings. Because adolescents have a reputation for giving minimal answers to adults' questions and can pose a challenge to traditional therapeutic methods, our therapists initially assumed that adolescent groups required formal structure and a preset agenda. They tended to revert to this assumption at times when they questioned their own skill level. In retrospect, the desire for formal structure appears to have been more for the comfort of the therapists than because it was needed for the clients.

Adolescents, we soon learned, were very vocal when the therapists were curious about their ideas, wants, and priorities. In fact, we found that preset agendas of activities and exercises actually inhibited the clients' conversations and therefore limited the development of potential solutions. As our therapists gained confidence in their ability to actively and effectively utilize the SF approach with their adolescent client groups, their previous need for a tightly controlled, preset agenda disappeared.

Over time, we have found that our group skeleton model (described in Chapter 3) provides all the necessary structure to guide the therapists and ensure that each client interaction is purposeful and useful. As a result of this more individualized approach, our adolescent clients frequently tell us that they feel heard and understood, which is the greatest compliment they can give adults.

LIMIT SETTING AND THE SOLUTION-FOCUSED APPROACH

On the surface, limit setting and solution-focused therapy can appear contradictory. Early in our transition to using the SF approach with our adolescent groups, the therapists went through a phase of allowing disruptive client behaviors, such as side conversations, disrespectful gestures (such as rolling of the eyes when a peer was talking), and flippant answers to questions, to go unchecked.

Again, in retrospect, the therapists' inexperience in applying solution-focused therapy temporarily shattered their confidence in their ability to apply basic group skills. Eventually the therapists resumed setting limits. Without a basic shared understanding of when one speaks and listens, the group process becomes chaotic and the therapists cannot hear what is important to the clients. Furthermore, each group has its own personality. Group members tend to become emotionally guarded and engage in disruptive behaviors if the group leader does not provide sufficient limits to ensure a safe space in which to explore and discuss what is truly important.

The therapists on our team learned to set limits gently while maintaining a solution-focused stance. This meant that limits were given as a means to address the goals expressed by the group members, rather than as a judgmental or punitive reaction. The following interaction demonstrates how limit setting is done in our adolescent groups:

CLIENT: This is stupid [rolling her eyes]. I don't need to be here and group is not helping. [This client had been referred to our agency by her probation officer after she had stolen a car with her friends while under the influence of alcohol and marijuana. Her mother was very concerned yet was unable to control her daughter's behavior.]

THERAPIST: Hmm. Tell me whose idea it was for you to be here.

CLIENT: My mom's. She thinks I have a problem, but she doesn't know anything. This is dumb and isn't helping anyone! Why aren't you teaching us anything? I thought we were going to watch a video or something.

THERAPIST: Is there something in particular that would be helpful for you to learn about?

CLIENT: No. I just thought that was what you were supposed to do. I don't need to learn anything from these groups.

THERAPIST: OK. How about you and I take some time together and figure out what would be the most helpful for you? It is very important to me that you are not in group if it is not helpful to you.

The therapist would then take the client out of group (if a cotherapist was present) or wait until after group and discuss with the client what would be helpful. It is important to immediately address client complaints about group not being useful. This communicates the therapist's intent to make every group interaction helpful rather than a meaningless experience of "doing time" to satisfy a legal or parental requirement. This further assures the other clients that the group setting is a productive environment in which to discuss important issues, and that everyone present is working in a similar direction.

Many times client concerns about the usefulness of groups can be effectively addressed immediately in the group setting. This is because the SF approach typically results in a strong group norm that results in other clients responding to a concern about the usefulness of the group by spontaneously expressing how it has been useful to them:

CLIENT: This is stupid [rolling her eyes]. I don't need to be here and group is not helping.

THERAPIST: Hmm. Tell me whose idea it was for you to be here.

CLIENT: My mom's. She thinks I have a problem, but she doesn't know anything. This is dumb and isn't helping anyone! Why aren't you teaching us anything? I thought we were going to watch a video or something.

THERAPIST: Is there something in particular that would be helpful for you to learn about?

CLIENT: No. I just thought that was what you were supposed to do. I don't need to learn anything from these groups.

SECOND CLIENT: I used to think that too. The questions are sorta weird, but once you get into it, it makes you think. I even think about their questions after I leave here. It's important to think about future stuff.

THERAPIST: Really! How has it been helpful?

SECOND CLIENT: Well, now I see how important going to school and getting along with my parents are. It's just not worth all of the stuff I was doing before.

THERAPIST: How did you go from the place where you thought group was stupid to this place of seeing how helpful it is?

SECOND CLIENT: I guess just listening. I don't know. Those questions, like that one about the miracle, just make you think.

Occasionally groups are vulnerable to becoming negatively influenced by a member's complaint or by an outward disrespect for the group process. In such situations, the complaint is best addressed individually. The following example illustrates how the therapist would address this client's concern individually (the therapist could use this same approach in the group setting if a positive group norm exists):

THERAPIST: Thanks for being willing to talk to me. It's really important to me that you aren't wasting your time. I'm sure you have other things you would rather be doing. I'm a little confused why you came today if you don't think you need to be here.

CLIENT: I have to come! I hate everyone telling me what to do all the time!

THERAPIST: Wow! That sounds tough. Let me ask you a weird question, OK?

CLIENT: OK [said with an exasperated tone while rolling her eyes].

THERAPIST: I want you to imagine that tonight a miracle happens and the miracle is that your mom isn't worried about you anymore. She knows that you are going to make good choices and she doesn't have to tell you what to do. But because you were asleep, you don't know that the miracle happened. So, when you wake up tomorrow what will you notice that will let you know that something is different?

CLIENT: This is a stupid question.

THERAPIST: I know it's strange, but just play along with me.

CLIENT: Well, she wouldn't be banging on my door telling me to get up for one thing.

THERAPIST: What would she be seeing in you to know that she didn't need to do that this morning?

CLIENT: I would be getting up on my own and getting ready for school.

THERAPIST: Wow! What else would she see?

CLIENT: That I took the time to talk to her before I left for school. Maybe even had breakfast with her and my sister [said with increased eye contact and a serious tone].

THERAPIST: And what difference would that make to your mom this morning?

CLIENT: Well, she would be happy. She wouldn't have to yell at me.

THERAPIST: What is she like when she is happy?

CLIENT: She makes stupid jokes and is more laid back.

THERAPIST: And what difference would that make for you?

CLIENT: I guess I would leave the house in a good mood. I probably wouldn't mind coming home on time. I might even get my homework done since I would be home.

THERAPIST: Would that be different?

CLIENT: Yeah! It would be totally different!

THERAPIST: So, on a scale from one to ten (ten being that it is extremely important, and one being that it isn't important at all), how important is it to you that things be like this between you and your mom?

CLIENT: About a nine.

THERAPIST: That's pretty high! OK. On another one-to-ten scale (ten being that how you described your miracle morning is how it is now, and one being the opposite), where would you say your relationship with your mom is now?

CLIENT: About a two.

THERAPIST: Where would you like it to be?

CLIENT: At least an eight.

THERAPIST: So how can I help with this?

CLIENT: I guess coming to group will help.

THERAPIST: How?

CLIENT: I think it will help me to remember that this is important to me. It will remind me that there are things I can do that might help my mom not to have to yell so much.

THERAPIST: OK. But . . . if group is ever not helpful, I want you to let me know because this is important stuff you are working on. All right?

CLIENT: OK. See you next week.

This interaction typifies the shift we see in adolescents when we listen attentively and respectfully to what they really want. Meeting with the therapist individually was not intended as a punishment, and the client was not reprimanded for her questioning in the group setting. Her statement that group was not helpful was honored, and she learned that the therapist was there to ensure that every interaction is useful in helping her get where she wants to be. This client wants her interaction with her mother to be different, yet she initially saw group as yet another forum for an adult to tell her what to do (e.g., teach, show educational videos). The therapist taking the time to find out how the client wanted her life to be vividly communicated that group could be an opportunity for change. She now sees purpose in participating. This purpose and relevance to the desired future engages clients and results in meaningful, lasting change.

As our therapists gained the ability to listen to what our adolescent clients really wanted and mastered the ability to include gentle limit setting, the treatment groups stabilized and positive norms of productivity were established. We discovered that the adolescent group process was no different from that of our adult client groups. All clients (irrespective of age) had unique wants, desires, and imagined miracles, and by focusing on the individual details of their desired futures, the stereotypical problems of working with adolescents became irrelevant.

"Life Groups"

Our adolescent clients frequently describe our future-oriented questions as "hard" because they "make us think" (similar comments are heard from our adult clients as well). They often tell us that they continued to think about the questions we asked them in group even after they left the agency and that our way of thinking became common between sessions. Although the problem that resulted in the clients' referral to our agency was always alcohol or drug related, our treatment groups have been more accurately described by our clients as "life groups" due to their future orientation.

RELATIONAL QUESTIONS WITH ADOLESCENTS

Adolescents tend to be keenly aware of how others perceive them. This makes the use of relational questions (see Chapter 1) especially useful. Although adolescents are not always aware of what they would be doing differently after the miracle occurs, they can often identify what other people will be doing differently or noticing in them. They are frequently able to accurately describe other people's perceptions and responses to the changes precipitated by the miracle. By using this line of questioning, clients are then able to identify what difference these changes will make for them.

Although adolescents often pretend to ignore their parents' (or other important adult figures') words of wisdom, we find that they have stored the information and can readily recall it as needed. By using relational questions, therapists can access this information to ensure that client decisions and responses include all aspects of their current reality. This serves to ensure that client goals are transferable to their environment and are reality based.

The following interaction shows how we use relational questions to assist clients in including all aspects of their world:

This client was referred for services by the legal system after he was charged with possession of cocaine and with theft. He had not been attending school, and his parents were concerned that he had joined a gang.

THERAPIST: What are you hoping will be different as a result of coming here?

CLIENT: That my parents will get off my back and leave me alone.

THERAPIST: What will that look like when it happens?

CLIENT: They would let me make my own decisions.

THERAPIST: What kind of decisions would you be making?

CLIENT: When to come home, who to hang out with. You know, that kind of stuff.

THERAPIST: What are your parents hoping will be different as a result of you coming here?

CLIENT: That I'm home all the time and don't want to hang out with my best friend.

THERAPIST: It sounds like you guys don't agree on a lot of stuff. I'm wondering if you would be willing to imagine with me that it is the end of treatment and, somehow, you and your parents are all happy and agree that this has been worth your time. What is different?

CLIENT: They would be letting me make my own decisions about who my friends are.

THERAPIST: OK. What are they seeing that lets them know that they can let go a little and trust your judgment about your friends?

CLIENT: That I'm being responsible.

THERAPIST: How would they know that?

CLIENT: I would be going to school, getting good grades, and doing what I was asked around the house.

THERAPIST: Hmm. Would that be different?

CLIENT: Yeah, I guess so.

THERAPIST: How would that make your life better?

CLIENT: It would make it a lot better. I wouldn't have to worry about getting in trouble all of the time. It would probably be calmer around the house.

THERAPIST: What would your parents tell me about how these changes made their life better?

CLIENT: They would say that I wouldn't be a bad influence on my brother anymore and that they wouldn't be so stressed out because of me.

THERAPIST: How about your brother? What would he tell me?

CLIENT: He would say that he was happy that my parents would let him spend more time with me. He really likes it when we hang out together.

THERAPIST: How about you? What difference does it make to you when you get to spend more time with him?

CLIENT: It's sorta cool. He's a cool kid, even though he gets on my nerves.

THERAPIST: So, how would his life be better from hanging out with you?

CLIENT: He would learn that you could still have fun and stay out of trouble.

THERAPIST: How would he learn that from you?

CLIENT: By going bike riding, swimming, and stuff like that.

Adolescent clients (as well as many adult clients) often begin by talking about how other people's behavior would be different, as the previous excerpt illustrates. This can be easily utilized by asking the clients what they did to precipitate this positive response in others. In the previous example this is demonstrated by the client's initial statements, "My parents will get off my back and leave me alone" and that his parents would be "letting me make my own decisions." Through therapist questioning, the client identified that his "being responsible" precipitated his parents' change in behavior. It is understandably tempting to point out to clients that they cannot change other people's behavior and then to refocus the clients on what behaviors they would like to change in themselves, but we do not find this expert-based response helpful. It often results in needless power struggles due to the client not believing that the therapist understands the importance of others changing as well.

Conversely, by asking questions that explore the systemic aspect of change, clients readily discover what behavioral changes they can make that would naturally result in a change in those around them. By using this technique, the clients discover the interconnectedness of human behavioral change. As Miller and de Shazer (1998) point out, "This different behavior [referring to the client] will prompt other people to respond to her differently. These different responses can come to serve as reinforcements for the client's different behaviors, thus also reinforcing the inner changes" (p. 366).

RELATIONAL QUESTIONS AS A WAY TO WORK WITH FAMILIES

Family usually plays a significant part in adolescents' lives (McCollum and Trepper, 2001) and family members are often affected by the adolescent's problems. Through relational questions, the therapist can incorporate the opinions, concerns, and feedback of family members even when they are not present during the therapy session.

Relational questions can help clients to incorporate other family members' opinions into the desired solution, thereby increasing family cohesion and increasing the likelihood of reaching a solution that is acceptable to all.

Nevertheless, sometimes working directly with the adolescent's family members is the best course of action. We find it most useful to ask clients when family members should be involved in treatment, for they are the best judge of who should participate to obtain the desired solution.

We utilize the same relational questions and other interventions (described in Chapter 1) when working with adolescents' family members that we use with individuals and groups. However, when working with family members, our primary initial goal is to assist the family members in describing a miracle upon which they all can agree. The following interaction demonstrates how we would work with the previously mentioned client in a family session to develop a family miracle:

THERAPIST: So, what are you hoping will be different as a result of coming here today?

MOTHER: We just want to know that Sam is going to stop using drugs and is going to be OK. We are worried sick about him.

FATHER: He has been associating with friends who are a bad influence on him. His attitude is poor and is getting worse.

THERAPIST: It sounds like you both love Sam a lot. Is it OK if I ask him a few questions?

MOTHER: Of course. That's why we are here. We want you to tell us what we should do to get him to stop using drugs.

THERAPIST: Sam, my guess is that you know your parents pretty well. Would you agree?

SAM: Yeah.

THERAPIST: Well, I'm curious about something. On a scale of one to ten (ten being that your parents are very confident in your decisions and know you will make the best decisions for yourself, and one is that they have no confidence at all and they are very worried about you), where would you say your parents are now?

SAM: About a two.

THERAPIST: OK. Mom and Dad, where would you rate yourselves on that same scale?

FATHER: I think Sam is about right. I probably would have said about a three.

MOTHER: I agree. I think I would have said a two.

Using scaling in this fashion is often helpful in demonstrating to the parents that the adolescent has heard their concerns, for often the problem has been made worse by the parents' belief that the adolescent has not heard anything they have said. This intervention begins the process of building a bridge of understanding between the generations and provides a common language with which to explore a possible solution.

THERAPIST: OK. Sam, where would you like your parents to be on that scale?

SAM: At least an eight. Things would be much more comfortable at an eight.

THERAPIST: And how about the two of you [addressing the parents]? Where would you like to be?

MOTHER: I would be fine with an eight. Of course I would love a ten, but I don't think that is realistic right now.

FATHER: An eight would be great!

THERAPIST: Wow! So everyone agrees that an eight on this scale would be a worthwhile goal. So, I want all of you to imagine with me that tonight, when you go home and go to bed, a miracle happens. The miracle is that you are now an eight on that scale. However, because everyone was asleep, you don't know that this miracle happened. So, what do you notice when you wake up that lets you know that this miracle happened?

SAM: Well, I guess I would get up and come downstairs for breakfast. Everyone would be in a good mood and we would get off to a good start.

MOTHER: Yeah. That would be nice. We would have a few minutes together in the morning before everyone rushed off to work or school.

THERAPIST: What else would be different about this morning together?

MOTHER: Sam would be willing to answer my questions about his plans for the day.

SAM: And it wouldn't feel like I'm being quizzed!

THERAPIST: What would be different about the questions on this morning that makes them more comfortable to answer?

SAM: Mom would trust that I'm doing what I'm supposed to and it would be more casual conversation rather than looking for me to mess up.

THERAPIST: And what would Mom see is different about you this morning to know that she can trust that you are doing what you are supposed to be doing?

SAM: Probably that I am willing to answer her questions, and that I might even volunteer what I'm up to.

THERAPIST: So when you have this time together in the morning to talk, what difference will this make for the rest of your day?

FATHER: I will be able to focus on my day without having to worry about whether Sam is going to get into trouble.

MOTHER: I will look forward to seeing him in the evening and won't be so stressed out all day.

SAM: I guess I wouldn't be so angry when I go to school. It would make it easier to go to class and stay out of trouble.

THERAPIST: Who would notice once you got to school that something was different this morning?

SAM: My teachers. They would be shocked that I was actually on time and paying attention.

Family members and clients most often want the same thing. The therapist's challenge is to listen carefully enough to identify the commonality within the family members' descriptions. In this case, all family members want the parents to worry less and to be more confident about Sam's decisions. This would decrease the stress on the parents and increase the amount of freedom that Sam is given. Significantly, Sam is clearly able to identify what he needs to do differently in order to decrease his parents' worry. By asking him to scale his parents' confidence level in front of his parents, the therapist gives Sam the opportunity to demonstrate that he is aware of his parents' concerns and that he also wants life at home to be different. This understanding of the needs of other family members is often the first step in mending family conflict.

When working with family members, it is important to quickly redirect family members when they begin to drift into blame or conflict, lest this further exacerbate family strife. Fighting is not a productive use of therapy sessions. We assume that family members come to treatment because they want to discover a solution. They have already perfected the art of argument and do not need our guidance in this area! We have discovered that family members frequently use the solution-focused techniques they learn from the therapist outside of the treatment sessions to refocus on the common goal and to identify times in which they are achieving parts of their miracle. This positive focus serves to reinforce change even during potential conflict.

SCALING AND THERAPEUTIC ANALOGIES TO KINDLE HOPE

Our adolescent clients often tell us that they are discouraged because their parents seem to have lost hope that they will change their behavior. At these times we have found analogies and the use of scaling questions to be most helpful in sustaining the client's hope that they will be able to regain their parents' trust. The following example demonstrates how this is done:

This excerpt is from a session with an adolescent male who was removed from his parents' custody by social services due to his violent behavior against family members, legal problems, and not complying with family rules such as curfew and no drug use. His parents remain uninvolved and angry.

CLIENT: There is no point in this. My parents don't notice any of the changes that I have been making. Why bother?

THERAPIST: I can understand why it would be really discouraging. When you were talking I imagined this guy in a really deep hole. His goal is to get to the top of the mountain, before he can even begin to climb up the mountain, he has to get out of the hole at the base of the mountain. He's climbing and climbing, yet no one notices because he is still in the hole. You know what I mean?

CLIENT: Yeah! That's what I'm talking about. I'm in a really deep hole!

THERAPIST: So, on a scale of one to ten (ten being you are at the top of your mountain, and one is you're at the bottom of your hole at the base of the mountain), how far would you have to climb before you get out of your hole so someone notices all of the hard work you are doing?

CLIENT: Probably about a five.

THERAPIST: Where are you now?

CLIENT: About a three.

THERAPIST: Hmm. That means you don't have that much further to go before you hit daylight.

CLIENT: Yeah!

Scaling and Analogy As a Means to Elicit Hope

Clients often lose hope as a result of all-or-nothing thinking. Scales are instrumental in assisting clients to discover the progress they are making and to connect their current efforts to the desired goal. The previous analogy demonstrates to the client that it is normal for people not to notice his tremendous efforts because he is "digging out of a hole." This also serves to eliminate any blame since those around him could not possibly notice the hard work he is doing because he is figuratively hidden from sight in his "hole."

Typically, clients' predictions about when others will begin to notice are quite accurate. Clients often report excitedly in subsequent sessions that someone has begun to notice their hard work. When we then ask them to scale where they are on the previously mentioned scale, they soon discover they are at or above the number that signifies they are "out of the hole."

WORKING WITH YOUNGER CHILDREN

There is a wonderful systemically based trend in substance abuse treatment to include children of all ages in the parents' treatment. Professionals have become more aware that children and adolescents are often significantly impacted by the parents' struggle with substances or other life problems. Substance abuse treatment agencies have traditionally provided services for adolescents, due to the adolescents' use of substances, yet have neglected the possible need for services related to the impact that their parents' use or other problems have had on them or their younger siblings. This new trend of including children and adolescents in this manner can pose a unique challenge for professionals whose training is more traditional and does not include the necessary knowledge of how to work with younger children in this manner. Professionals often believe that children are unable to identify what is important to them or to think in a logical manner due to lack of life experience and normal cognitive development. When therapists have training in child therapy it is most often in play therapy or in other forms of treatment that appear contradictory to solution-focused therapy. Despite these challenges, we explored with good success the idea of using the SF approach with our youngest clients.

I (TP) have often been asked about the effectiveness of using solution-focused therapy with young children (age five and older), and my response is frequently to ask, "Who is having the problem?" I typically discover that the parents are concerned about the welfare of their children. In this sense, it is the parents' problem, although it is being experienced by the child. For example, the parents' concerns may be due to the child's behavioral problems or exposure to potentially traumatic events such as divorce, domestic violence, or substance abuse. In such cases, parents may seek professional help in response to feelings of confusion or helplessness about how to respond to their child's need. Unfortunately, this helplessness is often inadvertently reinforced by the expert-based approach of the services they receive. All too often, parents walk away from such consultations believing that the "right" answer can come only from an "expert."

Although childhood mental illness does exist and can have devastating consequences, I have found this rarely to be the cause when parents inquire about services for younger children. As a result, we find it most helpful to use a family approach with the goal to assist the parents in discovering how they can be the best possible resource for their child in overcoming the current difficulty. This simultaneously reassures the parents and empowers both the parents and the child by accessing the best possible resource for the child. A significant advantage of this approach is that the parents are placed in the expert role for their child which increases their ability to assist their child in future crises. The following example illustrates one of the ways that we address parents' concerns about younger children:

FATHER: I'm really concerned about the girls. Their mother left them a few months ago, and Karen [age seven] cries for her all of the time. Susan [age six] doesn't follow directions and needs to be reminded to do chores that she used to do without being asked.

The father had sought services after the children's mother had disappeared. He described her as a "drug addict," and he was very concerned about the probable neglect and abuse to which the children had been exposed.

THERAPIST: I'm really impressed by your concern for your children. You must love them very much to seek services so soon to prevent future problems! [Turning to address the children] I'm really impressed both of you are here too! I bet you miss your mom. How have you both been doing so well without her?

SUSAN: I don't think about her much [playing with her doll].

KAREN: I go to school and keep busy. I still cry [starting to cry].

THERAPIST: What is it that your dad does that helps you get through this even though you miss your mom so much?

KAREN: I like it when he holds me when I cry and reads me stories until I fall asleep.

SUSAN: Me too. Dad spends more time with us. He even plays games now, even though he isn't very good. [Both girls are giggling now.]

THERAPIST: What else should your dad know he should keep doing to help?

KAREN: Making my lunch with little notes inside helps. It makes it easier when other kids talk about their moms since I keep the notes in my pocket to look at.

THERAPIST: [Addressing Dad] Did you know that made a big difference?

FATHER: No, I didn't even know that she noticed.

THERAPIST: How about the other things? The holding, stories, and games?

FATHER: I do notice that Karen doesn't cry at night when we spend time together like that. She has even talked about her mother to me more when we have time together.

THERAPIST: How about Susan? What difference do you see in her when you do these things?

FATHER: Things go smoother. I guess I hadn't thought about it before, but she does go with the flow better and follow directions when we have time together.

Over the years we have learned that children and adolescents (even very young children) tend to be very proficient at identifying what their parents do that makes a difference. I (TP) have even discovered that children (similar, believe it or not, to adolescents) give very accurate information about which disciplinary measures are effective and which are not. When we ask children these types of questions in front of their parents, we find that the parents are often amazed at the wisdom of their children. The parents become aware of the positive impact of asking their children what difference their parenting efforts are making.

This leads parents to take a discovery approach to parenting and to notice what behaviors result in positive responses from their children. As a result of this noticing, parents become more flexible and responsive to the unique needs of their children (one of the primary skills of effective parenting). I have had parents tell me that they have learned lessons through this approach that therapists once thought were learned only through an expert-based approach. Child problems that once seemed insurmountable frequently return to proper perspective as parents learn to listen to the wisdom of their children.

SUMMARY

In order to effectively apply the SF approach to our adolescent program, we had to reexamine some of our old assumptions based on the tradition of using expert-based, problem-focused approaches and preset group agendas with this population. Over time, we realized that the SF approach does not preclude limit setting, and as a result it adapts well to adolescent groups and the individual needs of adolescents. Although adolescents' problems are likely to be related to their developmental stage, their solutions tend to be unique to them as individuals. Not surprisingly, our adolescent clients readily embraced the SF approach, as it utilizes the tasks of differentiation and exploration of possible future roles characteristic of their developmental stage.

Chapter 7

The Art of Speaking "French": Interagency Diplomacy

Most people see what is, and never see what can be.

Albert Einstein

In order to best serve their clients and keep their jobs, solution-focused therapists need to communicate effectively in a problem-focused treatment world. This chapter describes how we found ways to communicate respectfully and collaboratively with colleagues who have philosophies different from ours.

Once we had experienced the therapeutic rewards of solution-focused therapy, we were unable to work in a problem-focused manner. Our referral sources, other treatment providers, and governing agencies, however, all continued to communicate in problem-focused language.

At this point, we made some mistakes. Still new to the SF approach, we (TP and team) became hypervigilant about identifying and changing our own problem-focused thinking patterns. We began to think of the problem-focused approach as a sort of enemy. Realizing that problem-focused talk did not help us produce the results we were seeking, we became determined to eradicate it from others' vocabularies as well. We do not recommend doing this! Besides being ineffective, it resulted in needless power struggles and conflict with our colleagues; worse, we risked permanently alienating them.

Fortunately, we eventually remembered the solution-focused axiom, "If it's not working, do something different." A useful shift occurred when we learned (or in some cases remembered) to carefully listen to the meaning behind our colleagues' problem-focused words.

Often, their meaning was very similar to our own. We were simply speaking a different language.

In order to be effective as an agency, we needed to describe our work in words that our problem-focused colleagues could understand and appreciate. Fortunately, this did not necessitate a change in the clinical work with clients, only a change in how we explained this work to others. Insoo Kim Berg helped us make this shift when she metaphorically described the ability to communicate effectively with the problem-focused world as "speaking French" (personal communication, 2000). As Insoo pointed out to us, one can speak "French" without becoming French.

We began to see that speaking a common language with listeners was simply a matter of showing courtesy and respect, and not an indication that we were abandoning the method of working we valued. In order to move forward, we learned to translate the solution-focused concepts we were using into problem-focused words, so that those whose primary language is problem focused could understand what we meant. This was an important turning point for our team. At this point in our journey we realized we could apply solution-focused concepts not only to our work with the clients but also to our work in the community.

WORKING WITH OTHER PROFESSIONALS

Remaining Neutral

Since a high proportion of our substance abuse treatment referrals come to us via outside agencies such as social services or probation departments, our therapists must be able to communicate effectively and productively with representatives of these agencies. Without this, our clients would be caught in the middle and treatment services compromised.

Since most of our clients come to us via referrals, we naturally hear two sides of every story. Our referral sources often emphasize information that the client may minimize or not tell the therapist at all. Conversely, our clients often complain that their referral source does not have all the necessary information or that their referral source is "out to get" them. It would be all too easy for us to fall into siding with one or the other; however, we know that would be counterproductive.

Insoo Kim Berg and Norm Reuss (1998) compare the relationship between the client and referral source to that of a married couple whose marriage was arranged by relatives. For the good of the couple as well as the extended family system, both parties need to be treated respectfully and experience their needs being met. We have found this metaphor especially meaningful in our work with mandated clients, because, as in conjoint family therapy, the therapist must perfect the skill of remaining neutral.

Any time that a therapist works with more than one party, the work becomes more complex. The therapist must "understand the importance of conceptualizing and identifying with two clients simultaneously" (Shulman, 1992, p. 217). Therapists must listen to both parties and refrain from emotionally identifying with either, so they can assist both in identifying common ground for an agreeable solution.

Solution-focused questions help both the referral source and the client to clarify the desired outcome. In the process of doing this, the information being presented typically becomes more factual and less influenced by personal opinion. Often this leads to the discovery of an initial, shared goal. Since conversations with referral sources frequently take place by telephone, the clients are usually absent when they take place. Therapists may be tempted to become informal during such private discussions and to focus on shared biases about the client. However, this is best avoided because it can result in negatively prejudiced thinking, which may interfere with working effectively with the client. The following case excerpt exemplifies the advantages of remaining neutral when speaking with a referral source:

THERAPIST: What are you hoping that Susan will gain by coming to treatment?

REFERRAL SOURCE: Well, she needs relapse groups. She keeps relapsing on methamphetamine, and I don't know if she will be able to keep it together long enough to keep her kids safe. She used to use meth every day and she just can't seem to stay away from the stuff.

THERAPIST: She no longer uses meth daily? What happened?

REFERRAL SOURCE: No. She has made some significant changes. She said that she realized how much of a problem it was for her. Now she uses probably once a month or so. Each time her urine screen comes back dirty she tells me that it was a "slip" and it will never happen again, yet it just keeps happening. I can't be sure her kids will be safe. I don't know what to believe!

THERAPIST: What would you need to see her doing differently that would let you know that she does indeed have the necessary relapse prevention skills?

REFERRAL SOURCE: She would have to stop hanging around her ex-boyfriend. I know that he is a drug dealer, and I can't believe she is really serious about staying clean as long as she continues to be with him.

THERAPIST: What else?

REFERRAL SOURCE: She would start looking actively for jobs so that she could support herself and the kids. That would let me know that she really wanted to get them back.

THERAPIST: If Susan was here, what would she tell me that you need to see in order to be more confident in her abilities?

REFERRAL SOURCE: She would say I need to see clean urine screens.

THERAPIST: What else?

REFERRAL SOURCE: I guess she would probably say that I am concerned about her ex-boyfriend. We have talked about it, and she has acknowledged that he is a negative influence on her.

THERAPIST: On a scale of one to ten (ten being that you have complete confidence in Susan's ability, and one being that you have absolutely no confidence in Susan at all) where would you put yourself right now?

REFERRAL SOURCE: About a four. I have seen her do it before, so I know she can if she puts her mind to it.

THERAPIST: Where on this scale would you need to be to trust that Susan can do the rest on her own without treatment?

REFERRAL SOURCE: At least a seven. She will always be at risk, yet at some point I will have to let her try it on her own, maybe with a support group such as AA or something.

THERAPIST: As we go through treatment, I really would appreciate your feedback to both Susan and me about what you are noticing that she is doing differently. You are much more knowledgeable about her personal life than I am, and you will probably be the first to notice progress. I need you to let me know your concerns and what you are seeing.

There were several opportunities in this example in which the therapist could have drifted into problem talk with the referral source (e.g., exploring why Susan keeps associating with her ex-boyfriend, what triggers her to relapse, why Susan is not a fit parent). Rather than clarifying what the referral source needs to be different, problem talk could have caused the therapist to become unnecessarily pessimistic about the case. By remaining focused on what additional changes the referral source needs to see, the therapist was able to transform the otherwise vague concept of "confidence" into a useful, measurable goal. This process is also helpful to the referral sources, because it elicits a clear description of the behaviors they need to see in their clients. This facilitates an objective view and often results in the referral source recognizing previously unidentified signs of progress in the client.

This method of working allows us to communicate respect for the concerns of the referral sources, and invites them to actively participate throughout treatment by monitoring and describing the changes they are noticing in the client. Furthermore, this allows us to acknowledge and utilize the referral source's expertise.

In collaborating simultaneously with clients and referral sources, solution-focused therapists cocreate a usable description of what will be entailed in creating a life without the problem. The input of all involved parties is valuable and necessary in order to create a future vision that will be meaningful, respectful, and accurate for all involved. Asking relational questions (see Chapter 1) is especially useful in situations involving multiple agencies or family members because it elicits information from the perspective of the various other people. The following case illustrates how this is done with a client:

THERAPIST: We have been talking about how your life will be once your miracle has happened. I'm curious what your caseworker would say she needs to see in you that will let her know that you can do this on your own, and that she can step out of your life.

CLIENT: Well, she would probably say that I wouldn't be hanging out with my ex-boyfriend.

THERAPIST: What difference would she say that would make?

CLIENT: She would say that I wouldn't be so likely to relapse and go back to drugs, but we don't always do drugs together!

THERAPIST: What else would she say?

CLIENT: She would say that I would have a good job and a place for my kids.

THERAPIST: What difference would that make?

CLIENT: I would be more stable. Remember? That was part of my miracle too.

THERAPIST: So they overlap in some ways.

CLIENT: Yeah. I want to be stable, have a job, place to live, and all that. I guess I even agree that my ex-boyfriend isn't a good influence. I can never keep everything together when I'm with him.

THERAPIST: Wow! Does your caseworker know how much you two have in common?

This example demonstrates how clients and referral sources often view the solution similarly. The therapist's role is to gently explore what each person wants, while listening carefully for commonalities in what each describes. Even when the goals initially appear different, the motives behind the goals are most often the same. In this example, both the client and referral source want "stability" for the client and her children. The client does not initially agree that she should stay away from her ex-boyfriend, but she does agree that stability would be difficult to maintain otherwise.

Although a therapist may be tempted to defend the client when a referral source appears to be overly critical or unjustly negative, we have learned that this response tends to polarize the therapist and referral source. It can also prevent the therapist from hearing important information the referral source has to offer. Caseworkers and other referral sources (as can any professional) can succumb to burnout, but we find it productive to assume that they have valuable ideas about how we can both be helpful to our shared client.

Referral sources who are actively involved in their clients' cases and therefore collaborate with us as treatment providers are likely to be aware of their clients' potential. Our hunch is that sometimes they become frustrated or disappointed due to the clients' apparent lack of living up to that potential, and this is often expressed in their primarily problem-oriented language or problem talk. Whether our hunch is true or not, this stance allows us to remain curious to learn what potential the referral source sees and what will convince the referral source that the clients' changes are positive and likely to last.

Referral sources often refer clients for evaluation, and therapists' opinions are essential to court reports and other legal documents. This can be an especially confusing role for a therapist who has just recently made the paradigm shift from thinking of "therapist as expert" to "client as expert". To make issues more complicated, court-mandated clients often do not believe that they have a problem, yet problem-focused therapists and other professionals are recommending services for them.

How can solution-focused therapists maintain credibility with the problem-focused community yet respect their client's viewpoint when making recommendations? On the surface, this role requires the therapist to decide whose story is correct.

This can be a difficult dilemma. I (TP) once heard a therapist say, "There is solution-focused treatment, and then there is case management." We respectfully disagree. Solution-focused case management is definitely possible. (We say this not only because we do it, but because successful diplomats have been doing it for hundreds of years!)

SOLUTION-FOCUSED CASE MANAGEMENT

Solution-focused case management requires the ability to accurately hear the opinions of everyone involved and then to carefully and respectfully combine (and sometimes reword) these into a useful professional recommendation. This results in the client's and referral source's views and ideas being respectfully reflected in the "expert's recommendation." Ironically, we have noticed over time that this process often results in recommendations that are very similar to those that would be made by our problem-focused colleagues, except they are worded proactively. The following example demonstrates how this can be done:

THERAPIST: Before I tell you my recommendations, I want to make sure that I have all of the facts. Tell me what you are hoping will be different for Jim as a result of coming to treatment here.

REFERRAL SOURCE: Well, he needs to understand that he has a problem!

THERAPIST: You know . . . I've worked with a lot of clients who would say whatever they thought their referral source wanted to hear, even when they didn't really believe it. It doesn't sound like that is want you are wanting from Jim. You really want him to get it! How will you know that he really understands this and is not just telling you what you want to hear?

REFERRAL SOURCE: Yeah, I know what you are saying, and that's a tough one. I guess I would know if he started making some changes in his life.

THERAPIST: Like what?

REFERRAL SOURCE: Following through. Going to groups, holding down a job, keeping all his appointments.

THERAPIST: What else?

REFERRAL SOURCE: His attitude would change.

THERAPIST: How so?

REFERRAL SOURCE: He wouldn't be fighting all this, and would take responsibility for what got him in this mess.

THERAPIST: How would you know that he was taking responsibility?

REFERRAL SOURCE: By him doing all of the things the court ordered.

THERAPIST: OK. Anything else I should know before I let you know my recommendations?

REFERRAL SOURCE: Just that he needs help.

THERAPIST: I hear that. I would agree that he has had considerable difficulty with consistency and with doing what he needs to do. When I look at the facts (sporadic urine drugs screen, inconsistent attendance at required appointments, etc.), it doesn't look very good. I can see why you would be concerned. Treatment will give him another opportunity to work on this consistency and provide some positive evidence for you and the court. This issue of consistency and helping him to think about how his current actions influence his future is something that I would recommend that we work on during treatment. In addition, I am going to recommend that he work very closely with you during this treatment episode so that he really understands the larger picture and what he needs to do. Is that all right with you?

REFERRAL SOURCE: Yes. That is what I have been trying to tell him.

By gently challenging the referral source to operationalize her initial statement that the client must "understand that he has a problem," the referral source is able to identify that it is the client's current behavior that will serve as a barometer of successful treatment. This shifts the focus to something that the client can change and creates the possibility of agreement between the client and referral source. Once this is in place, the therapist listens very attentively to what is important to the referral source (that the client understands or "gets it" and that he demonstrates this through his behavior by complying with the court order and being consistent).

The therapist also notices that the referral source believes that treatment is necessary for these changes to take place and connects this to measurable facts and behaviors that can be addressed by the client. The therapist then words the recommendations to reassure the referral source that her concerns will be the focus of treatment. Ironically, these same aspects (understanding how current behaviors can positively impact the future, and taking responsibility for creating the desired future) are the foundation of SF treatment.

Both clients and referral sources report a greater sense of satisfaction with the recommendations when they play a pivotal role in forming them. Both believe that compliance with these recommendations is necessary to assist in resolving the problem.

In addition to addressing the stated needs of all parties involved, we try to incorporate all other available information when making recommendations. This is necessary to maintain credibility with the legal system and with other community agencies. In addition, we have discovered that utilizing testing instruments in combination with urine screens is useful to provide objective evidence of the client's current level of progress.[1] Evaluation instruments and urine screens allow the therapist to simultaneously gather necessary evidence for credibility in the problem-focused community while continuing to address the client's goals.

These instruments, along with face-to-face interviews with our clients, demonstrate to our governing agencies that we have indeed collected the necessary evaluative data to ensure that we maintain state credentials. The results of these instruments are presented to the clients, and the clients are encouraged to let the therapist know whether the information is correct.

If the client says that the information is not accurate, client and therapist explore together what behaviors and test results others will need to see in the future in order to be convinced that the client's view of the situation is accurate.

IDENTIFYING EVIDENCE OF A CLIENT'S POTENTIAL FOR SUCCESS

SF therapists are often erroneously thought to overlook negative aspects of the client's life in their quest for solutions. Because of this inaccurate belief, SF therapists have been viewed as naively optimistic or "Pollyannaish." More accurately, SF therapists seek to be neutral in order to truly listen to the client without any preconceived ideas. This stance encourages clients to explore the facts and to make well-informed decisions, which are solidly grounded in evidence. This evidence-based approach is well suited for the task of evaluation. Whereas traditional evaluations uncover evidence that a problem exists, solution-focused evaluations simply record facts or evidence that is present in the client's life. This evidence is gathered through face-to-face interviews, testing instruments, and reports from third parties, such as the referral source or parent. The evaluating therapist works in partnership with the client to record the evidence to objectively substantiate that the client is working toward a predetermined goal (often this goal is defined or heavily influenced by the referral source), while not ignoring evidence to the contrary. By maintaining this neutral stance, the therapist can remain curious to understand the client's current reality and desired goal.

We are not looking for additional evidence of the client's problem. In fact, this would be counterproductive since the client would most likely disagree with our assessment. This would contribute to a needless power struggle instead of facilitating movement toward a common goal. Instead, almost paradoxically, we examine the testing information for evidence that demonstrates that the client is at low risk for a current substance abuse problem. Of course, initially, we are unlikely to find this, or the client would not have been referred to us.

If insufficient evidence is found to demonstrate that the client is currently at low risk for having a problem with substance abuse, the therapist shares this information with the client and asks what he or she would like to do. This empowers and motivates our clients to work to create positive evidence during both the initial evaluation and throughout treatment. As long as the referral source is not convinced that the client is at low risk of having future problems, the involuntary court-mandated relationship between the client and referral source is likely to continue.

Because clients typically want to rid themselves of involuntary court-mandated relationships, they are usually eager to explore ideas about what needs to happen to legitimately justify terminating that relationship as well as what their life will be like afterward. Since this places the responsibility for success squarely on the shoulders of the client, resistance is quickly deflected. Furthermore, a growing body of evidence indicates that substance abuse clients who are allowed to have an active voice in treatment decisions are more likely to succeed and are less vulnerable to subsequent relapse. In addition, those who have a voice in treatment decisions demonstrate increased motivation for change. The Bruges model, developed at the Alcohol Treatment Program at St. John's Hospital in Bruges, Belgium, offers clients choices and responsibilities in a manner similar to Teri's program.[2] This has yielded high success rates, which appear to be directly related to empowering clients to have a voice in their own treatment. A recent survey of outpatients treated with the Bruges model suggests that having their own goals and being able to choose the approach to reaching these goals is crucial to the treatment of problematic drinking (Isebaert, personal communication, 2001).

The following dialogue with a client, Susan, illustrates how clients can be given a voice in their own treatment and recommendations generated from exploring the client's needs:

THERAPIST: What do you hope will be different as a result of coming here?

CLIENT: Nothing. I just want my caseworker to see that I don't have a problem with meth anymore. I used to use meth every day, and I quit. I don't need treatment. I know that my caseworker thinks I do. She thinks I'm going to keep relapsing or something.

THERAPIST: What will she need to see from you to be confident that you have quit for good?

CLIENT: She just needs you to tell her. That's why she sent me here.

THERAPIST: Let's look over some of those instruments you completed and see what I will be telling her. Remember those?

CLIENT: Yeah.

THERAPIST: This one [holding the SASSI-3] indicates that you felt pretty comfortable answering the questions. Is that right?

CLIENT: Yes.

THERAPIST: It confirms what you told me—that you have used drugs other than alcohol rather extensively. It also confirms what you told me about having a hard time when people tell you what to do.

CLIENT: I told you I was telling you the truth. No one ever believes me.

THERAPIST: This is nice evidence to back you up when you say you have been telling the truth. I'm very impressed that you have been so open. This instrument confirms what you have said. Unfortunately, it is not able to confirm for sure that you won't relapse in the future, which is what you mentioned your caseworker is worried about. That is where we are going to have to get creative on how we can provide the evidence you need to demonstrate that. I have another question for you. On a scale of one to ten (ten being that your caseworker has complete confidence in your ability to stay away from drugs, and one being that she has no confidence at all), where would you put her?

CLIENT: About a two.

THERAPIST: Has it ever been lower?

CLIENT: Oh yeah! I've gone to a zero. That was when she took my kids.

THERAPIST: How did you go from a zero to a two?

CLIENT: I worked very hard! I'm not hanging around the same people that I used to. I don't stay up late with that crowd and party anymore. I'm much more responsible.

THERAPIST: Wow! It sounds like it has paid off. Your caseworker has even noticed these changes.

CLIENT: Yeah, that's why she is willing to not go for terminating my parental rights yet.

THERAPIST: What does she see in you that lets her know that there is hope and that she shouldn't give up on you yet?

CLIENT: She has seen me pull myself up before. I really do want this to work. My kids are very important. She knows that getting away from old friends was very hard, and I think that was a big deal to her when I broke away.

THERAPIST: So, what do you think she's looking for in you now?

CLIENT: I think going to group is going to be important. She keeps saying that I need to get some skills to not relapse. It is really tough. I think she also is hoping that I will not hang out with my ex-boyfriend and that I will get a stable place to live and a job.

THERAPIST: What do you think about those things?

CLIENT: I guess group wouldn't hurt. It might even help to get some ideas on how to handle tough times. I have also been thinking that I need to stop hanging out with my ex-boyfriend. I have always been with him when I have slipped and used meth. And I want to get things stable for me and my kids.

THERAPIST: If you did attend some groups, got some ideas on how to prevent relapse, and thought some more about what you want to do with your relationship with your ex-boyfriend, where would this put your caseworker on our scale?

CLIENT: Probably a six.

THERAPIST: It would make a big difference!

CLIENT: I think it would. She would be more confident in me, and it might help me sort some stuff out.

THERAPIST: OK. Here are the treatment recommendations that I am leaning toward. Tell me if you think this will get you closer to where you want to be. It sounds like attending a group that focuses on relapse issues would be helpful in addition to providing urine screens to get some evidence that you aren't using methamphetamine anymore. I would recommend that we start with that and go from there. What do you think?

CLIENT: All right.

Not surprisingly, most treatment programs require treatment plans. Furthermore, local, state, and federal regulations and licensing boards typically require that these treatment plans be completed within a set number of days from the date of intake and that these plans be measurable and specific. This results in much paperwork for caregivers, but it is an understandable requirement intended to ensure that treatment is purposeful and goal directed. Without clearly defined goals, the therapist and client would not know when the problem is solved and treatment is complete, and treatment could continue endlessly (de Shazer, 1988). Unfortunately, treatment plans tend to become therapist driven and prescriptive in nature as a result of the therapist being required to complete them at the onset of treatment, often before it has been possible to fully collaborate with the client.

The commonly used treatment plan models identify the problem, state the desired goal, and list the steps that will be taken by both the client and the therapist to resolve the problem. Treatment plan goals are often closely related to the problem behavior (e.g., "The client will learn to cope with depressive symptoms without the use of alcohol" or "The client will gain the ability to discipline his children without the use of physical punishment"). These plans often stem from problems that the therapist has identified in the client, and are frequently not areas that the client has identified as needing change.

SOLUTION-FOCUSED TREATMENT PLANS

Despite the practical purpose behind it, this problem-focused requirement of treatment planning created a significant challenge in our initial attempts to move toward a solution-focused approach. This was not surprising because solution-focused therapy utilizes the client's ability to imagine and describe the problem from a context in which the problem does not exist and to identify and enact the small changes that are meaningful to the client.

It was difficult to assist the clients in predicting the steps that they would find necessary during treatment. Our early attempts created a problem-solving mentality, which failed to access the potential power of our approach. Even the ability to update the content of the treatment plans did not accommodate the creative power of solution-focused therapy.

Although we shared the commitment to goal-directed treatment, we needed to create a written plan that was client driven and that provided the needed session-to-session flexibility that our approach demands. Our solution was to broaden the language of the treatment plan. Our solution-focused treatment goals often resemble our former problem-focused treatment plans (e.g., "The client will gain the ability to manage her depression effectively"), but typically the client steps are more inclusive, more accepting of our clients' needs to experiment with change, and more in line with our approach (see Figure 7.1 for a sample treatment plan).

INDIVIDUAL TREATMENT PLAN

CLIENT NAME: CLIENT #: 73770

COUNSELOR NAME: DATE: 3/20/01

****

GOAL: The client will identify and practice the skills necessary for her to live life substance free.

SHORT-TERM OBJECTIVE: The client will identify the skills necessary for her to live life substance free.

DUE DATE: 5/10/01

CLIENT'S STEPS:

1. The client will answer the miracle question 1x.
2. The client will make a list of the things she is currently doing that assist her in living her life substance free 1x.
3. The client will make a list of the things she will be doing once the miracle occurs that assists her in living her life substance free 1x.
4. The client will explore what will be different in her life when she is confident in her ability to remain substance free 1x.

SHORT-TERM OBJECTIVE: The client will practice the things she has listed that would assist her in living her life substance free.

DUE DATE: 5/10/01

CLIENT'S STEPS:

1. The client will continue to do the things she is currently doing that assist her in living her life substance free and discuss with the group 1x per week for six weeks.
2. The client will practice one new thing each week from her list of things she could do and share her progress with the adult group 1x per week for six weeks.
3. The client will discuss her progress on her miracle with the group 1x per week for six weeks.

COUNSELOR'S STEPS:

1. The counselor will facilitate group 2x a week for six weeks.
2. The counselor will monitor the client's progress 2x a week for six weeks.
3. The counselor will assess the client's progress 1x at the end of the six-week episode.

_______________ _______ _______________ _______

CLIENT SIGNATURE DATE COUNSELOR SIGNATURE DATE

****

_______________________ _______________________

DATE CLIENT COMPLETED GOAL COUNSELOR SIGNATURE

FIGURE 7.1. Sample Treatment Plan #1

Most people are surprised to hear that our treatment plans rarely mention alcohol or drug use. Since our clients are working toward a future in which these elements are no longer present as a problem, they are seldom a part of the client's future. As experienced solution-focused therapists, we have come to expect that using our approach will make a significant impact on the clients' lives. Many of our clients report that their entire miracle has come true during the course of treatment.

However, in an effort to work within the problem-focused community and to be specific and accountable to our referral sources and governing agencies, it is often necessary to break the client's miracle into smaller goals that can be more readily communicated to other professionals. In addition, the goals often come directly from the clients' statements about their miracle day.

We listen attentively to what the client states will be different once the miracle has occurred, and we listen for parts of this miracle that are something that the client would like to specifically address during treatment. The following interaction demonstrates how the therapist works with the client to identify a goal from a miracle question discussion:

THERAPIST: I am going to ask you a strange question, OK?

CLIENT: OK.

THERAPIST: Imagine that while you are asleep tonight, a miracle happens. The miracle is that all of the problems you have mentioned today are resolved. However, because you were asleep, you don't know that the miracle has happened. So, when you wake up tomorrow morning, what will be different that will let you know that a miracle happened?

CLIENT: Wow! That is a strange question. Let's see . . . I guess I would notice that I have energy and want to get out of bed. My eyes would open because I felt like I had enough sleep. I wouldn't have that heavy depressed feeling I usually have. I would probably not hit the snooze button, and just get up and take a shower.

THERAPIST: What else would you notice?

CLIENT: Well, after my shower, I would go to the kitchen and eat some breakfast. I would probably actually spend some time with my husband, and it would be a pleasant conversation.

THERAPIST: What kinds of things would you be talking about?

CLIENT: Just about what we were both going to do during the day. You know . . . catch-up stuff.

THERAPIST: What would your husband be noticing about you this morning?

CLIENT: He would be shocked that I was up and eating!

THERAPIST: What difference would that make for him that you were there with him?

CLIENT: I think he would be happy. He is always trying to get me to get up. I think it would get us both out the door on a good note. Maybe our whole day would go better.

THERAPIST: If we could fast-forward your life just to the end of treatment and there was one thing that was different in your life that made all the difference in the world, what would it be?

CLIENT: That I wasn't depressed anymore.

THERAPIST: Really? What difference would that make for you?

CLIENT: It would make a huge difference! I would get along better with my husband. I would be able to get and keep a job. I would be happy!

THERAPIST: It sounds like that might be something worth working on while you are here. What do you think?

CLIENT: That would be good.

This client's resulting treatment goal (written in treatment planning language so it is readily understood by our colleagues) would be as follows: The client will gain the skills to manage her mood.

The following are some of the steps that might be written on a treatment plan in regard to this goal:

- The client will complete the miracle question (the miracle is that her mood is not problematic), one time.
- The client will make a list of things that she is currently doing to manage her mood.
- The client will scale her mood (ten being that her mood is not problematic, and one is that her mood is incapacitating her) one time per day for five weeks.
- The client will write down five things each day that she does that increase her rating on this scale (for five weeks).
- The client will ask her husband one time each week what differences he sees in her (for five weeks).

See Figure 7.2 for an example of this treatment plan.

Translating the client's miracle into a treatment plan in this way allows the therapist to communicate more easily with the referral source as well as with other professionals in the client's life. These other treatment professionals may choose to diagnose the client and work from a more traditional stance. Incorporating the miracle into the treatment plan allows us to provide a measurable treatment update as needed to these professionals without becoming involved in diagnostic language. We ask these other professionals for their assessment of the client's progress and often ask them also to scale this progress so that it becomes measurable.

Our clients often report positive changes in many areas of their lives as a result of completing their treatment plan. Frequently no additional services are needed, yet other times clients or referral sources identify another area that they would like to be different prior to terminating services.

TERMINATION

Services are finished when all parties involved agree that the client has accomplished the necessary changes. The therapist's role is to assist all parties to define progress in definable, measurable terms, avoiding vague concepts. This is done by using scaling and often focuses on all caregivers giving their current views of the client's progress and contrasting that with what they saw at the time of admission. The following interaction demonstrates how we use scaling with both the client and referral sources to determine when treatment is finished:

THERAPIST [talking to the referral source by phone]: What have you seen that is different in Karen since she began coming to treatment?

REFERRAL SOURCE: Well, she has followed through with everything. That is something she has not been able to do before. Has she completed everything that you are recommending?

THERAPIST: She has attended all eight scheduled groups. We originally set the treatment goal for her to gain the necessary skills to manage her mood. She has completed her treatment goal. She is

INDIVIDUAL TREATMENT PLAN

CLIENT NAME: CLIENT #: 314073

COUNSELOR NAME: DATE: 2/13/01

****

GOAL: The client will gain the skills to manage her mood.

SHORT-TERM OBJECTIVE: The client will identify the skills necessary to manage her mood.

DUE DATE: 4/5/01

CLIENT'S STEPS:

1. The client will answer the miracle question 1x.
2. The client will generate a list of things she is currently doing to manage her mood 1x.
3. The client will make a list of things she will be doing to manage her mood once the miracle has occurred 1x.
4. The client will explore what will be different in her life when she is able to manage her mood 1x.

SHORT-TERM OBJECTIVE: The client will practice the skills necessary to manage her mood.

DUE DATE: 4/5/01

CLIENT'S STEPS:

1. The client will scale her mood 1x per day for five weeks.
2. The client will write down five things each day that she does that increase her rating on the above scale (for five weeks).
3. The client will ask her husband 1x each week what differences he sees in her (for five weeks).

COUNSELOR'S STEPS:

1. The counselor will facilitate groups 1x per week for five weeks.
2. The counselor will monitor the client's progress 1x a week for five weeks.
3. The counselor will meet individually with the client following the five-week period to assess her progress and need for additional treatment services.

CLIENT SIGNATURE	DATE	COUNSELOR SIGNATURE	DATE

****

DATE CLIENT COMPLETED GOAL	COUNSELOR SIGNATURE

FIGURE 7.2. Sample Treatment Plan #2

reporting that she is now able to get up each morning within five minutes of her alarm going off. She is stating that she now eats breakfast each morning and has found and maintained steady employment as a result. Before I give you my recommendations, I would like to ask you a couple of questions to make sure that I have all the information that I need. On a scale of one to ten (ten being that her mood is not problematic, and one is that her mood is incapacitating her), where would you have put her on that scale at the time of admission?

REFERRAL SOURCE: About a three. She was having a really hard time. That might have been why she was missing so many appointments.

THERAPIST: Where would you put her on that scale today?

REFERRAL SOURCE: An eight. She is much more consistent.

THERAPIST: How high on that scale would you say she needs to be before you would feel confident that she can do the rest on her own?

REFERRAL SOURCE: An eight is fine. I think she can handle it as long as she continues the work she has done. I don't see any need for additional services unless you do.

THERAPIST: I need to meet with Karen prior to making any final recommendations, but since you are comfortable with her progress, I would like to create an aftercare plan with her and discontinue treatment as long as she is also comfortable with those recommendations. I will call you after my session with her.

Therapists must know what external requirements exist prior to meeting with the client to make treatment termination decisions. Without this knowledge the therapist and referral source may be at odds, for treatment cannot be finished as long as the referral source has an unmet need. This does not mean that treatment should continue for an indefinite period of time. Sometimes referral sources request that treatment continue indefinitely because they are not clear what they hope will be different in the client once the need for treatment is resolved. In this situation, the therapist should assist the referral sources in clarifying what they will see in the client once the need for treatment is resolved. Once the input from the referral source is obtained, the therapist can make accurate decisions with the client.

THERAPIST: How is your life different now that you have done so much work?

CLIENT: Everything is different! I'm getting along better with my husband, I have more energy, and I'm working. I can't believe the changes!

THERAPIST: On our scale of one to ten (ten being that your mood is not problematic, and one is that your mood is incapacitating you), remind me where you would have put yourself when you started treatment.

CLIENT: About a two.

THERAPIST: And now?

CLIENT: A nine. Most days I don't even think about my mood. It's not an issue. It hasn't been a problem for over two months. (I guess I did have difficulty getting out of bed last month, yet I was even able to get over that fairly easily!) I have been going to work, hanging out with friends and my husband. You know. All the normal things.

THERAPIST: If we could fast-forward your life one year from today and you were telling me what you did over the past year to maintain the changes you made, what would you tell me you did?

CLIENT: Got up even when I didn't feel like it, exercised, ate a good breakfast, and stayed focused on what is really important to me.

THERAPIST: What do you think you need from me at this point?

CLIENT: I think I'm done.

THERAPIST: What do you think your caseworker would say about your progress?

CLIENT: She is pretty impressed. I don't think she would think that I need to do any more treatment either unless you recommended something else.

THERAPIST: Well, here are my recommendations. I am going to recommend that you continue to do those very things that you discovered make a difference. If our paths ever cross again, I'm going to be curious to learn how you remembered to keep doing those things that worked so well.

The client's personal expertise about what she needs to continue is incorporated directly into the aftercare plan. The therapist often has the client write this advice down to take home in order to make it more formal, but this is not always necessary.

HOW CLIENT CHARTS CAN BE HELPFUL TO SOLUTION-FOCUSED THERAPISTS

The client chart is key to explaining the solution-focused work in problem-focused language. As much as many therapists detest paperwork, it is vitally needed in order for therapists to thrive in a problem-focused treatment culture. The good news is that any solution-focused intervention can be described in problem-focused language that is readily understandable to colleagues who use other approaches, so that they can understand and appreciate the work that was done. For example, the chart note for the previously mentioned client's individual session to review the progress on her treatment goal would read:

> Data: The client attended an individual session to discuss treatment progress. The client stated that her depressive symptoms have subsided. She reported no vegetative symptoms for 30 days and no suicidal ideation for over 60 days. The client reported that she is able to maintain her active lifestyle (work, recreational, and social interactions). We reviewed the client's relapse plan. She demonstrated appropriate knowledge of the importance of exercise and nutrition in the prevention of a relapse. The client rated her progress in managing her mood as a 9 on a 10-point scale (10 equals that her mood is no longer problematic). She stated that this is sufficient for discharge. This has been confirmed with her referral source. It was agreed that she has completed her treatment plan and that no further services are needed at this time.
>
> Assessment: The client appears to have the necessary skills to manage her mood and does not appear to be currently experiencing any depressive symptoms. The client's aftercare/relapse plan appears sufficient, and she appears to have the skills to manage a mild to moderate recurrence of symptoms if needed. In addition, she appears willing to seek additional services as needed in the future.
>
> Plan: Discharge client. Client to contact agency if additional services are needed.

Although the therapist did not initiate the problem-focused language (e.g., assessment of vegetative symptoms), the client provided this information as she enthusiastically described her progress in treatment. The therapist is then able to translate this progress into a problem-focused assessment. The bad news is that this often increases the amount of paperwork. A more detailed chart is needed in order to make clear connections between the solution-focused interventions and the problem-focused requirements. In order to achieve the clarity that is so crucial to success, all of our clinical staff members needed to understand the relevance of charting in problem-focused language and be sufficiently familiar with that approach to do so accurately while continuing to work from a solution-focused orientation. This can sometimes be a tall order, and having the support of a strong solution-focused team is often vital to success.

VIEWING GOVERNING AGENCIES AS CLIENTS

Although it is easy to become frustrated with governing regulations that appear to directly oppose solution-focused therapy or with those that create more work for the therapists in order to comply with their mandates, we believe it is important to mentally step into the governing agency's shoes in order to understand what goals it views as important. This requires us to refrain from judgment, and to be willing to incorporate the goal of the governing agency into our treatment vision. This stance helps us to see respectfully the governing agency as yet another "client" with valid needs, rather than as merely an impersonal agency with arbitrary requirements.

This learned skill of viewing the governing agency as a client and applying solution-focused concepts to all areas of the job are frequently the most difficult tasks we ask our therapists to do. Yet without this, their risk of burnout and frustration increases because often through this process a common goal is identified.

This common goal then becomes the opportunity for solution-focused therapists to work in conjunction with the problem-focused governing agency while remaining true to their philosophy. (Often, we find that the governing agency's goals are similar to our own, yet the steps identified to achieve these goals are frequently quite different. See Boxes 7.1, 7.2, and 7.3 for examples of how the necessary solution-focused and problem-focused steps often differ despite similar goals.)

BOX 7.1. Content Knowledge

Requirement: Specific content/topic areas are to be covered in group sessions

Goal of both solution-focused and problem-focused approaches: Ensure that all clients demonstrate that they possess the knowledge and ability to apply this knowledge in the designated areas

Therapist steps:

Problem-Focused Approaches	Solution-Focused Therapy
1. Create a clear, topic-based curriculum and provide predetermined educational sessions to ensure that all clients know the required information.	1. Listen carefully to what the clients say during solution-focused structured group and individual conversations that indicates that they know the information covered in the designated topics.
	2. Correct misinformation as clients bring up designated topics naturally. Provide access to resources that clients identify are lacking and/or provide additional facts when needed to correct the misinformation.
	3. Ask specific questions during group and individual conversations that address topics that clients may not otherwise initiate.
	4. Ask specific questions during group and individual conversations about the client's application of these content areas. Questions are asked from the client's perspective as well as from the perspective of those who are involved in the client's life (e.g., caseworker, child). This serves to ensure that the client's answers are realistic, holistic, and accurate.
	5. Ask additional questions to assist the client to identify ways to change behavior to further integrate information learned.
	6. Ask the referral source if any additional areas of concern are noticed that need to be addressed through education, and confirm that the client's perspective of the areas addressed are consistent with the referral source's perspective.
2. Document that the required educational areas were covered.	7. Document all of the above.

BOX 7.2. Evaluation and Treatment Planning

Requirement: Ensure that all clients receive comprehensive evaluation and treatment planning as appropriate

Goal of both solution-focused and problem-focused approaches: Ensure that all clients receive the most appropriate and efficient services to address all biopsychosocial areas of concern in order to resolve the current problem and prevent the recurrence of the problem

Therapist steps:

Problem-Focused Approaches	Solution-Focused Therapy
1. Provide a thorough assessment addressing biological, psychological, and social aspects.	1. Provide a thorough assessment addressing biological, psychological, and social aspects.
2. Develop a problem list of all areas of concern developed from the evaluation.	2. Develop an issue list of all areas of concern developed from the evaluation.
3. Determine which issues are most urgent and develop treatment plans in collaboration with the client. Treatment plans may address issues that the clients may not agree are important.	3. Determine which issues are most urgent through a collaborative conversation with both the client and the referral source.
	4. Identify a minimum of one issue that the client sees as most urgent and develop a treatment plan about this as a starting place.
	5. Ask the client questions throughout treatment that assist the client in evaluating what other issues need to be addressed and what other behaviors need to change. Questions are asked from the client's perspective as well as from those who are involved in the client's life (e.g., caseworker, child). This serves to ensure that the client's answers are realistic, holistic, and accurate.
4. Review, update, or add treatment plans as needed throughout treatment.	6. Update and add treatment plans as clients identify additional issues and express a desire to address these issues.

(continued)

(continued)	7. Clients often report issues that they spontaneously resolve between sessions, resulting in no formal treatment plan needing to be created on these spontaneously resolved issues.
	8. Ensure that all issues on the issue list have been resolved to the satisfaction of the client, referral source, and all of those involved prior to discharge.
5. Document the status of all client issues at the time of discharge.	9. Document the status of all client issues at the time of discharge.

BOX 7.3. Individualized Services

Requirement: Ensure that services are individualized and sensitive to client's gender, culture, sexual orientation, etc.

Goal of both solution-focused and problem-focused approaches: Ensure that all clients receive highly individualized treatment services that are sensitive to the unique needs of each client, thereby increasing the client's chances for long-term success

Agency/therapist steps:

Problem-Focused Approaches	Solution-Focused Therapy
1. Ensure that all staff members are knowledgeable about the unique needs of client subpopulations and how to integrate these general facts into the clients' treatment as appropriate.	1. Ensure that all staff members are knowledgeable about the unique needs of client subpopulations. Ensure that all staff are well trained in how to listen to the degree to which the client identifies with his or her subpopulation and for what each client needs and wants in regard to his or her culture, gender, sexual orientation, etc.
2. Ensure that each client receives services that are consistent with the client's identified subpopulation.	2. Assist all clients in developing a clear picture of how they want their lives to be once the presenting problems are resolved. Pay specific attention to and ask specific questions about the degree to which clients include changes relative to their subpopulation.

(continued)

(continued)	3. Ask questions throughout treatment about the client's desired amount of inclusion of areas specific to the client's subpopulation.
	4. Provide any desired resources or information regarding the client's identified subpopulation.
	5. Ask questions to the clients throughout treatment that assist the client in evaluating what other subpopulation issues need to be explored. Questions are asked from the client's perspective as well as from the perspective of those who are involved in the client's life (e.g., caseworker, child). This serves to ensure that the client's answers are realistic, holistic, and accurate.
	6. Ask questions to the clients throughout treatment that assist the clients in evaluating the positive impact that the clients' decisions in regard to subpopulation issues will have on their ability to achieve their desired goals.
	7. Document the status of all client subpopulation issues at the time of discharge.

For example, a recent trend requires therapists to cover predetermined topics in substance abuse treatment groups. Although using topics that were predetermined without the input of the clients would not be characteristic of the solution-focused approach, we recognize that all groups should have purpose and that topics that are common to clients who abuse substances should be addressed. By agreeing with the underlying concept that clients often share common themes (the problem-focused term for theme is "topic"), the therapist can now document the specific topic and work that the client identified and addressed during the group session.

Although this process does not necessarily require that the therapist modify treatment, the therapist must be sufficiently aware of the requirements of the governing agency in order to accurately describe the treatment that was done in problem-focused terms when charting this client interaction. This will ensure that the work is clearly understood from a problem-focused perspective. Ironically, we have consistently observed that the required topics are naturally covered in the group process as a result of our carefully incorporating the themes brought up by the clients, since the governing agency has done an excellent job of understanding what clients naturally need to address. Although we do not explore the required "topics" from a problem-focused perspective, clients nevertheless leave the group with a solid understanding of how the client-initiated "topic" applies to their miracle and how it can enhance their long-term success (the problem-focused phrase for miracle is "long-term goal"). This is consistent with the governing agency's goal to ensure that the clients understand how the predetermined topic has or could negatively impact their recovery.

We find it helpful to remind ourselves that the purpose of a client chart is to provide documentation and summarization of the results of treatment, and to communicate key information to the reader. Solution-focused therapy and problem-focused approaches result in the same issues being addressed by the clients. The only difference is the *process* by which the issues are resolved. We find that as therapists become more adept at understanding the governing agencies' needs, they are better able to answer the questions that these agencies have. They are able to ensure that these answers are present in the chart and are in a language that the reader can readily understand. This results in quality treatment for the clients and clear communication of this treatment to those who are monitoring that quality.

SUMMARY

Providing solution-focused therapy in a problem-focused world requires dedication, skill, and, often, the ability to be ideologically bilingual. If we fail to communicate effectively and respectfully with colleagues from other disciplines and approaches, we will not only lose credibility with them, we will compromise our ability to help our clients. We work in a world in which problem-focused terms are still the dominant language for many helping professionals, so we owe it to our clients to be "bilingual," incorporating both solution-focused and problem-focused languages into our communication as needed in order to communicate respect and to foster common understanding. When we want to remind ourselves of the value and importance of this form of interagency diplomacy, we refer to it as the art of speaking "French."

Chapter 8

Solution-Focused Supervision: Leading from One Step Behind

What you expect to happen influences what you do.

Steve de Shazer

This chapter will describe the structure and principles of the solution-focused approach to supervision we developed at our agency. The phrase "leading from one step behind" comes from Cantwell and Holmes (1994).

WHY DO SOLUTION-FOCUSED SUPERVISION?

The short answer is "because it works!" Nevertheless, critics of this approach sometimes ask, "Since you are the boss, why don't you just make a decision and let them deal with it?" Experienced solution-focused supervisors know that working alongside people, being curious, and listening is always more effective than telling them where they are going. They know the importance of investing the time to see beyond a problem to a time in the future in which it does not exist. Team members support decisions that they understand and in which they see relevance to the future.

The skills needed to excel at management are often seen as vastly different from those required for clinical work. Because management is seldom viewed as theory based, managerial theories and clinical theories are often thought to be worlds apart, and the effective application of "theory" within an agency begins with the work with clients rather than management. *This is a myth.* In order for an agency to become purposeful and theoretically congruent, the management staff must share the same value system and theoretical constructs as the line staff. Therefore, in order to have an agency that truly utilizes solution-focused therapy, the supervisor and management team must espouse the approach as well.

Furthermore, practitioners of solution-focused therapy see the wisdom of investing time in understanding the clients' miracles rather than focusing solely on today's problems. Although it may not initially seem efficient, the power of assisting clients to actively envision where they want to go is amazing. Therapists are no exception.

ADAPTING SOLUTION-FOCUSED SKILLS TO A SUPERVISORY CONTEXT

The skills of a solution-focused supervisor resemble those required for a solution-focused therapist. Similar to a solution-focused therapist, the solution-focused supervisor values an environment of discovery, curiosity, and accountability. The initial task for the supervisor is to help the therapists to clarify their professional goals. This can be extremely difficult, because it requires investing time in each individual therapist in addition to embracing the tasks of agency leadership.

This mandates a proactive stance that many supervisors complain is too time consuming given their hectic schedule. However, as with solution-focused therapy, solution-focused supervision is all about taking the time to listen, setting aside personal agendas, and respecting the employee's unique solutions. Without a supervisor's time commitment and willingness to listen in a disciplined and respectful manner, solution-focused supervision cannot take place.

New therapists are often skeptical of the solution-focused supervision style. At first it may seem almost "too good to be true" because this approach leads to a genuine interest in each therapist's vision of the future, regardless of whether this involves long-term plans to continue working at the agency. This means that the supervisors must set aside their own fears of potential problems that losing the therapist may bring to the agency. This stance is often initially surprising to therapists since historically most problem-focused supervisors' primary interests were the needs of the agency. Staff members were often viewed as replaceable and interchangeable rather than unique.

Solution-focused supervisors assume that each staff member possesses unique talents, goals, and interests that compose an invaluable resource for the whole agency. The solution-focused supervisor is simultaneously committed to both the agency and each individual staff member. The challenge is to assist staff members in discovering a unique and meaningful way that they can fit into the agency, assuming they want to be there.

Questioning plays an important role in solution-focused supervision. Just as clients are encouraged to question how their daily life can become a part of their miracle, staff members are invited to question how their work at the agency can be fashioned to fit into their professional miracle. Staff members feel a strong commitment to the agency because they create the connection between their present employment and their long-term goals. As a result, solution-focused supervision unleashes staff members' passion for their work, and the agency benefits from increased creative energy and dedication. This passion and creativity, coupled with purposeful goals, produces a work environment in which accountability and therapeutic effectiveness are highly valued.

In this atmosphere of openness, therapists' ideas and challenges are welcomed. This results in a psychologically safe environment in which all decisions are expected to be made purposefully and thoughtfully. In short, all questions are carefully considered and answered respectfully. By seeing a supervisor modeling a purposeful discipline in decision making and openness to scrutiny, therapists similarly learn to be purposeful and disciplined in interactions with their clients.

Questions are viewed as welcome and a valuable link in accountability, rather than as a threat to uncover incompetence. The inclusion of the staff in decision making whenever possible is empowering and fosters mutual respect. The resulting ability of the supervisor to lead from one step behind the therapists is more productive than a hierarchical model, because therapists and supervisor are united in a common purpose.

Because the ability to be proactive and to plan effectively is a crucial skill of management, solution-focused therapy's strong emphasis on goal setting (e.g., defining the miracle) makes this approach readily applicable to supervisory tasks. This future-focused stance provides an effective vehicle for strategic planning or changing the agency culture from one of crisis management to a more proactive environment. Furthermore, the same solution-focused questions that work effectively with clients can be adapted to help clinical staff develop goals and document change. For example, the miracle question could be modified for the use with staff as follows:

> Imagine that while you are asleep tonight, a miracle happens. The miracle is that this agency is the best place to work that you could imagine despite all of the outside restrictions that impact your work. However, because you are asleep, you don't know that the miracle has happened. So, when you wake up tomorrow morning and come to work, what will be different that will let you know that a miracle has happened and that this is a great place to work?

Although staff members smile knowingly as they recognize the intervention, they begin thinking in a proactive manner. In response to the miracle question they may identify valuable elements such as increased trust, teamwork, or communication that subsequently have a profoundly positive effect on the degree of team functioning. Once the team's collective miracle has been established and the details have been identified, the supervisor then asks the team members to scale where they see the team in relation to this miracle by asking the following:

> On a scale of one to ten (ten being that this miracle is how life is now, and one being completely the opposite), where would you say we are as a team?

The supervisor then asks the members to share the number they picked and what aspects of this miracle they are currently seeing on the team. The next step is to ask the team members to say what they will see when the team is just one number higher than it is now. This is helpful in assisting each team member to identify what small steps would make a large difference in making their team's miracle come true.

This same approach can be employed for five-year strategic planning by asking the miracle question in the following manner:

> Imagine that while you are asleep tonight, a miracle happens. The miracle is that it is five years later, and this agency has

> grown in a wonderful direction and is the best place to work that you could imagine despite all of the outside restrictions that impact your work. However, because you are asleep, you don't know that the miracle has happened. So, when you wake up tomorrow morning and come to work, what will be different that will let you know that a miracle has happened and that this is a great place to work?

In response, staff members are able to share their hopes, dreams, and ideas about the agency's future. Because this process incorporates each staff member's creative vision, it results in a far better work product than one completed independently by the supervisor. It also allows the supervisor to understand how the staff members envision themselves fitting into the larger plan, and how each person sees the agency fitting into the larger community.

Some examples of themes that have emerged in our own agency from this type of strategic planning include increased family services, children's groups, expansion into other communities, and increased referrals from specific community or population groups. When such ideas emerge, the supervisor can then initiate team discussions to learn how the team envisions they would have accomplished these things in the miracle.

I (TP) have been amazed by the ideas and solutions that come from this future place! Even more amazing are the significant changes that the staff members spontaneously make as they work toward achieving the team miracle, meanwhile benefiting from the camaraderie and hope for future change.

In order for this type of planning and change to have lasting cultural impact on an agency, the supervisor must regularly revisit the staff's miracle and ask them to scale the progress. Whether used with clients or staff members, the miracle question will be far less effective if it is used only as a passing intervention rather than as the unifying foundation for current and future supervisory interactions. This frequent revisiting of the team's goals and ideas is crucial to effectively demonstrate that staff members' goals and ideas are important to the supervisor, that change and team evaluation are part of the team culture, and that small differences are valued.

Periodically scaling specific areas of concern (such as trust or level of teamwork) is often helpful in clarifying and understanding team members' goals for these elements. Our team members report that this process is not only useful for team building and planning but also enhances their understanding of how to apply the miracle question and scaling with clients. Furthermore, this provides a congruent demonstration of the importance and value of ongoing evaluation in the work with clients and with one another. In addition, this type of work creates a sense of hope for the future, which results in increased energy, enthusiasm, and excitement for the tasks ahead.

Even while using the solution-focused supervision model, the supervisor will need to make some decisions independently, primarily those requiring an immediate decision or those that would negatively impact the team if they were prematurely involved. For example, when a team member is questioning whether the agency is the best fit for him or her and is contemplating leaving, the potential negative impact of including the team (e.g., the fear of being short staffed) would be unnecessary, for it is not a team issue until the therapist resigns. In addition, if team members were prematurely involved they might understandably not invest the needed energy to challenge and teach the questioning team member. This would result in the questioning team member's internal process being negatively influenced by his or her peers' response. At the same time, it would be prudent of the supervisor to be devising a backup plan for coverage just in case the therapist does resign.

However, even these decisions are open for scrutiny by the team once the decision has been revealed. Solution-focused supervisors ensure that they are also held accountable by those who are impacted by the decisions that are made. The solution-focused supervisor routinely asks the team how much information they want about outside factors and how much involvement in decision making they would like. Naturally, the answers to these questions vary according to the individual personalities and long-term interests of the team members. Therapists who envision themselves in future supervisory roles tend to be very interested in learning about outside political factors.

On the other hand, those who are not as interested in the political arena are often simply grateful that their input is respected. This type of supervisory model requires that the supervisor help the staff members explore potential decisions from a multitude of angles to ensure a solid grasp of the issues before any final decision is made.

As therapists gain an understanding of the political and financial factors that affect the agency, they are better able to make decisions about the degree that they would like to be involved in those areas. Some may want a minimal role; others may become excited at the prospect of learning more about the challenges facing the team. This is a valuable topic for therapists to explore in individual supervision as they continue to work toward their professional miracle.

Once staff members experience agency goals as relevant to their own life, they are committed. Once they have committed their hearts, the agency cannot help but benefit from their resulting passion, enthusiasm, and energy. Even though it does require more time up front, the results are excitement in the shared journey, minimal power struggles, and fewer future problems. Staff members who feel valued and respected are much more willing to fight for the agency in public and make fewer political blunders. They are more confident, for they are a part of the agency's plan, and this results in a culture of accountability and purpose.

THE PRACTICAL STRUCTURE OF SOLUTION-FOCUSED SUPERVISION

Individual supervision, group supervision, daily group process, and impromptu supervision compose the structure of solution-focused supervision.

I (TP) cannot sufficiently emphasize the importance of committing time to meeting with the therapists because they are the agency's most important assets. Without them, there would be no agency. Any time invested in their development, support, guidance, and growth will benefit the agency tenfold. Unfortunately, however, any neglect will return 100-fold.

Individual Supervision

Regular individual supervision (weekly is strongly recommended even for seasoned therapists) is valuable in providing the necessary time for each therapist to privately explore both clinical and professional issues that arise from using this approach. In the beginning of learning solution-focused skills, often therapists believe that they have a strong grasp of the solution-focused approach. However, as they become more familiar with the approach, they frequently go through a period of soul-searching in which their core beliefs are challenged, and they consequently discover that this approach is not as easy to implement as it first appeared.

Over the years we have heard many therapists confide that the more they were exposed to the solution-focused approach, the more they realized how much they did not know. For example, therapists are typically taught in school how to become "experts." They are trained to extensively evaluate and form opinions. Conversely, the solution-focused approach requires that all of that teaching, evaluating, and formulating opinions be set aside so that the therapist's primary skill is that of objective listening. The therapist's challenge is to become an expert on the process of change rather than on what is best for the clients.

Although this concept initially appears simplistic, paradoxically, it tends to be one of the most difficult for people to master. Typically this process is time consuming and requires a safe environment that congruently models the solution-focused approach at both the management and supervisory levels.

Individual supervision provides an appropriate context for teaching team members to discriminate between individual and team issues. When work environments do not make this distinction, a negative culture of repetitive complaining or emotional "venting" results. Individual supervision should provide a safe environment for the therapists to say what they want to say, but this should not be misunderstood as an invitation to catharsis.

First popularized by Freud, emotional venting usually takes on the form of an unstructured monologue in which one seeks to accomplish the "emptying of emotional reservoirs" through activities such as crying, angry words, or destruction of objects (McKay, Rogers, and McKay, 1989). It is still mistakenly thought that unexpressed feelings will become repressed, resulting in the utilization of unhealthy defense mechanisms. In therapy settings, the accepted solution would be to assist the client to begin to feel and accept the repressed emotions (Wegscheider, 1981).

First, supervision is not a therapy session! Second, research does not support that the cathartic release of emotions has a significantly beneficial response (Ebbesen, Duncan, and Konecni, 1975; Feshbach, 1956; Straus, 1974; Tavris, 1982). In fact, the opposite may be true. Not only does yelling, talking, or acting out an emotion not reduce the feeling, it actually serves as a rehearsal for "more of the same" (McKay, Rogers, and McKay, 1989, p. 21). McKay, Rogers, and McKay (1989) further note, "expressed anger tends to make you even angrier and solidifies an angry attitude" (p. 22). When this is allowed in the team setting, a negative culture results (similar to the results of venting in a client group setting).

The supervisor gently challenges staff members' complaining or venting behavior by assisting the therapists in identifying what outcome they want and by asking what behavior they will be doing when this desired outcome is achieved. This focus on the desired outcome and accountability assists the therapist in evaluating the value of venting, identifying personal responsibility, and refocusing on what is important.

This approach to venting is not only valuable to the team by minimizing the damaging effects of venting and complaining on team morale but also directly demonstrates to the therapist how to respectfully respond to venting by clients as well. Once the therapist has clarified and resolved the personal issues, any remaining team issues can be effectively brought to the appropriate team members. Team members are assured that each person will address personal issues that arise in the workplace in an appropriate manner and setting, which results in a more effective use of time and leads to increased trust within the team.

Both task and process issues arise during supervision, and achieving a balance of these two elements is important to produce a well-functioning team. Some therapists focus on their work tasks to the exclusion of team dynamics and process-oriented issues; others may become so preoccupied with process issues that they struggle to complete their tasks.

Individual supervision provides a safe place to explore how staff members view these two elements and to discuss how they see themselves regarding these crucial elements. Once the identified issue is resolved, staff members typically express a desire to achieve a balance of task and process. This individual focus of the staff members, coupled with an awareness of larger system issues, creates a safe environment when combined with group supervision, for each person is accustomed to identifying what he or she would like to be different. This decreases blaming and criticism of others and strengthens the culture of accountability.

Group Supervision

Regular group supervision (weekly to biweekly is recommended) is helpful to address overall team issues (both task and process oriented). This is also a good setting in which to practice solution-focused role-playing and to have theoretical discussions. Group supervision is also a valuable setting in which the supervisor can gently question pathology-oriented assumptions that are counter to solution-focused therapy.

As a team solidifies and gains trust, these core assumptions become more evident and the therapists become more eager to explore the subtleties of the approach. Since learning this approach results in the therapists challenging their professional beliefs, there is often a strong need for the sharing of thoughts, struggles, experiences, and ideas in a group setting. Therapists report that these conversations often help to prevent burnout, and lead to increased enthusiasm and respect for the approach. Group supervision can also be effectively applied to smaller subgroups of a team. For example, staff members who work specifically with adolescents often find it helpful to form an "adolescent team" and meet on a regular basis to discuss the specific needs of this population.

Daily Group Process

Another type of group-oriented supervision is daily group process. In traditional settings, therapists are expected to perform their job duties and seek guidance as needed. Therapists who use this traditional model often find themselves having difficulty separating from the work environment at the end of the day and increasing their risk of burnout. We have found it more effective to meet as a group for thirty minutes each evening to briefly discuss how each therapist's clinical sessions went that day.

This provides a proactive structure that allows the therapists to receive support from their supervisor and peers, receive immediate ideas and feedback about their work, and learn from other peers as they work as a team to apply this approach. It also provides the supervisor with daily information about the quality of client care and any individual or team issues that need attention in other supervision settings. The therapists also frequently identify various clinical issues that arose that day (e.g., how to address client venting, how to apply solution-focused therapy to the group setting) that they would like to address in more depth in future group or individual supervision sessions.

Impromptu Supervision

Last, impromptu supervision is invaluable. Therapists need to know they are not alone when handling difficult situations. They are not always able to plan when supervision is needed, and "hallway supervision" or an open-door policy can lessen the likelihood of reverting to old, less productive thought processes during times of stress. Often, a five-minute conversation can prevent a political blunder or a needless clinical mistake that would afterward need to be corrected. Taking the time to do this as needed provides the staff with the support to continue to learn and experiment in the work setting.

PRINCIPLES FOR INITIATING SOLUTION-FOCUSED SUPERVISION IN AN ESTABLISHED AGENCY

I (TP) have often been told, "This is all great, but I have an established agency and don't have the luxury to start over!" Rest assured, these concepts are extremely powerful, and have the ability to turn the direction of virtually any agency, regardless of size. The only requirement is that the person initiating the changes has the primary responsibility and authority over the group of therapists. This is not an approach that can be arbitrarily dictated by upper management to be implemented by lower management.

However, upper management can use this approach with their direct subordinates, and larger agencies can be strongly influenced by individual supervisors initiating this approach with their individual treatment teams. The solution-focused approach is contagious, and once higher management experiences the positive impact of this approach, they become curious and eventually supportive. Nevertheless, changing the philosophy of an agency can be overwhelming. Here are the most poignant administrative lessons I have learned from our agency's journey:

- Make your expectations clear to the staff.
- Set the standards high for yourself and your staff (expect a miracle).

- Go slow.
- Question everything.
- Make making mistakes safe.
- Avoid debating or defending solution-focused therapy.
- Ask for feedback even when it hurts.
- Listen; don't react.
- Focus on the miracle even when the present seems overwhelming.
- Always have a "mighty plan."

Make Your Expectations Clear to the Staff

It is often thought that the solution-focused therapist will do and work toward whatever the client wants, and not give direction. This is also sometimes assumed of the solution-focused supervisor. *This is a myth.* The solution-focused practitioner is an expert on the process of change, and seeks to guide the client or staff member through the use of questions to a way of thinking that will lead toward change. These questions encourage the inclusion of the client's or staff member's reality, and this results in good decision making that is reality based. However, the solution-focused practitioner is not an expert on what is best for the individual. It is up to those individuals to decide how they want to cope with these realities.

The solution-focused supervisor must not shy away from giving information or feedback about what environmental realities are not negotiable in the workplace. For example, complying with regulatory requirements is not negotiable, no matter how arduous and time consuming doing so may be. The supervisor must ensure that staff members understand these requirements and then assist them in exploring the aspect that is under the therapists' control (how they will comply in a manner that is workable to both the therapist and the agency). By assuring that staff members know the agency limits and the expectations of the supervisor, they are able to make good decisions for themselves.

Staff members need to know that the supervisor will be honest with them about the existing realities, and that their answer is genuinely wanted when a question is asked. This results in a strong trust between the staff and supervisor that there are no surprises.

Especially in the beginning, staff members need specific information and ideas about how to apply the solution-focused approach. A solution-focused supervisor needs to be comfortable serving as a mentor for those learning this approach and be available to answer questions about the specific interventions and purpose behind the methods used. Effective supervisors must acquire the ability to determine when they need to provide information and when simply listening to the staff members will be more productive.

Set the Standards High for Yourself and Your Staff (Expect a Miracle)

This approach leads to amazing results, so do not be afraid to envision high standards for your agency. Staff turnover can be very low, staff morale can be extremely high, and the work quality can exceed the neighboring agency's standards. It just might take some time.

The decisions that the supervisor makes today will be the direct result of where that supervisor sees the agency in the future. This is reflected in Steve de Shazer's (1985) statement, "What you expect to happen influences what you do" (p. 45). Solution-focused therapy begins with the miracle and works backward, and solution-focused supervisors must take this stance. This means that the agency risks being shortchanged if miracles are not perceived as possible.

It is a common mistake for agency administrators to make nasty decisions in response to a crisis rather than from a context of expectation and purpose. Even staff members at times would prefer that the supervisor made a decision that would result in the immediate resolution of a problem rather than taking the extra effort to seek lasting change (e.g., hiring a staff member who would not be a good fit just to have a "warm body" when short staffed). Unfortunately, this usually leads to continued crisis and minimal growth. If a supervisor makes decisions based on where the agency will be in the future, these decisions will be congruent with the long-term goal. This results in fewer reactive decisions and an increase in purposeful changes. This will also increase the support from staff, for they will trust that there is a reason for the changes, and that change is part of the larger plan toward an agreed-upon miracle.

Go Slow

Solution-focused therapy values taking small steps, and solution-focused therapists recognize that a "small change in one person's behavior can make profound and far-reaching differences in the behavior of all persons involved" (de Shazer, 1985, p. 16). It can be very overwhelming to staff if a supervisor rapidly implements significant changes. Beginning by gradually targeting small, specific areas would be a more effective approach. Then, once the staff members have incorporated the one change, gradually move to another area.

For example, one of the first changes that I (TP) implemented at our agency involved improving the quality of the discharge summaries. I read each summary before they went out, and I began to question how therapists knew the information they had stated in the summaries. This resulted in the therapist either removing unsubstantiated assumptions or citing the evidence that supported the statements. It was a small step, yet the impact of this gentle challenge to use facts to back up statements rather than relying on assumption or interpretation was far-reaching. It was the first step toward challenging the notion that therapists are the experts.

Supervisors must be sensitive to the needs of staff members. If staff members are overwhelmed by change, supervisors should slow down even more and listen to their needs. It is crucial that the supervisor leads from within and not from ahead. There will be times of rapid growth and times of plateau. If there is grumbling, take the time to listen to the staff members individually to hear their concerns and where they want to be. (Listening in a team setting will most often lead to negative venting and be counterproductive since grumbling is usually not a team issue, but rather an individual issue that has spread throughout the team.) When staff members feel they have been heard and share the agency's direction, they often resume their professional journey with renewed energy.

Question Everything

It is probably going to be difficult if not impossible to convince people that the solution-focused approach is the way to go if they have not discovered this firsthand. One of the most effective techniques to initiate this is to simply ask staff, "Did it work?" If the answer is yes, encourage them to continue. If the answer is no, listen to what they think might have worked better.

During the times when interventions have failed or their skills are taxed, therapists are often most curious about alternative approaches. These are the potential teaching moments that will most likely result in change. For example, during the initial months of implementing the solution-focused approach at our agency, I (TP) made it a point to casually chat with the therapists immediately following their groups. I would show up in their offices and ask, "So, how was group?" I was genuinely curious and enjoyed these evening discussions.

By being present and curious, I was able to recognize when these potential teaching moments surfaced and could pose questions that gently challenged the staff's assumptions about their methods. The therapists later confided that they subsequently began to mentally anticipate my questions even when I was not present. The culture of questioning had begun.

This questioning is a part of everyday supervision, for the role of the solution-focused supervisor is to pull the wisdom from the therapists rather than to tell them what to do. The therapists are most often in a much better place to make the best decision, for the supervisor would be making clinical decisions with secondhand knowledge at best. Therapists have said that this can be frustrating, for at times it seems easier if I would just tell them what to do. However, similar to working with clients, an expert-based approach would not be as effective as assisting the therapists to explore and find their own unique answers. An expert-based approach might provide more immediate answers, but it would not provide professional challenge and empowerment, which are the hallmarks of solution-focused supervision. My role as a supervisor is to ask the questions to assist them in exploring areas that they might have missed if they had not sought supervision, thereby assisting the therapists in making more clinically sound decisions.

Make Making Mistakes Safe

An environment of questioning quickly becomes overwhelming and threatening if mistakes are not seen as a valuable opportunity for learning. Unfortunately, most staff members have experienced an environment in which mistakes were viewed as a sign of failure and incompetence.

Because the solution-focused approach values learning and discovery, mistakes are not only expected but embraced as an opportunity for growth. This stance must be communicated congruently by the supervisor and must be genuine. This requires that the supervisor admits mistakes and strongly believes in the importance of acknowledging when a change of direction is needed.

Although I have heard supervisors express concern that staff members will decrease their expectations and become cavalier if mistakes are acceptable, our experience has been just the opposite. Our staff members acknowledge their mistakes because their priority is high-quality work. By discussing their mistakes and having an environment that explores how to correct mistakes without judgment, the expectation is that one person's mistake typically provides valuable learning for everyone. Emphasis is placed on the skill with which a mistake is resolved and on the learning that results rather than on the mistake itself. Once again, this further contributes to higher expectations and a culture of accountability.

Avoid Debating or Defending Solution-Focused Therapy

This has been by far the most difficult and painful lesson for me (TP) to learn. I am passionate about this approach, and I become uncomfortable when I hear the approach being presented incorrectly or criticized by people who are ignorant of its basic tenets. Someone once said, "The most worthless answer is that to an unasked question." This could not be more true than in this instance! I have found that the strongest critics of the changes we have made at our agency were not the higher administrators, the therapists, the clients, or the referral sources, but outside governing bodies and other treatment agencies.

In my initial naïveté and excitement about the results of the changes we had made, I (TP) often volunteered the answer to the unasked question. I mistakenly thought that everyone would appreciate hearing how wonderful the changes were once they truly understood the approach and its impact on the quality of care. Unfortunately, this resulted in me being perceived as arrogantly trying to fix problems that were not seen by others. I had inadvertently jumped in front and tried to get our challengers to follow rather than remembering to lead from one step behind.

This has taught me the importance of waiting until people become curious about what we have accomplished at our agency before offering this information. Even then it is important to slow down and answer only the question that is being asked. There are means to carefully and quietly comply with the myriad problem-focused regulations while implementing a powerfully solution-focused approach. It takes considerable dedication, patience, creativity, and belief in the power of the approach, for challenging the norms is never without risk.

Ask for Feedback Even When It Hurts

Some of the most useful information I have received has been from my staff during very difficult moments. I have learned to trust their input regarding my supervisory skills. (Who else is truly in the position to evaluate them?) During times of stress it is often tempting to make an "executive decision." It is easy to justify this when you are the boss. However, at these times listening to staff members and focusing on the team's miracle are much more effective choices.

For example, I have learned to periodically ask my staff members how I come across during staff meetings or individual sessions. This provides valuable information and insight about what I am or am not doing when difficult team dynamics arise. My staff members have learned that I am truly curious about what I could be doing differently and what team members need that I am not hearing. As a result, I learn from my team, and they learn it is a safe place to express concerns that might otherwise go unaddressed. Pride is not a useful emotion for a solution-focused supervisor because it prevents the supervisor from listening. The success of the agency is not the result of the supervisor but the result of the team.

Listen; Don't React

Listening to staff members when they are saying something that is unexpected or departs from the planned direction can be very difficult. By including and considering all of their input, solid decisions are made. Although on some days the "ostrich" (head buried in sand) approach may seem more comfortable, it doesn't work! Power struggles are most often the direct result of the supervisor not being available to listen.

Staff members will continue to say what they need to say until they are acknowledged or until they give up (very similar to clients). When staff members know that you want to hear them, they are more patient when their thoughts are not immediately understood. Only when a supervisor takes the time to listen and sets aside the fear of what the staff members might say will the staff solidify and move together toward a common goal.

Focus on the Miracle Even When the Present Seems Overwhelming

It would be misleading to say that this process is painless. Not all staff members want to answer questions about how they work or want to be held accountable for the work they do, and not all staff members want to relinquish the role of expert associated with the medical or traditional treatment model. These staff members will decide to leave at some point during the transition to this new approach. In some cases, their leaving may be the best move for them as well as for the agency.

Remember that a significant role of the solution-focused supervisor is that of assisting staff members in clarifying where they want to work and what role they want to have with the agency. Sometimes a therapist's decision to move on can be a sign that the supervisor has done a good job with that task.

We have found that therapists leave when they are no longer interested in the direction the agency is heading, and that in such cases their leaving then actually assists the agency in making and solidifying desired changes. Ironically, staff members who are key to an agency's development and growth at one point of the agency's journey may become an impediment at a later point due to conflicting goals.

Nevertheless, staff members leaving can evoke panic in even the most seasoned supervisor. This is precisely when it is crucial to stay focused on the overall goal. Reactive hiring to fill vacant positions or trying to convince someone to stay who no longer shares the agency's goals and has already decided to leave will actually make the situation worse. Instead, view staff leaving as an opportunity to find someone who will make a great solution-focused therapist. We have learned that these therapists are not always easy to find, but they are well worth the wait!

By focusing on the team's miracle during staff transitions and other times of stress, creative solutions often become obvious. For example, during our lowest point, I (TP) found that using a temporary agency to access qualified staff to help with the more mundane tasks allowed us to solidify a core team of therapists. By not hiring and by utilizing temporary help (who were not included in group supervision and team discussions), I was able to protect this core group from the negative influences of therapists who were not committed to the journey.

I did not hire anyone onto the core team until all our team members were convinced that the potential hire wanted to go where we were going. We also discovered that the best potential therapists for this model approached us after learning about our model and were not the result of standard recruitment practices. The qualities that we found to be most predictive of a good fit for this model were those of curiosity, strong work ethic, openness to feedback, awareness of their lack of knowledge, and desire for continuous professional growth.

Always Have a "Mighty Plan"

It has become a private joke on our team that I (TP) always have a "mighty plan." However, team members have also told me that the "mighty plan" is a source of comfort. Supervisors often are the bearers of bad news. Their role is to deal with the outside factors that impact the team to assure the team's survival. I have discovered that I need to have an idea of how to possibly address potential problems in the context of the miracle before presenting the problem to the team. This does not mean that the mighty plan is final; it means only that the staff members can be reassured there is always hope and a way to get through when bad news comes along. This allows them to set aside their sense of fear to begin to listen and make good decisions that will continue our journey toward our vision of the team's shared miracle.

GETTING STAFF TO STAY

Many books are available today that give ideas on how to reward staff in order to increase employee retention. High staff turnover is expensive and disruptive to client care. However, many of these books (Kaye and Jordan-Evans, 1999; Nelson, 1994) focus on getting employees to stay rather than on truly caring about the employees' professional "miracle." Ironically, many of the behaviors that these books recommend (flexibility of schedule, compliments, creating purpose and opportunities for meaningful projects) are naturally characteristic of solution-focused supervision.

Our agency's turnover rate has decreased from 64 percent to 18 percent since we implemented the SF model. Because they have a sense of ownership about our agency's treatment programs, our team members work together to ensure that staff coverage is always in place, that all necessary tasks are completed, and that deadlines are met. The more experienced therapists instinctively take the newer therapists under their wings and provide the necessary guidance to perpetuate this positive culture. This minimizes the need for supervisor intervention and mandates, which further increases team morale.

In addition, our community reputation has improved since implementing this model. This has resulted in increased referrals, increased revenue, increased employee morale, increased client satisfaction, and national recognition from our peers. We are creating challenging and purposeful projects such as writing this book, training graduate-level interns, giving national presentations about our agency, and designing and implementing research projects. All of these are meaningful to the therapists and help them to obtain their professional miracle. We have created an amazing sense of team, in which we are cocreating this model on a daily basis. All levels of management throughout our agency now embrace our model and believe in the miraculous impact on clients and staff. (This was not always the case!) Despite the many painful struggles, the journey is incredibly worthwhile.

SUMMARY

Solution-focused tenets are not only applicable but can be productively implemented in the service of change in even the most established and complacent of agencies. Valuing the uniqueness of each individual and the power of truly listening, respecting the abilities of the people with whom we work, appreciating the potentially large impact of small changes, and focusing on a future in which the problem no longer exists are invaluable in the task of supervision. When supervisors embrace these tenets, they are in the position to successfully lead from one step behind. This creates the opportunity for miraculous results because it releases the previously untapped creative energy of both staff and supervisor, leaving the agency and people who work there forever changed.

Chapter 9

Maintaining the Team's Miracle: Observations from Our Solution-Focused Team

Megan Shea
Diane Strouse
Calyn Crow

Openness is a precursor to curiosity.

Calyn Crow

Developing and maintaining an effective team environment is a challenging process composed of myriad factors. Although many agencies claim that their management supports a team environment, they are nevertheless vulnerable to pitfalls that can damage working relationships. This chapter shows how to avoid these pitfalls and describes how we have created an effective team environment.

We have worked hard to develop our team in a way that benefits all members personally and professionally. We generally enjoy going to work and have realized that this is a safe environment in which to learn. We are supportive of one another and are comfortable giving and receiving feedback from one another. We also respect one another,

---

This chapter is the product of hours of conversations among the team members as they explored what worked on the team and reflected upon how they achieved their "team miracle." Although every team member was instrumental in developing the content of this chapter, a special thanks to Darla Oglevie, Karen Nielsen, Jonathan Heitsmith, and Charlene Wilson for their additional input into the writing of this chapter.

which results in our mutually high expectations and confidence in the skills of our team members and ourselves. Team members are encouraged to identify who they are and what they want from their careers, in essence, answering their own miracle question.

We have all discovered firsthand that the solution-focused approach is more than a theory and is, in fact, an entirely new view of the world. This new worldview has transformed each of us personally and helps us to strive for our own miracles. The SF approach also assisted us in creating and maintaining an agency of which we truly want to be a part, and it makes this more than just a job because our hearts are attached to our work. Our commitment to this team results in forward thinking, excitement, playfulness, and laughter. We all have a great deal of pride in being a part of this team and are dedicated to ensuring our team's successful future.

THE IMPACT OF OUR SUPERVISION

Applying the solution-focused approach to a team requires a conscientious effort by management to make specific changes. Creating a sense of a nonhierarchical environment, effectively modeling the approach, and allowing staff members permission to work on their goals at their own pace are all essential elements of a well-functioning, solution-focused team. Together, these elements result in an environment that values quality, dedication, peace of mind, well-being, patience, acceptance, and togetherness. Included in this environment are a sense of exploration, energy, and adventure, and a culture of personal and professional growth.

A Nonhierarchical Environment

What we mean by a nonhierarchical environment is that the input of each team member is valued and expected. At the same time, each team member also recognizes and accepts the chain of command. However, unlike the traditional top-down management style, we have cocreated a work environment in which decisions and responsibilities are shared. This is reflected in the following examples:

Regardless of each team member's level of expertise, each team member's contributions are considered equally valuable. Although different positions are available within our team, these are considered individual achievements and do not affect the team structure or the individuals' status on the team. Although advanced positions on our team are seen as personal goals toward which to work, they do not interfere with our sense of egalitarianism.

Another example is that the majority of decisions affecting the team are made by the team as a whole rather than made and implemented by management without the team's input. We are continually informed of the political issues that may affect the team and are given the option to learn as many of the details as we request and with which we are comfortable. This results in the team investing in each decision that is made and taking responsibility for the outcome.

Modeling

We believe that a supervisor's modeling of the solution-focused approach is very important. This contributed significantly to the transformation of our team; in fact, our trust and confidence in solution-focused therapy first developed from experiencing solution-focused supervision. Our supervisor not only encouraged the team to try this new approach but also congruently and consistently modeled what it meant to be solution focused.

This showed up in many ways. Flexibility in our work schedules is one example. Our agency's flexibility allows each team member not only to develop professional goals, but also to provide room for our own personal miracles, that is, a structure for identifying what we want and a plan for making it happen. Our flexibility and respect for one another allow us to achieve what is important to us outside of the workplace.

Striving to match each team member to the specific client population with which he or she enjoys working, and attempting to enhance one another's strengths and improve our weaknesses are other examples of our program's flexibility. It is also important to us to remain flexible with one another so that we can all take time off when needed, and that we respect the choices each team member makes when attempting to balance our personal and professional lives.

Work Environment

Whether it be school, family, friends, career, or all of these combined, our team's application of the miracle question has resulted in an environment in which each person is allowed to identify and work to achieve what is most important to him or her. This allows us to connect the work we do today with the goals we would like to accomplish in our personal and professional lives tomorrow, and evaluate how well this is working.

Significantly, this kind of thinking closely resembles what we ask and expect of our clients. We expect that through using a solution-focused approach and with our support, in their own time, our clients will find what works best for them just as we do. Our team always expects to be learning and gaining new insight, and we have found that we must allow patience for ourselves and for others as well.

This method of working keeps us from experiencing burnout. How can we really burn out when working on a future in which we are truly invested? Being invested in our teammates has also been very rewarding. We have learned firsthand that everyone has his or her own personal as well as professional miracles, and we have created a place where we value and expect that all team members will pursue what they desire. This has resulted in our team members being willing to give more than 100 percent.

On our team, each new team member must be aware that questioning assumptions and therapeutic practices is a useful and valuable means for developing clinical skills. We have learned to apply the solution-focused approach through respectful ongoing questioning from both our supervisor and our team members. In order to be beneficial, this questioning needs to be asked in a spirit of genuine curiosity.

At times, this is as simple as asking how a particular intervention was helpful for our clients. Holding one another accountable in this manner has taught our team that it is okay to make mistakes and that there is purpose in the way we work. New team members need to know that we all make mistakes regardless of our previous training and experience, and that these mistakes can be addressed and corrected with the help of our team members or supervisor. Mistakes are viewed as part of the learning process, and since we are continuously learning as part of our journey, these mistakes are expected and corrected as needed.

Ensuring the availability of our supervisor and experienced team members whenever needed has been another important component of our team's implementation of this approach. Remaining available to one another further contributes to an atmosphere in which we are supported, and no one is left to make difficult decisions alone. We accomplish this by leaving our office doors open when possible to encourage questions and by carrying pagers during office hours. This not only enhances availability of all team members but also results in consistency for our clients.

Goals

Envisioning and describing our team's shared miracle has led to our team setting goals for our agency, and team members' envisioning their individual miracles has led to defining professional goals. Our supervisor respects these goals and recognizes that team members will work at the process of achieving them at their own pace and in their own manner.

Not only are we committed to utilizing the solution-focused approach with our clients, we believe firmly in using the approach with our team. We repeatedly ask ourselves and then answer the miracle question. When times are tough, we believe in focusing on how things will be when the problem no longer exists. Scaling is used frequently in our staff meetings in order to get everyone's perspective on how we are functioning as a team.

Using the approach with the team is not only helpful in setting personal and team goals, but has also given us insight into the potential impact of the approach, and contributes to our continued training. It also helps foster our shared commitment to the same journey, and enhances our trust that what we have chosen is the right path for us all. Like most valuable skills, developing this has taken time and effort, and it has truly been worthwhile.

TEAM NORMS

The team norms (behaviors that we eventually came to perceive as normal and expected from one another) that developed as we learned to use the solution-focused model have become the backbone of our team culture. These norms include honesty, boundaries, respect/value for one another, questioning everything, work ethic, and trust. Our team continues to develop and discover means to function more effectively, so we realize that we will always be developing new norms that will aid our team to grow while continuing to carry on the norms that are already in place.

Honesty

We have learned from experience that we can be open and honest in offering feedback to our team members (although this is a personal challenge at times). This directness is an essential element in our growth as therapists and on our journey toward implementing the solution-focused approach. Team members are open with one another and give direct feedback about their skills as therapists, how the solution-focused approach is being utilized, and how the clients are benefiting from each therapist's skills. Feedback from team members is offered and received with mutual respect.

By listening to team members' feedback we can each mature and develop our skills as therapists. This has resulted in a constructive, systemic accountability within our team. In our busy and often stressful work world, sometimes it would be easier not to take the time to point out something to peers that they may not know. However, we want each team member to have a clear understanding of the how and why of the solution-focused approach. So, the long-term benefit is well worth the initial energy spent.

Boundaries

We believe that maintaining professional boundaries with one another contributes significantly to our ability to genuinely care for one another. The professional peer relationships we share as team members include caring for and respecting one another, being able to help one another, and truly being interested in each person's personal and professional growth.

However, we believe that fostering friendships outside of work would not be beneficial to our team because this could easily lead to cliques of team members, or the development of personal contexts that might hinder our ability to focus on what is important to the team. Furthermore, this could result in a less professional atmosphere in which complaining or venting about work feels natural and acceptable.

Some people might view our team boundaries as unnecessarily constricting, but experience has taught us that they are helpful for our team. Perhaps paradoxically, not having team member friendships outside of work actually seems to forge a stronger shared bond among our team members.

We have created an open and honest work environment in which we are readily able to address our work-related concerns, so we do not find it necessary or desirable to complain to one another about our work. We have no need to slip off into a corner to criticize or complain to one another.

We know from experience that if we bring concerns to the attention of our supervisor, they will be addressed promptly and will be handled objectively in a sincerely caring manner. However, we should emphasize that our supervisor helps us develop solutions rather than solves the problem for us. For example, help us to prioritize tasks, communicate more effectively with peers, and discover different options for solutions. By leaving the final decision to the therapist, our supervisor ensures investment and commitment to the solution selected.

Another key aspect in maintaining our team boundaries is the expectation that we all take care of our personal needs and issues privately rather than at work. This is supported by our shared expectation that we will each do what is needed to take care of ourselves and that (to whatever degree possible) we will be given the flexibility and freedom to do so.

Respect/Value

The respect and value that we have for one another play essential roles in the relationships we share with our teammates. Everyone on our team knows that we genuinely care about one another as individuals and are willing to do what we can to help in times of need. Mutual respect and consideration for one another is reflected not only in our willingness to adjust work schedules when needed, but also in the courtesies we show one another.

For example, we all leave together in the evenings so we can be certain that each person gets to his or her car safely. We also do what it takes to give one another enough flexibility in scheduling to attend school, complete internships, participate in training opportunities, take care of medical issues, care for children, etc.

Perhaps because we value and respect one another, our team is able to be playful and laugh frequently. People observing our team often comment about our team's obvious ability to laugh and be playful without underlying negative connotations. We see the fact that our team can be playful with one another, without anyone becoming mean spirited, as a sign of the health of our shared relationships. Our shared humor is vital to our team's dedication because we enjoy one another's company and can have fun in the midst of our commitment to excellence.

The respect and valuing we share with fellow staff members further extends to our clients and referral sources. We believe it is very important to listen carefully to what our referral sources need when it comes to serving our mutual clients, and we make sure that our referral sources are kept up to date about the clients' status throughout their involvement with our agency. As for our clients, we respect and value them as individuals, and we strive to be accepting and nonjudgmental. Our goal with our clients is to find what will truly make a difference in their lives and then to collaborate with them to build treatment plans around those goals.

We trust that each person on our team is committed to our standard of excellence and is genuinely curious about how to achieve this excellence. Every day at our agency is a challenge that opens the doors for growth. We have learned that being humble is the key to our continuous growth. No one assumes that he or she has all the answers. Instead, we all can recognize our strengths and weaknesses, be humble in our knowledge, and respect the knowledge of others. We believe that this stance of intentional humility contributes to our further growth.

Work Ethic

Everyone on our team agrees that we all have a very high work ethic. To us, the work we do is not just a job; it is our career. In addition, we implement what we do (the solution-focused method of interacting with the world) in our daily lives. There is a shared team commitment to excellence in all that we do, which new therapists who have joined our team have told us is obvious from the first day they began their work at our agency. This commitment begets respect as all team members communicate their knowledge by example.

We have learned to be meticulous in our training of new therapists, so we are careful to maintain an open forum for questions. Our training of new therapists does not end after one or two weeks. It is a shared philosophy at the agency that we are all continuously in training, striving to be the best that we can be. New therapists are consistently supported as they are learning how to do their job, and are not left alone to fulfill their positions until they feel confident in their skills.

An amazing atmosphere of caring is exuded in our staff training process. Constructive feedback is given with genuineness and sensitivity. Each member is expected to maintain attention to detail and accountability for work, and it is understood that there is a purpose in everything we do. Part of our work ethic stems from knowing that all team members are doing all that they can every day to maintain the professionalism and quality of work that is expected.

Trust

Above all, a sense of mutual trust provides the foundation for all of the team norms we have discussed. This trust has been earned over time and is valued by every team member. We as a team can trust the intentions of each team member and ask one another for clarification if there is some misunderstanding. The old days of wondering who was or was not doing more work or who was or was not committed to learning and applying the solution-focused approach (early in our transition to this approach) are long gone. In their place is a trust that each of us is doing all that we can do, and that each of us is committed to learning and applying this approach. It is a good feeling.

MAINTAINING THE TEAM MIRACLE

As the earlier part of this chapter demonstrates, developing an effective team is a complicated yet extremely rewarding process. The challenge comes in not only developing the team but also in maintaining the progress when adding new team members, facing stressful times, or having problems related to a lack of appreciation or dedication to the team. One way in which we have learned to maintain the great team we have developed is to consistently evaluate where we are as a team and to self-correct when necessary.

We have learned that giving team issues priority prevents problems from getting out of control. We do this in a number of different ways. For example, we pay close attention to our peer relationships within the team in order to address and correct issues that develop. We avoid deterioration of our peer relationships by taking the time to discuss issues with one another as they develop. Facing problems directly by talking with one another saves us time in the long term. On occasion, when larger issues arise that cannot be handled on a one-to-one basis, the supervisor addresses it. Many times in the past few years we have delayed team projects or discussions to address team-related issues. Postponing these other plans and projects to talk about team issues reminds us all of the importance our team places on maintaining an effective work environment.

We have also learned to hold one another accountable for the things we do and say. This is done with respect and care, and is crucial to keeping our team intact. This is possible because of the genuine respect we have for the opinions of each team member. Accountability also requires us to be forgiving of one another's shortcomings or weaknesses. This can be a difficult balance to achieve.

Over time, our team has become aware of the differences among team members, and we have learned to use one another's strengths to help us limit the impact of our weaknesses. We recognize that we all have things that we tend to do really well and enjoy doing, as well as things that we do not do as well. Balancing our strengths and weaknesses has become a continual process of challenging ourselves to grow individually and as a team.

Self-Correcting

We would be remiss to imply that we do not struggle with old patterns and issues at times. Our team is not immune to normal issues that impact teams, and our team is far from perfect. However, our team has learned that we have the ability to address these problems directly and refocus on our miracle. The problems are then placed into perspective, which makes them more manageable. Our team achieves this by maintaining ongoing focus on how we, as individual team members, impact one another, fit into our agency, and how our agency fits into the rest of our professional world (our governing agencies, the community, our referral sources, solution-focused therapy, etc.). We call this the "big picture." Occasionally we have to remind one another of what this big picture consists of and the role we play in achieving our longer-term goals.

The amount of paperwork we are required to complete and the time it takes to complete these seemingly mundane tasks is frustrating. However, we are very aware of the importance of documenting the work we do. Although these tasks may seem pointless and irritating at times, we remind one another that we must do the documentation in order to continue with the clinical work and to peacefully coexist within the problem-focused world.

In light of this, we have learned to redirect one another when needed in a nonjudgmental manner, and to be proactive in recognizing potential problems within our team. We do this by checking in with one another on a regular basis and by taking the time to discuss issues or concerns. For example, we may notice that a peer has a sudden lack of tolerance for the mundane, a poor attitude, a tendency to isolate, etc. We have learned the importance of not only holding our team member accountable for the behavior but also reaching out to see how we can help. At times, this means simply taking the time to go to lunch together and talk. This serves to remind our team members that we notice and care while it also provides an opportunity to offer a word of guidance. It is also common during these times to encourage the struggling team member to utilize individual supervision to further address the problem.

As a team, we have accepted that we will always be learning new techniques for working with our clients. This has been a difficult lesson for those of us who are used to perfecting tasks and then moving on. We have all agreed that we are on a journey and that we will never "arrive"; we will always be training and learning new methods to work with our clients. These never-ending lessons change as we become more proficient with using solution-focused interventions, and we just continue to learn on a new level.

Appreciation for What We Have

We are motivated to work as hard as we do by our appreciation for our program and our team. Many of us have had the opportunity to compare our team to other work environments through internships or other community involvement. This reminds us of what is different at other agencies and why we are willing to work as hard as we do to maintain this environment.

Keeping our team miracle in mind also reminds us of what we are working toward and helps us to take ownership of the team. We continue to fight to ensure that we do not lose what we have developed. We are all incredibly invested in this team and our program, which results in motivation to continue our hard work.

Incorporating New Team Members

One challenging part of maintaining our close-knit team is incorporating new team members. We reduce the potentially negative impact of this by hiring those who appear to value the norms our team has developed. Each qualified applicant is interviewed by the team, and the team as a whole then decides if the person would fit into our agency. The decision to hire someone must be a unanimous decision, and if one person hesitates, the search for a new team member continues. This process results in each team member being invested in the training and success of the new team member.

As we mentioned earlier in this chapter, we make sure that new team members are supported and not left alone during their training process until they are confident about their ability to do the job. Because this directly impacts how the cohesiveness of our team is maintained and continued, we now go into further detail.

Initially, new employees accompany or "shadow" a more experienced team member to observe our work with clients. This allows them to learn the basics of our approach (as described in previous chapters) before being expected to apply them on their own. This is the beginning of learning how to generalize our solution-focused model and subsequently being able to apply it to a wide variety of specific situations.

These situations may include assisting clients, working with peers, benefiting from supervision, communicating effectively with referral sources, etc. As they begin to learn the basics of our approach, new team members are shadowed by more experienced colleagues until they demonstrate that they are ready to perform the task on their own.

They are given feedback to help ensure that their work reflects the consistency and accuracy necessary for them to be effective team members. This provides room for new team members to develop their individual style while working within the tenets of the solution-focused approach. This training allows for questions to be asked as they arise, and then these questions can be discussed at length if necessary.

This process continues until both the new team member and the more experienced colleague agree that the new member is ready to work independently. This training process continues as long as necessary, because time invested early in training new team members ensures that everyone has a basic understanding of how to perform tasks as required.

In addition, new team members need to see the big picture, that is, our shared vision and how our work fits within the larger community. Our team's expectation of high-quality work requires newer team members to devote a great deal of energy to learning our approach, and it can be difficult to keep the big picture in mind. However, it can be detrimental to the team and to the well-being of the new team member to forget or overlook the big picture, and a reminder of this can ensure that tasks are completed correctly. For example, countless details must be completed. When these details are viewed independent of the big picture, they can appear arbitrary and perfectionistic. However, once the new therapist understands the details' role in translating our solution-focused work into the more mainstream problem-focused language, the details become more meaningful.

We have learned that taking the time to train our new team members carefully and thoroughly pays off in the long term. We do not put specific time frames on learning new tasks or on training in general. New therapists take on additional tasks as they become ready. We have created an environment in which mistakes are seen as a learning experience rather than as a failure. Established team members point out mistakes but assume that the mistakes were made because the newer team member did not know the correct way to complete the task. Therefore, blaming others for mistakes is not an issue. The focus remains on what needs to be done to correct the situation.

We also recognize that people have different learning styles and, whenever possible, we try to accommodate these styles. We have found that the entire team benefits from the energy invested in training our new team members well. This has resulted in our previously mentioned open-door policy. Everybody feels comfortable knocking on one another's door and asking questions regardless of the circumstances.

In order to truly understand what makes our team continue to be successful, it bears repeating that we not only value but also *encourage* questions. We have discovered that we save much time by addressing these questions at the beginning rather than having to correct mistakes later. Newer team members (as well as more established team members) are encouraged to use their individual supervision time to discuss problems they are experiencing.

Team Dedication

As we mentioned earlier, one of the factors that drew us to this team and this approach is the high standard we have for our peers and ourselves. We are all very dedicated to this team and to our program; however, we occasionally need to be reminded of this. We can become overwhelmed by all that is expected of us. This can result in "tunnel vision" and us being more concerned about ourselves rather than the team or the big picture. We are aware that each of us has this potential and have found that gentle reminders to one another can quickly resolve this issue.

Our dedication to this team and this approach has been a natural result of becoming solution focused. As we see the solution-focused approach work with our clients and one another, we become excited to continue in this growth process. This excitement is contagious to our new team members and to others who work closely with our team. It is easy for each of us to be dedicated to our team and solution-focused therapy because we see the positive results on a regular basis with our peers and our clients.

SUMMARY

Team members must have respect for one another and be supportive of each team member's goals. It is also helpful for the health of a team that members are able to laugh together, although we are not sure exactly how this develops. The values and norms of the team not only are passed on by our training process and our supervision but, more important, are inspired by each team member who views them as an integral part of a successful future.

Continual effort is required to maintain an effective team, and remember that the team will never reach perfection. However, a great team is worth the effort put into it, in that it leads to dedication and commitment to growth. We know from our own experience that there cannot possibly be a more supportive and nurturing environment than a well-functioning, solution-focused team.

Chapter 10

Case Examples of Clients Who Changed Their Lives and Our Way of Working

> You are never given a wish without also being given the power to make it true. You may have to work for it however.
>
> Richard Bach

This chapter examines some of the obstacles we initially encountered in applying the SF approach to a wide range of clients who came to our (TP's) agency, and demonstrates through case studies how we apply this approach with a variety of multiproblem clients, many of whom have been court-ordered into treatment.

A CASE OF QUIET REBELLION

Over the years we (TP and YD) had been repeatedly cautioned by well-meaning colleagues that solution-focused therapy could be effective only with simple cases, those involving mild family or marital conflict, substance abuse (not dependence), or situations in which the client obviously has ample support and resources. It was an approach, according to these therapists, for clients with mild, transient symptoms.

I (TP) was told that this approach would not work with the more challenging cases, such as those with panic disorder, borderline personality disorder, narcissistic personality disorder, major depressive disorder, schizophrenia, or post-traumatic stress disorder.

I (YD) was told that it would not work with cases involving physical, emotional, or sexual abuse.

These conditions, we were told, required the more traditional approaches. Unfortunately, the traditional approaches did not seem to be working with these clients either. Since neither of us had seen any actual evidence to prove that solution-focused therapy would not work with these populations, we quietly rebelled and tried solution-focused therapy. Fortunately, the alleged limitations of solution-focused therapy turned out to be untrue (see Dolan 1991, 1998; Berg and Dolan, 2001). In fact, our clients kept getting better.

Some of the therapists at our (TP's) agency also grappled with this myth, repeatedly questioning whether solution-focused therapy could be effective with our especially difficult cases. Although they had read studies that demonstrated the effective use of this approach with severe mental illness and other difficult populations (Eakes et al., 1997; Lindforss and Magnusson, 1997), they initially remained skeptical. Despite well-intentioned words of caution from colleagues unfamiliar with the solution-focused approach, and despite the initial skepticism of some of our own staff members, we successfully applied this approach to our work with all of the clients at our agency. The significant therapeutic results our therapists witnessed over time gradually convinced even our most vocal critic.

Although all of our clients are initially referred to us because of substance abuse or dependence, a large portion are also diagnosed with various co-occurring mental health diagnoses. For example, many of our clients have a concurrent diagnosis of a mood disorder (either bipolar disorder or major depression), borderline personality disorder, and some form of substance dependency (such as cocaine or alcohol).

These multiproblem, multidiagnosis clients have often received prior psychiatric evaluation and have been or are currently receiving mental health treatment. Although our agency does not diagnose mental health disorders and does not use these labels in treatment planning or service delivery, we are frequently presented with the clients' mental health symptoms and are challenged to assist with these issues in addition to symptoms of substance abuse/dependence.

Although we support clients obtaining traditional mental health services, our clients frequently decide that the traditional methods alone are not helping them to obtain the desired results. Often they utilize the skills and future focus that they are learning at our agency to address their mental health issues, with amazing results.

Not surprisingly, the most challenging cases have taught us the most. These clients have taught us to suspend our judgment and to honor the clients' paths, no matter how treacherous those paths may appear. Our clients have shown us that they have the resources to make their miracles a reality. We have selected a handful of these cases (those from which we have learned the most) to share in this chapter. We hope that these client stories touch your heart and enrich your understanding of the treatment potential of solution-focused therapy just as they did for us.

JIM

Jim's diversion officer referred him to our agency for help with stopping his use of marijuana. Jim had recently resumed his use of marijuana following the suicide of his best friend. Not surprisingly, Jim demonstrated symptoms of depression and grief upon admission. He repeatedly cried, tearfully explaining that he had lost interest in all the activities he had previously enjoyed, lost motivation, slept excessively, and did not have much of an appetite. He said he had been using marijuana to try to cope with his intense feelings of grief and loss. He really missed his friend.

It is often thought that clients who have suffered a significant loss need time during therapy to talk about their pain, specifically when the loss is this devastating. Clients often report that spending time talking with family and friends who also knew the loved one is extremely healing. We agree that this time of remembrance and introspection is healing during times of intense grief, but we question whether therapy time is best used this way.

We suspect that the experience of shared understanding and empathy which occurs with a close friend or loved ones is a unique, highly personal and meaningful event that cannot be simply replicated with a therapist during an individual therapy session. Our hunch is that clients seek professional help only in instances when this natural healing process is somehow not sufficient or when their accustomed coping methods are no longer working. This was the case with Jim: his grief symptoms were not subsiding despite the fact that he had spent a significant amount of time with family and friends. Furthermore, his continued use of marijuana to cope with his grief had failed to give him relief, and it now was putting him at risk for being terminated from the diversion program. (Diversion is a legal program in Colorado that allows clients who have received a deferred sentence from the courts to have the charge dismissed if they comply with closely monitored, treatment-focused requirements.)

As with many clients who are overcome with grief, Jim did not need services to help him remember or acknowledge the loss of his friend. In fact, memories and pain had become overpowering and had a debilitating effect on him. He needed help to figure out how he could continue on with his life despite his loss, for he could not imagine a future without his friend.

Using the miracle question, the therapist asked Jim to describe a future in which he had been able to integrate meaningful aspects and memories about his friend:

> Imagine that while you are asleep tonight, a miracle happens. The miracle is that even though you have lost the person most important to you, you know that he will always be a part of you and have a powerful impact on your life. However, because you are asleep, you don't know that the miracle has happened. So, when you wake up tomorrow morning, what will be different that will let you know that a miracle has happened and that your friend will always be a part of who you are?

This question offered Jim the first glimpse of hope that his friend could be not only a part of his past but also a meaningful part of his future.

Over a relatively short period of time (approximately one month), Jim discovered his own solution and his depressive symptoms and use of marijuana subsided. When the therapist asked how this had happened, Jim explained that one day he had decided to draw a picture that depicted his friend's life. The image that he drew was of his friend snowboarding (an activity they had often done together).

Subsequently, Jim had shown the drawing to his friend's family, and they decided that the image should be made into the headstone for his friend's grave. Jim explained that through this process, the memory of his friend had become a meaningful part of his current and future life as well as his past.

This case illustrates how healing interventions (such as rituals) from other theories are readily integrated into our program's solution-focused work with clients. The primary distinguishing characteristic is that these interventions are initiated and designed by the client rather than by the therapist.

Rituals can be extremely healing, and the most effective ones are often highly personalized. The therapist could never have designed a cathartic ritual that was as effective as the one that Jim initiated for himself. Jim's idea to make this drawing came from his ability to see a future in which his friend still played a part. This allowed him to design an individual ritual that was specific to his needs and to access the healing power of sharing this memory and drawing with his loved ones. This resulted in Jim's drawing becoming a meaningful part of his friend's family's future as well. Once clients are able to envision a desirable future, their pain becomes more manageable. Answers that were always present often become visible, allowing clients to move forward, out of the pain.

TRACY

Tracy's diversion officer referred her to our agency for substance abuse services. In addition to a history of substance abuse-related issues, Tracy had prior mental health treatment for bipolar disorder and panic attacks. Upon admission, she confided that she was no longer taking psychotropic medication or receiving mental health services because she could no longer afford these services. She told us that she had been abusing prescription pain medications in order to cope with panic attacks. She told us that she had stopped using the drugs due to her resulting legal problems and that her primary concern upon admission was her frequent panic attacks.

She explained that she was reluctant to leave her house for fear that she would "do something stupid and people will see." She said that this fear made it difficult to hold down a job or to enjoy doing things with her son. For example, she avoided going into stores and avoided being in public alone by only leaving the house with her boyfriend. In addition, she complained that she frequently experienced sweaty palms, rapid breathing, rapid heart rate, and a dread of social situations.

Despite her fear of leaving the house, Tracy came to our agency and attended the treatment group. Several times she experienced these symptoms (rapid breathing, rapid heart rate, and sweaty palms) during the group treatment sessions. Each time, the therapist gently encouraged her to take a break and pay attention to what helped her to feel more calm.

The therapist also introduced Tracy to using scales to rate her emotional state (ten meaning that she was completely calm, and one meaning her state was the worst it had ever been). On the first occasion that this scale was used when the symptoms arose during the treatment session, the client rated herself as a three. After Tracy took a break, focused on what made her feel more calm, and then returned to the group session, she rated herself as an eight. Once Tracy was able to manage her symptoms and stay in the room, the therapist's interventions then focused on assisting her to imagine life without the problems that brought her to our agency (similar to the work we do with all of our clients).

Less than one month later, Tracy came in for a treatment session and reported that she had gone Christmas shopping with her boyfriend and then went to another store on her own without experiencing any anxiety! When the therapist asked how she had accomplished such a feat, Tracy explained that she had "practiced going into stores until it didn't bother me anymore." Upon further questioning, Tracy spontaneously described a process that was strikingly similar to the behavioral technique of systematic desensitization (Barlow and Durand, 1999) in which clients are gradually introduced to situations that evoke increasing levels of anxiety while they do something incompatible with fear (such as relaxation).

Tracy had independently discovered and implemented a traditionally therapist-based intervention for resolving social phobia! Furthermore, she did not experience any other symptoms of panic or anxiety while at our agency. When asked further about her progress in this area upon discharge from our agency a couple months later, she answered, "It's just not a part of my life anymore."

We have found that solution-focused therapy is a natural fit for addressing anxiety-based disorders. Not surprisingly, when clients are encouraged to concentrate on a time and place in the future in which the problem is resolved, they are able to experience a sense of calm and relative well-being. As the clients combine this future focus with scaling, they gradually identify increased periods of time in which the problem is no longer present.

The clients are then able to identify what they are doing during these periods of calm that prevents the panic response or stops the feeling if it begins to occur. This process empowers clients by demonstrating undeniably that they have the ability to control their response to external stimuli, thereby dissipating the anticipated negative response. The clients gain a sense of mastery and are able to live their lives without fear.

JULIE

Julie was referred to our agency by social services to rule out a current substance-related problem. She had a history of past drug use. Julie was very angry about being involved with social services and protested adamantly that she did not have a problem that would warrant social services' referral to our agency.

She had recently been detained on a "mental health hold" following a domestic violence incident. (This is a legal process used in Colorado when a client is determined by a qualified professional to be at imminent risk to harm himself or herself, or others. The client is then detained for up to seventy-two hours to obtain a psychiatric evaluation and to determine the need for additional services to ensure safety.) The hold had been put into place by a mental health staff member who assessed Julie as being a potential threat to the safety of other people. Julie protested, claiming that "she lied to get the hold." Julie's presenting story was difficult to follow, and many parts seemed contradictory. She repeatedly blamed other people for her problems and referred to her child as a "wicked little kid."

After consultation with the referral source and review of Julie's evaluation and testing results, we explained to Julie that because the results of her evaluation were inconsistent, we were recommending a brief period of treatment to allow her to provide evidence that substance use is not a problem. Although Julie initially told the evaluating therapist from our agency that she agreed with these recommendations, subsequently both she and her husband telephoned me (TP, as the therapist's supervisor) repeatedly, complaining that she was being treated unfairly and protesting that the recommendations were incorrect. After each telephone conversation, Julie would say that she thought treatment would be helpful in demonstrating to her caseworker that she did not have a problem. Later, she would reverse her position.

During a supervision session, the evaluating therapist confided that she was frustrated with Julie because she kept making inconsistent statements and because the case was requiring excessive time and energy to answer the client's repeated phone calls and questions. She questioned whether Julie could benefit from our treatment groups because of her tendency toward angry outbursts, inconsistent statements, and propensity for blaming others.

At this point, the therapist was far from neutral; she dreaded any contact with Julie. Nevertheless, I encouraged her to listen carefully to Julie during each conversation, to try to understand what Julie really needed and what she was willing to do. I stressed the importance of resisting the assumption that future interactions would necessarily go poorly simply because they had in the past.

Despite the difficulties we had experienced working with Julie during the evaluation process, we agreed to be consistent in our solution-focused approach. We decided that Julie deserved a fresh start. In order to foster this, the evaluating therapist intentionally refrained from talking to the group therapist about the difficulties she had experienced with Julie prior to beginning the group.

At the end of Julie's first group, the group therapist came to my office and expressed frustration about Julie's behavior in her group that day. She reported that Julie had blamed social services for "traumatizing" her child by removing her from the home and insisted that she did not need to be in treatment. When I asked the group therapist how she handled the situation, it became clear that the therapist handled it well despite her frustration. She had spoken to Julie privately and explained that blaming social services is not acceptable in the group setting, and had subsequently encouraged Julie to think about how she wanted her life to be once she was past these current problems.

As we mentioned in Chapter 8, supervision (impromptu and scheduled) provides an opportunity to help therapists refocus on listening to the client and regain a position of neutrality and objectivity. Similar to many of the clients we see, Julie triggered frustration. Nevertheless, the therapist evidenced the discipline to remain in the moment, set and enforce gentle limits, and invite Julie to envision and describe how she wanted her life to be different in the future.

We have learned that it is impossible for us to accurately predict ahead of time who will benefit from treatment. Therefore, we adopt a neutral stance. Inherent in the solution-focused approach, this neutrality empowers our clients to make changes without losing face and allows the therapist to acknowledge the positive changes the client makes.

Initially, our clients are often surprised at this approach and defend why they do not have a problem, and therefore do not need to change. Once they realize that we are not going to label them as having a problem, they often change their stance and adopt the future focus. We have seen very challenging clients change, and supervision served an important function in reminding the therapists in this case that Julie could very well be one of those clients who would also change. We agreed to trust the change process and to continue with our approach with Julie in a group setting. However, if Julie was unable to abide by the limits, as a "fallback" position we would offer individual sessions to assist her in identifying how she wanted her life to be in the future while minimizing the potential negative impact on the group norms.

Although she continued to appear unhappy about having to attend treatment, during Julie's second group session she was no longer disruptive to the group process. The group therapist carefully provided Julie with some psychological "space" by refraining from directly addressing her or asking her questions in the group setting unless Julie initiated conversation. (We often use this approach with clients who are angry in a group setting. This simultaneously demonstrates respect for the client's belief that they do not need to participate in treatment and allows the client access to the future-oriented conversation. This directly demonstrates that our focus is on the clients' desired future rather than on their past.)

During Julie's third session, as the therapist worked with the other clients in defining and working toward their miracles, she was surprised to hear Julie interrupt this group work and say, "You haven't asked me the miracle question yet." Julie had become curious.

From that moment on, Julie participated actively in the group sessions and eagerly worked toward obtaining her miracle. She became energetic and excited about a future that was within her control, and each week she reported various changes that she was making. Significantly, the anger that had once characterized all of Julie's interactions abruptly melted away as she embraced her future.

During her final session, Julie described herself as a nine on a ten-point scale (ten signifying that she was living her miracle, and one meaning the opposite). She told us that she had appreciated the flexibility of our staff, that her time in our program had been a positive experience, and that she had benefited from treatment. Working with Julie was a powerful reminder to our staff that all clients (even those who repeatedly trigger our frustration) want to move beyond their problems. They just are unsure how to get there. By remaining neutral and listening to our clients, we can understand what will make a difference for them.

CONNIE

Connie was referred to our agency by social services because of a history of alcohol abuse. Connie's two sons had been placed in the custody of social services after she was charged with sexually assaulting a child. Connie had received mental health treatment in the past and was given a diagnosis of major depression with narcissistic features. She protested to us that this prior treatment had not been helpful and that, furthermore, she was not depressed.

Because she was on probation due to the sexual assault charges, Connie was required to participate in offense-specific treatment. Her probation officer described her as "difficult" because she would not admit to the sexual assault or the alcohol abuse, and because she "whines a lot."

At first, Connie attended treatment only sporadically and often showed up drunk at our agency. She frequently came without an appointment, demanding to see her therapist. She gave inconsistent information to her therapist, her caseworker, and her probation officer.

On one occasion Connie disclosed that she was violating the restraining order placed upon her by continuing to have contact with the child who she allegedly sexually abused. In order to comply with the law, her therapist insisted that Connie immediately inform her caseworker of this violation prior to leaving our agency that evening. Connie served two weeks in jail as a result of this disclosure, and we wondered if the therapist's rapport with Connie had been irreparably broken.

However, Connie returned to treatment following her incarceration and started responding to the solution-focused questions. She answered the miracle question and began to identify a future that she viewed as worth achieving. She explained that she wanted to do things that helped her to feel good about herself because she was tired of feeling bad about her behavior. She told us that this desire was resulting in her choosing to avoid activities that would lead away from her goal.

Also, Connie appeared to have been especially affected by the therapist's compliments, because she repeatedly said that, in contrast, other professionals had told her that she was a "horrible person and will never change." Finding an environment in which positive change was the norm apparently was refreshing and offered her hope.

As Connie continued to work toward obtaining her miracle, people around her began to notice the changes and her probation officer described her as more cooperative. Most marked, however, were the changes that Connie's mother described one evening in a family group. (Our clients are encouraged to bring family members or other important visitors to their group sessions at their discretion on designated evenings. Connie brought her mother.)

Connie's mother was the person who originally contacted the authorities because of concern about the safety of Connie's children. She had also assumed custody of one of Connie's children once they were removed from her care. Her mother had previously stated that she did not believe that Connie could ever remain substance free and not "screw up her life." So it was quite significant and dramatic when, on this evening, she proudly declared that she had *no doubt* that her daughter would be successful, and that she deserved to regain custody of her children.

Just prior to her discharge from our agency, Connie's caseworker stated that the "permanency plan" was to return her children to her care, and that this was the result of the caseworker's confidence that Connie's changes were lasting. Eight months after her discharge, one of our therapists ran into Connie in the community and had the opportunity to obtain an update on her progress. Connie smiled happily as she reported that she was doing well, was working full time, and indeed had regained custody of her son.

Addressing Legal Responsibilities Involving Community Safety

Our therapists often struggle when they have to "wear a different hat" and step out of the therapeutic role and enforce community safety by reporting child abuse, etc. It is an uncomfortable task that runs the risk of damaging their rapport with the client. However, wearing this protection "hat" as well as the therapeutic "hat" is a requirement of being a therapist. Equally difficult is remaining neutral and listening to clients when they have been labeled child abusers. It is understandably tempting to judge the client and be appalled by the victimization of an innocent child, specifically when other professionals have taken this stance. However, this is counterproductive because this judgment typically results in the clients needing to defend their behavior rather than explore how they would rather be. Connie's case demonstrates the powerful impact of remaining neutral and believing in people's ability to change despite unacceptable behavior. It was this genuinely neutral and accepting stance that assisted Connie in questioning how she really wanted her life to be. By knowing that others believed in her, she was able to begin to believe that change was possible. It was this hope and future focus that assisted her to make her miracle a reality.

KERRY

Kerry was referred to our agency by diversion due to charges of prescription drug fraud. She had multiple physicians (approximately eight to eleven at one time) prescribing opiates for various ailments, and she had repeatedly frequented the hospital emergency room each month for additional shots of Demerol. She had been involved with mental health treatment due to a diagnosis of post-traumatic stress disorder due to a prior sexual assault. She also exhibited characteristic symptoms of borderline personality disorder. She blamed others for her problems, displayed intense emotions (from anger to depression in a short period of time), reported unstable relationships, had poor self-image, was suspiciousness of others, and gave inconsistent communication. She had a past history of suicide attempts and past hospitalizations, and she often presented herself in a melodramatic fashion.

Kerry resisted following the payment plan at our agency and frequently blamed her therapist for being unreasonable for not allowing her to submit a required urine screen when she did not pay for the service. She cried angrily and increased her agitated behavior when payment was discussed, accusing her therapist of causing her to be at risk of going to jail.

To avoid any confusion about payment and treatment expectations, we used written contracts in collaboration with her referral source. Soon after admission to our agency, Kerry was terminated from the diversion program because of an additional charge of prescription fraud. Her case was then transferred to probation.

We worked with Kerry in the same manner we work with all of our clients, gently interrupting Kerry's storytelling and blaming during treatment sessions by refocusing the conversation on how her life would be once the problem that brought her to us was resolved.

We were careful not to initiate discussions about emotions, except in reference to the client's future. Other clients appeared able to integrate emotions into their description of how life would be once their miracle became a reality, but Kerry typically became overwhelmed and distracted by discussions involving emotions, and struggled unsuccessfully to identify the behaviors that would be occurring in her desired future.

Sensitive to this difficulty, the therapist carefully and gently interrupted Kerry when she noticed her becoming overwhelmed. At these times, the therapist asked specific behavior-oriented questions to provide Kerry with necessary structure to succeed in envisioning a positive, hope-filled future. In response, Kerry became more focused, less overwhelmed by her emotions, and able to verbalize a clear future that she desired. We watched Kerry move from being a victim of her pain in need of prescription medications to taking responsibility for her actions.

In working with Kerry, the therapist often used an intervention in which the client is asked to imagine that she is watching a video of herself that depicts life once her miracle has come true (O'Hanlon and Wilk, 1987). The video does not have any sound, and the client is asked to describe what she sees on the imaginary screen that lets her know that the miracle has occurred. This intervention requires that the client pay specific attention to the behavioral cues that indicate change. The result is a heightened awareness of the role and meaning of behaviors in signaling change. Subsequently Kerry discovered that she could withstand difficult emotions by maintaining a focus on her behavior and her desired future.

Sometimes Kerry requested time in group for assistance in responding to difficult emotions and situations. Kerry would quickly drift into emotion-based stories when given the opportunity, and the therapist found that frequently interrupting and assisting Kerry to remain focused on what she needed rather than on the story or how she felt was very helpful. The following interaction demonstrates how this was done:

KERRY: I need some group time to help me resolve a problem that is really stressing me out.

THERAPIST: Sure. How can we help?

KERRY: I have something that I have to do by Thursday, and I keep avoiding it because it interferes with my social life. I feel really stressed about getting this done.

THERAPIST: Hmm. I'm wondering if you would imagine that it is next week and the problem is resolved.

KERRY: OK.

THERAPIST: So, here we are. It's next week and you are in group telling us how you handled this issue. How did you do it?

KERRY: I put some time aside to deal with what I had to do instead of giving all my time to my social life. I did it!

THERAPIST: Wow! So you did what you had to do! What difference did this make?

KERRY: Getting it done has reduced my stress.

THERAPIST: And reducing your stress made what difference to you?

KERRY: Well, getting done what I had to do reduces my stress and helps me increase my self-confidence. That's my miracle. That's what I want from being here.

How tempting it would have been to have gathered more information from Kerry about this task or to have explored why she was avoiding completing the task. However, this line of conversation would have only led to Kerry reexperiencing the stress and becoming overwhelmed.

Being assisted to view this problem from the perspective of a future time and place in which it had been solved empowered Kerry to find her own answer. She was able to put her difficult emotions into perspective rather than falling prey to their overwhelming potential. The therapist never knew what this difficult thing that Kerry had to do was, and this story was not relevant to Kerry finding the solution to the problem. Kerry left the session smiling, knowing what she needed to do and why. This new way of viewing problems and finding solutions was so powerful that it helped her to put her feelings into perspective and to manage her previously unmanageable emotions.

ELAINE

Elaine was referred to our agency because of her extensive history of substance abuse. She had a history of previous treatment (including eight to ten detoxification episodes), and had resumed her use of alcohol despite previous services. She had recently completed a residential treatment program and did not agree with her social services caseworker that additional services were needed. She reported a history of legal problems, domestic incidents, and suicide attempts while under the influence of alcohol. The client was pregnant during her treatment at our agency, and her older child was in the custody of social services. The client was Native American, and she demonstrated a strong mistrust of the "system" and was guarded in her disclosures.

Trust appeared to be a primary issue when working with Elaine. She expected her therapist to judge her, to not take the time to understand her, and to insist that she admit that she had a problem. Her mistrust needed to be respected. Solution-focused therapy's value of the individual and its focus on how the client wants life to be had an amazing impact on Elaine. Elaine's therapist did not do anything remarkably different with her than with any other client. The focus of treatment was on her future and what she wanted. The client's culture was not an overt part of her treatment, yet the individuality of the approach allowed her to integrate her culture into her treatment to the degree that she wanted. Elaine sensed the respect and safety that the approach offers, and she soon began to trust her therapist despite the cultural differences. She learned that her therapist was there to listen and learn from her, not to tell her how she should be. Elaine began to tell the therapist that she did not trust her previous therapist in the residential program and that this mistrust prevented her from using this experience. She began to call her current therapist when she was struggling and to be curious and eager to explore her future.

Elaine responded well to the miracle question and appeared to benefit specifically from focusing on her future goal rather than on her failures. For example, she wanted to keep her unborn child safe and to regain custody of her older child. She began to laugh and smile when she came to the agency, frequently eating corn chips in the waiting room as she playfully interacted with agency staff. Her comfort level at the agency was refreshing to all.

Solution-Focused Approach and Cultural Sensitivity

As a therapist, I was taught the importance of being sensitive to the client's culture, for without this sensitivity clients will not feel comfortable or benefit from even the best of services. In the problem-focused approaches, this sensitivity is often gained through therapist education of the unique aspects of the various cultures (Atkinson, Morten, and Sue, 1998; Davis and Proctor, 1989). This is very effective as long as the client shares the traditional views of that culture. However, problems arise when clients' individuality and varying degrees of cultural identity come into play. Many agencies address this potential problem by matching the client with a same-race therapist or by specializing in one particular culture, under the belief that the similarity between therapist and client will minimize any potential cultural differences. Although this approach does increase cultural sensitivity, the therapist's beliefs and culture (even though similar) still have a strong impact on the content and direction of therapy. In Elaine's case, she had received prior treatment from a Native American therapist at a Native American treatment center whose staff was familiar with her tribe's beliefs. However, she did not want to return to this agency due to the services not matching her individual needs even though this therapist's culture was more similar to her own.

Because solution-focused therapists intentionally maintain a stance apart from specific assumptions or preconceived beliefs about clients or problems, most cultural pitfalls are typically avoided. Differences in culture between the therapist and client do not serve as an impediment to treatment. Culture is valued and seen as another factor that makes each client unique. The therapist does not make any assumptions as to the degree to which the client's culture is important or a part of the solution. The therapist simply provides a safe environment and listens to the client's desired future. Through this respectful listening the roles that the client's culture, gender, and other unique factors play are revealed. This allows the therapist to figuratively walk beside the client through the journey rather than taking a leadership stance.

SUMMARY

Solution-focused therapy is sometimes erroneously viewed as not applicable to complex, long-standing, or difficult problems. Not only does the literature not support this view (Berg and Dolan, 2001; Berg and Miller, 1992; Dolan, 1991; Eakes et al., 1997; Lindforss and Magnusson, 1997), but repeated experience with clients at our agency directly contradicts it. Our clients have shown us the importance of providing them with the opportunity and necessary structure to discover their own unique solutions, and the importance of trusting that they have the ability to make these solutions a reality. We hope that the client stories in this chapter have touched your heart as they did ours, and have served to further enhance your awareness of the vast therapeutic potential inherent in the solution-focused approach.

Epilogue

The Parable of the Nomads

Once upon a time there was a band of nomads who were in search of the Promised Land. They wandered about in the Land of Khaos for many years and often became wearied by their plight. They watched as others discovered the path to the Promised Land, settled down, and discarded the nomad identity. This deepened the sense of hopeless doom that overshadowed this nomadic group. Many in this group had endured horrendous tragedies during their journey. Some outwardly displayed their wounds, yet others appeared unscathed. In an effort to survive, this group became a type of family, forming its own traditions and rules. Those who came into contact with this group often criticized its members for their lack of compliance with societal norms. Members were accused of being disorganized, lacking skills, and lacking direction. For fear of further criticism, the nomads became suspicious of outsiders and often declined assistance from others.

One day, some of the nomads discovered that eating black licorice quickly soothed their sore feet and tired muscles. Unfortunately, the nomads later learned of the toxic qualities of black licorice and the resultant loss of motivation to strive for the Promised Land. While under the spell of the toxic properties of the candy, nomads would lose their desire to escape from the Land of Khaos. However, despite this new knowledge some of the nomads continued to eat the licorice, arguing that the medicinal qualities were of greater value. This caused conflict and strife within the nomadic band, which slowed their journey. This served only to increase the criticism and scorn that the nomads received from the residents of the Land of Khaos. The nomads' disorganization, internal conflict, lack of progress, and continued consumption of licorice fueled the residents' beliefs that the nomads were incapable of change. The residents began an effort to force the nomads to hasten their journey. They enlisted the help of the Khaos

Enforcement Department to require that the nomads continue their journey out of the Land of Khaos. The nomads, desiring a more comfortable life, complied.

During the course of their journey, the nomads happened upon a mountain ridge that appeared to be insurmountable. The distraught nomads turned to their leaders to devise a plan. To their dismay, they found their leaders eating licorice and unconcerned about their dilemma. Without leadership, their short-lived progress appeared to vanish. The residents of Khaos again turned to their Enforcement Department to mandate the nomads to continue their journey despite the perceived obstacle. The Enforcers insisted that if the nomads wanted to get over the mountain ridge, they could. They ruled that the nomads' apparent lack of ability was only the result of overindulgence of licorice and lack of organization and desire. They proceeded to mandate that the nomads meet with the Mountain Experts in order to gain the skills to scale the mountain. This was the same mandate that had been given to previous nomadic groups who had passed through the Land of Khaos.

Now the Mountain Experts were well aware of the dilemmas that often faced nomads who were seeking to reach the Promised Land. The Mountain Experts used to be part of a larger clan called the Mountain Pioneers. The Mountain Pioneers used to be nomads themselves. They had wandered the Land of Khaos, eating licorice, and had also been highly criticized by the Khaos residents. However, the Mountain Pioneers had found a way to scale the mountain and travel to the Promised Land. They discovered that getting to the Promised Land was possible only if they did not consume black licorice to quell their sore feet and tired muscles. Once they learned these lessons, they returned to the Land of Khaos in an effort to help other nomads who were struggling with this same plight. However, the Mountain Pioneers would only help nomads who would agree to abstain from all forms of licorice. Once this agreement was made, the Mountain Pioneers would use explosives to blast the mountain to uncover the tool that the nomads needed to scale the mountain.

Although the Mountain Pioneers' methods were often effective, many nomads avoided their help. These nomads claimed that they did not need to give up their licorice and that the Mountain Pioneers blew up too many flowers and trees in the process. Because of this, some of the Mountain Pioneers began to question their methods and desired a more environmentally friendly approach. They left the Mountain Pioneers and formed the group called the Mountain Experts.

The Mountain Experts agreed that nomads needed to cease the consumption of licorice in order to get to the Promised Land. However, they discovered that refusing to help the nomads unless they agreed never to eat any form of licorice again was not the most helpful approach. However, they retained the belief that licorice was the cause of the nomads' dilemmas. They also discovered that an instrument called the Magic Telescope could be just as useful as the Mountain Pioneers' dynamite in uncovering the tool needed to assist the nomads in scaling the mountain. This Magic Telescope helped the Mountain Experts locate the needed tool in the nomads' own belongings. They often discovered that the nomads' past generations also frequently unknowingly possessed this tool. This Magic Telescope was environmentally friendly, and the nomads were often more comfortable with this way of locating the tool that was needed to scale the mountain.

The Mountain Experts were highly revered throughout the Land of Khaos for their wisdom and skill. However, many nomads remained skeptical of outside assistance. Some would become angry when the Mountain Experts searched their belongings for the tool, and some would become bored as the Mountain Experts searched for the tool on their behalf. Still others were brazen enough to question whether the tool the Mountain Experts discovered was really the correct tool to get them to the Promised Land. These nomads continued to eat black licorice and insisted that the Mountain Experts' help was not needed. They left the Mountain Experts' shack and continued to wander in the Land of Khaos. These apparent failures weighed heavily upon many of the Mountain Experts' hearts. Many began to question whether helping the nomads was worthwhile.

One day, one of the Mountain Experts, nicknamed the Curious Wizard, noticed a small button labeled "PL" on the Magic Telescope. The Mountain Experts never used this button, and Curious Wizard was told that the button's use was not important, for the Mountain Experts' skills were sufficient to locate the tool without any additional help. He secretly pushed the button and immediately noticed that the view from the Magic Telescope changed! The view of the Land of Khaos changed to a beautiful land. It almost looked like the Promised Land! In his excitement he allowed a nomad to hold the Magic Telescope and see the wonders that previously were only seen by him or other curious Experts. He began to allow all of the nomads with whom he worked to hold the Telescope, and he began to push this button while the nomads gazed through the Magic Telescope's lens. He felt a sense of wonderment and excitement as the viewing nomad described this desired land. The Curious Wizard soon became the brunt of the Mountain Experts' jokes since he allowed nomads to search for their own tools and he no longer valued what the Magic Telescope showed when the "PL" button was not activated. He was even chastised by the Head Mountain Expert due to his decision to stray from the expert role. Despite the criticism, he took walks with the nomads and asked them questions as they continued to explore this beautiful land through the lens of the Magic Telescope with the "PL" button activated.

During one such walk with a nomad, the nomad told the Curious Wizard that he had been packing his bags and getting organized for the trip to the Promised Land. The Curious Wizard was surprised, since the nomad had not mentioned during their walks that he had found the needed tool. Upon questioning, the Curious Wizard learned that the nomad had been gaining clues about the needed tool from his study of the Promised Land through the Magic Telescope. The nomad told the Curious Wizard that he was sure the tool would be found any day now, and he wanted to be ready to go the minute he found it. The next time that the nomad met with the Curious Wizard he was carrying a heavy sack. His voice was laced with excitement as he told the Wizard that he had found the tool and was heading to the Promised Land. He then handed the sack to the Curious Wizard. He said that he would not be needing its contents in the Promised Land and asked the Curious Wizard to give the sack to someone who could use it. The Curious Wizard watched in amazement as the nomad quickly scaled the mountain and jumped over to the Promised Land. Once the nomad had disappeared from sight, the Curious Wizard then stooped to open the sack. To his surprise, he found black licorice. "Wow!" thought the Curious Wizard. "We hadn't even talked about licorice yet. How did he know?"

As the years went by, word of the Curious Wizard's success spread throughout the Land of Khaos. Nomads came from all walks of life, and the Khaos Enforcement Department often mandated that the nomads go directly to him for assistance. Even some of the Mountain

Experts allowed their curiosity to get the best of them, and some asked the Curious Wizard to teach them his secret. They longed for the enthusiasm and joy that the Curious Wizard still had after all these years. The Curious Wizard often took long walks with his new students and frequently offered the Magic Telescope to them, with the challenge to activate the "PL" button. During one of these walks a student asked, "Why do you get such different results with this telescope? You use the same instrument as the Mountain Experts, yet you still hold your smile." The Curious Wizard chuckled appreciatively at the student's budding curiosity as they continued to walk up the path, clearly enjoying the journey. He then quietly revealed the secret. "It is not the telescope that holds the power," he said, "but the view within its lens. Without the view of the Promised Land, the nomads would never pack their bags."

Appendix

Reflections from Our Solution-Focused Treatment Team

Believing is seeing.

Unknown[1]

Throughout this journey the therapists and I (TP) have learned so much! We have had long conversations in both team and individual settings about the struggles and challenges that have been such a significant part of our past seven years. However, through these struggles some of the most poignant lessons have been learned.

I am frequently asked to speak to therapists and community agencies about our transition to using solution-focused therapy, and I enjoy bringing one of our clinical staff members with me to copresent. Initially, I brought them for self-serving reasons (e.g., to provide them with an opportunity to learn the skills of presenting and to provide helpful feedback to me about my own presentation style and suggestions to improve). However, I have come to learn that our audience often is eager to hear the more personal experience of a therapist who has experienced the journey. For example, Jonathan (a therapist who has been at our agency since the beginning of the journey) and I were recently presenting to a group of substance abuse therapists in the Denver area. I presented the more technical aspects of how to apply these concepts in the group setting, explaining the various stages of the group map while the audience members listened attentively, interjecting questions at various times during the presentation. At the end of the presentation, I asked what additional questions they had, and I was struck by their response. They turned to Jonathan and asked, "What would you add as a therapist?" Jonathan simply responded, "That it doesn't always go as smoothly as that."

Jonathan's genuineness about the process of learning these difficult, although simple, concepts added the necessary touch of humanity that is often absent as the approach is described. Although working with clients from a solution-focused stance is incredibly simple, paradoxically, the learning process can be equally frustrating.

This section contains thoughts and reflections from our clinical team. My hope in including this material is that you will hear the humanness that is the heart of this journey. When I first discussed the idea of writing about this journey with my team of therapists, I challenged each of them to identify what lessons they would consider to be imperative to share with the readers. Here are their thoughts.

Why Endure the Struggle to Become Solution Focused?

Patience and determination are required to change from a problem-focused approach to a solution-focused one. For me (Megan), this meant that I had to learn an entirely new way of looking at therapy. Many of the therapeutic interventions I had been taught were no longer useful. It is difficult to take everything you have learned about doing therapy and set it aside to learn a new approach, but this is exactly what I needed to do in order to use solution-focused therapy.

I learned in the past that my job was to be the "expert" for my clients and their referral sources. Giving up this role was difficult, as it was much easier to tell my clients what they needed to do rather than listen to their needs and help them to determine their next step. This meant developing creative methods to deal with clients who asked for advice. It took awhile for me to realize that giving advice often led to a solution that did not work for my clients, and that listening to what they were already doing or had done in the past that worked was much more effective in developing solutions.

Soon after I began at this agency, a client clarified this for me. She had asked for my "advice" many times, stating that I was the "expert" and should be giving her advice. I gently refused to do this and attempted to persuade her to listen to what was already working for her. However, she continued to ask for my advice and I had not yet discovered more subtle techniques of getting her to do this herself. What did work for her, though, was an exercise in which she wrote a letter to herself from the future. Her "older, wiser self" (Dolan, 1991, p. 36) from twenty to thirty years in the future, gave her all the advice she needed to continue on the path she desired. Her letter included how she should handle relationships with others as well as coping with cravings to use substances, deciding where she should live, and ways to deal with some very difficult situations she was facing. This client reinforced for me that she already had the answers she was seeking, but that developing creative ways of uncovering these answers is essential in using this approach.

Accepting the Journey Rather Than the Destination

Perhaps the greatest struggle I (Jonathan) have faced on this journey, a struggle that also combines personal and professional issues, is my desire to achieve a finished product. This journey on which I have embarked challenges that longing to its core. The ability to master something so that I can practice it effectively with as much care as possible, without always having to question myself, is an ability for which I long. Yet in the process of working within this approach, the self-questioning has become a necessary component. It is a component that prepares me for the questioning from others, which is guaranteed to happen. I have come to know this as accountability.

When I started in this field, I knew that my work did not allow me to see a finished product, for the people I work with will leave and continue to grow and be different people. The finished product I desire to see is in my own development. I want to have "arrived," as Teri puts it. I know that this will not be the case, however, at least as long as I continue to use this approach and work with this team. The challenge is constant, the accountability is high, and the lessons learned are invaluable. I continue the journey, knowing that I will never reach an end, yet am always able to justify where I am today.

What I now know is that I will never have "arrived." This is a tough concept for me to accept, a concept that I believe will guide me into whatever direction I eventually take. I know that I will always continue to learn. I know that I must have purpose in my methods, know the purpose of the interventions that I use and when to use them, and truly listen to my clients. I also know that I must try to quell my desire to understand and be good at everything all at once, which means taking one step, becoming solid in that, and then moving to the next. After having used this approach for the last five years, I know where my comfort level is and that I must continue challenging myself to move outside of the comfort level. I must keep in my head that I have the ability and the constant frame of reference that this approach requires. I have seen the many benefits for the clients from having been exposed to this approach and am confident that it is effective. When I now discuss the solution-focused approach, I am confident in what I talk about because it is becoming a part of who I am and how I operate both personally and professionally.

Using Every Opportunity for Possible Change

Being held accountable has also helped me (Megan) realize that every contact with a client is an opportunity to make a difference. Even a few words when passing in the hallway or waiting room can help clients refocus on their goals, review their progress, or highlight successes they are experiencing. One client in particular illustrates this for me. I had done an evaluation with an adolescent client but had little contact with her during her treatment. I heard some things about her progress from her primary counselor but little information had been passed on. This client had cried in my office during her evaluation as she told me that she did not believe she could stop using marijuana. She informed me that she did not have other skills to cope with stress and with difficult situations. However, she desperately wanted out of some legal difficulties she was experiencing, and remaining substance free was a requirement for her. We discussed some steps she could take to avoid using marijuana until she began attending group therapy the next week. The client developed a specific plan to cope with urges to use marijuana between her appointments. Her case was soon transferred to another therapist and I had no contact with the client for several weeks. When I did see her next, she grinned, and with a proud look on her face she informed me that she had not used marijuana since she had met with me. I asked her how she had done this, and she quickly named several things she had been doing to help her. She also informed me that her school grades had improved and that she was bettering her relationship with her parents.

My clients have continuously let me know that highlighting their successes is important in their remembering why they are working so hard to make changes in their lives. I had been taught in the past that focusing on the positive aspects in a client's life would result in "relapse" due to our ignoring the problems. However, not focusing on the problems is what provides solutions and the motivation to work toward the client's miracle.

Setting Aside Assumptions

Prior to my (Darla) introduction to solution-focused therapy, I ascribed to assumptions found in the problem-focused approach. The major assumption that I held was that self-disclosure was the most efficient way to build rapport with a client. I previously viewed self-disclosure as a powerful tool to assist clients in changing their behavior. I believed that self-disclosure created the therapeutic bond between a client and the therapist. Through practicing solution-focused therapy I have come to believe that what is most important in creating that therapeutic bond is the ability to truly hear and understand what is important to the client. This is best achieved through listening to the client rather than sharing my own experience.

Having had fifteen years of experience in the substance abuse field and hearing about SF therapy, I believed the solution-focused approach to be a simple form of therapy. Despite its simplicity, this has been the most difficult approach for me to implement. Part of what makes it more difficult for me is that I now have to answer my own questions. This can be frustrating, yet it has resulted in more lasting answers and professional, and surprisingly personal, growth.

Reflections from a "Once Skeptic"

I (Karen) would not begin to tell you this approach is "easy" or that it was simple for me to make this transition. It was very difficult for all of us. Being solution focused sounds so simple, yet it is so difficult to master. It is extremely easy to fall back on what you know, or on what you felt comfortable doing before. As a therapist using this approach, you must always keep these three elements in mind:

1. Never assume anything.
2. Ask yourself whose agenda it is.
3. Never rush to judgment.

It is even better if you have a team and a supervisor who constantly question your purposefulness. One of the biggest lessons that we learned as a team is that once we began to learn the solution-focused approach, we had a long way to go to master it.

What convinced me the most about solution-focused therapy is that the client is the expert. I never want to pretend to be the expert, for it is a difficult place to be. Our team has a very strong work ethic and is dedicated to meeting our clients' needs. So much of our time is spent on understanding our miracles and our clients' miracles. It has been extremely difficult at times to go against what my past training has taught me. I have spent hours soul-searching, and I know that this approach it not something you can read about and understand. It is something you have to practice and experience. I can now see the bigger picture and how utilizing this approach benefits others. It is truly magical and the "skeptic" in me has vanished. Miracles still do exist, even in the substance abuse counseling field.

Evidence of the Power of Solution-Focused Therapy

I (Calyn) know the power of what this approach can do and how people respond, for I see the way clients respond. I have seen the amazed looks I get when clients have just discovered what is most important to them and, when I take the time to make sure I really heard what they truly meant, they say "Yeah!" with a sigh of relief. I know it is genuine because an adolescent will be the first to tell you when you are wrong.

I have evidence that people feel respected and honored when they sit upright in their chairs with a proud look on their faces, when clients are so engaged in a group that they are waiting on the edge of the seat to hear the next question. This lets me know the clients are invested and ready to speak because they feel listened to and heard. I have had clients tell me they have left here feeling listened to and understood. They have told me they leave group pondering the questions they have been asked.

On one occasion I asked a client what he expected to get out of life. He thought hard about the question and then just went on and on about what he wanted to do with his life. When he finished, he took a deep breath, sighed, and said, "Wow, I have never said that before." Another time an angry adolescent came to my office ready to "give it" to me. Somehow, he was able to refocus on what was important to him, see past the problem to a time when the problem no longer existed, and tell me play by play how he was able to make the change occur. You know it means something to your adolescent client when just before he leaves your office he turns to you, looks you in the eye, and offers a handshake.

Preventing Burnout

I (Charlene) am certain that, even if you are not in the counseling field, you know how draining it can be to listen to someone's problem. The more complicated the problem, the more it can zap your energy. Along with listening to and trying to understand the problem, the listener is most often thinking very hard about what the person who has the problem should do about it and will probably offer some advice. How many times at the end of all of this listening and problem solving do you find that the people did what they wanted to do anyway? When they discarded the well-intentioned advice, do you recall a sense of disappointment? After awhile, perhaps after several attempts to guide this person toward what you believed to be the right solution, what was the opinion or the judgment you formed about this person?

Using the solution-focused approach, I do not ever have to put myself in this frustrating position again, unless I choose to do so. I know that guiding clients toward becoming invested in how their lives will be once the problem is solved is a much more productive route for clients to pursue in therapy and, as a fringe benefit, a much less draining route for me. The rewards of witnessing clients leaving our agency feeling empowered and invested in continuing to resolve their issues in their own way is amazing. Not only is the client energized by this work, but so am I.

Another beauty of this approach is that the clients walk away believing they have done it all themselves, and I believe they have too. I have not taught the clients "how" to fish, but rather I have shown them that they already know how.

The Professional and Personal Impact of SFT

You may be asking yourself right now, "Is it really worth such a challenging and personal struggle?" My (Diane) answer to you is yes. I have seen that this approach is so incredibly worth the difficulties and frustration not only for my own professional career but also for the clients I serve. I know that I am a better person and therapist for this experience and I absolutely love my job. I can also see the clients walk away from the experience with a different view about therapy and about themselves. I cannot count the number of times I have seen the clients shift during their evaluations when they realize that I am not there to judge them.

I have seen clients physically let their guards down (by relaxing their posture) when they "get" that I am there to help them by giving them the opportunity to provide the evidence they need for their referral sources. It is also a joy to see clients bloom in the groups. I completed an evaluation on a gentleman who was not too forthcoming with information. He appeared somewhat distrustful of the system and me in general. I was not sure how he would respond to groups; however, I saw a man come alive. He shared more and more in every group and at the end verbally expressed to the counselors how helpful the experience was to him. I truly believe that he was as surprised as I was of how much he benefited from the entire process.

I have discovered that this approach has been filtered into my daily life at work and in my personal life. I believe that I have been blessed with a new view of life and of the profession of counseling. I must conclude that having the opportunity to work at this agency has truly made all the difference in my life and has been the challenge that I had no idea I would enjoy so much. You might ask me, "Who else has noticed this difference?" My response is, "My husband, friends, and family."

Summary

When I (TP) meet with professionals who are interested in learning about solution-focused therapy, I often warn them that learning this approach will "get under your skin." I tell them that they will never be able to think in the same way again, for this approach has a tremendously powerful impact on both the therapist and the client. They often smile, thinking that I must be joking. However, once they begin the journey they begin to understand; they have found a path that leads to miracles.

Notes

Chapter 3

1. The "yes set" is described in full in de Shazer (1982), Dolan (1985), Erickson and Rossi (1979), and Erickson, Rossi, and Rossi (1976).

Chapter 7

1. A few of the instruments that we have found useful include the Substance Abuse Subtle Screening Inventory (Miller, 1985), the Adolescent Self Assessment Profile (Wanberg, 1992), the Adult Substance Use Survey (Wanberg, 1997), and the Beck Depression Inventory (Beck, Steer, and Brown, 1996).

2. This returning the locus of control and responsibility to the client is similar to that of the Bruges model (de Shazer and Isebaert, in press), a solution-focused alcohol treatment program developed at St. John's Hospital in Bruges, Belgium, where court-mandated clients and others are allowed to choose whether to participate in a program for abstinence, controlled drinking, or no treatment. They are provided with educational information about alcoholism and advised that abstinence is the recommended treatment for patients who fail in the controlled drinking program. A recent four-year follow-up study of seventy-one patients revealed a continued success rate of 50 percent for clients who chose the abstinence program and 23 percent for those who chose the controlled drinking program.

Appendix

1. Research has uncovered that this quote was most likely coined at the Brief Family Therapy Center in Milwaukee. However, the specific author is unknown, even to those at the center.

Bibliography

Alcoholics anonymous (Third edition) (1976). New York: Alcoholics Anonymous World Services.

The American heritage college dictionary (Third edition) (1993). New York: Houghton Mifflin.

Anderson, H., and Swim, S. (1995). Supervision as collaborative conversation: Connecting the voices of supervisor and supervisee. *Journal of Systemic Therapies, 14*(2), 1-13.

Atkinson, D. R., Morten, G., and Sue, D. W. (1998). *Counseling American minorities* (Fifth edition). Boston: McGraw-Hill.

Barlow, D. H., and Cerny, J. A. (1988). *Psychological treatment of panic.* New York: Guilford.

Barlow, D. H., and Durand, V. M. (1999). *Abnormal psychology: An integrative approach* (Second edition). Pacific Grove, CA: Brooks/Cole.

Bass, E., and Davis, L. (1988). *The courage to heal: A guide for women survivors of child sexual abuse.* New York: Harper and Row.

Beck, A. T., Steer, R. A., and Brown, G. K. (1996). *BDI-II Manual.* San Antonio, TX: Psychological Corp., Harcourt Brace.

Berg, I. K. (1994). *Family based services: A solution-focused approach.* New York: Norton.

Berg, I. K. (1995). Solution-focused brief therapy with substance abusers. In A. Washton (Ed.), *Psychotherapy and substance abuse: A practitioner's handbook* (pp. 223-242). New York: Guilford.

Berg, I. K., and Dolan, Y. M. (2001). *Tales of solutions: A collection of hope-inspiring stories.* New York: Norton.

Berg, I. K., and Gallagher, D. (1991). Solution-focused brief treatment with adolescent substance abusers. In T. C. Todd and M. D. Selekman (Eds.), *Family therapy approaches with adolescent substance abusers* (pp. 93-111). Needham Heights, MA: Allyn and Bacon.

Berg, I. K., and Miller, S. D. (1992). *Working with the problem drinker: A solution-focused approach.* New York: Norton.

Berg, I. K., and Reuss, N. H. (1998). *Solutions step by step: A substance abuse treatment manual.* New York: Norton.

Beyebach, M., Morejon, A. R., Palen, D. L., and Rodriguez-Arias, J. L. (1996). Research on the process of solution-focused brief therapy. In S. D. Miller, M. A. Hubble, and B. L. Duncan (Eds.), *Handbook of solution-focused brief therapy* (pp. 299-334). San Francisco, CA: Jossey-Bass.

Bloom, M., and Fischer, J. (1982). *Evaluating practice: Guidelines for the accountable professional.* Englewood Cliffs, NJ: Prentice-Hall.

Bobele, M., Gardner, G., and Biever, J. (1995). Supervision as social construction. *Journal of Systemic Therapies, 14*(2), 14-25.

Bradshaw, J. (1988). *Bradshaw on: The family.* Deerfield Beach, FL: Health Communications.

Brown, L. N. (1991). *Groups for growth and change.* White Plains, NY: Longman.

Budman, S. H., and Gurman, A. S. (1988). *Theory and practice of brief therapy.* New York: Guilford.

Burns, D. D. (1999). *The feeling good handbook* (Revised edition). New York: Plume.

Cade, B., and O'Hanlon, W. (1993). *A brief guide to brief therapy.* New York: Norton.

Cantwell, P., and Holmes, S. (1994). Social construction: A paradigm shift for systemic therapy and training. *Australia and New Zealand Journal of Family Therapy, 15*(1), 17-26.

Colorado Department of Human Services (1999). *Alcohol and other drug abuse/dependence treatment standards.* July. Available from Colorado Department of Human Services, 4055 S. Lowell Drive, Denver, CO 80236.

Compton, B. R., and Galaway, B. (1989). *Social work processes* (Fourth edition). Belmont, CA: Wadsworth.

Corey, M. S., and Corey, G. (1987). *Groups: Process and practice* (Third edition). Pacific Grove, CA: Brooks/Cole.

Coulton, C. J., and Solomon, P. L. (1977). Measuring outcomes of intervention. *Social Work Research and Abstracts, 13*(4), 3-9.

Davies, D. L. (1962). Normal drinking in recovered alcohol addicts. *Quarterly Journal of Studies of Alcohol, 23,* 94-104.

Davis, L. E., and Proctor, E. K. (1989). *Race, gender, and class: Guidelines for practice with individuals, families, and groups.* Englewood Cliffs, NJ: Prentice-Hall.

de Shazer, S. (1982). *Patterns of brief family therapy.* New York: Guilford.

de Shazer, S. (1985). *Keys to solution in brief therapy.* New York: Norton.

de Shazer, S. (1988). *Clues: Investigating solutions in brief therapy.* New York: Norton.

de Shazer, S. (1991). *Putting difference to work.* New York: Norton.

de Shazer, S. (1994). *Words were originally magic.* New York: Norton.

de Shazer, S. and Isebaert, L. (in press). A solution-focused approach to the treatment of problematic drinking. *Journal of Family Psychotherapy.*

DeJong, P., and Berg, I. K. (1998). *Interviewing for solutions.* Pacific Grove, CA: Brooks/Cole.

Department of Health and Human Services (DHHS) Substance Abuse and Mental Health Services Administration (1999). *Brief interventions and brief therapies for substance abuse: Treatment Improvement Protocol (TIP) Series 34.* (DHHS

Publication No. SMA 99-3353). Rockville, MD: Center for Substance Abuse Treatment.

Dolan, Y. M. (1985). *A path with a heart: Ericksonian utilization with resistant and chronic clients.* New York: Brunner/Mazel.

Dolan, Y. M. (1991). *Resolving sexual abuse: Solution-focused therapy and Ericksonian hypnosis for adult survivors.* New York: Norton.

Dolan, Y. (1998). *One small step: Moving beyond trauma and therapy to a life of joy.* Watsonville, CA: Papier-Mache.

Donley, R. J., Horan, J. J., and DeShong, R. L. (1989). The effect of several self-disclosure permutations on counseling process and outcome. *Journal of Counseling and Development, 67*(7), 408-412.

Dryfoos, J. G. (1990). *Adolescents at risk: Prevalence and prevention.* New York: Oxford University.

Duncan, B. L., Hubble, M. A., and Miller, S. D. (1997). Stepping off the throne. *The Family Therapy Networker, 21*(4), 22-33.

Eakes, G., Walsh, S., Markowski, M., Cain, H., and Swanson, M. (1997). Family-centered brief solution-focused therapy with chronic schizophrenia: A pilot study. *Journal of Family Therapy, 19,*145-158.

Ebbesen, E., Duncan, B., and Konecni, V. (1975). The effects of content of verbal aggression on future verbal aggression: A field experiment. *Journal of Experimental Psychology, 11,* 192-204.

Edelwich, J., and Brodsky, A. (1992). *Group counseling for the resistant client.* New York: Lexington.

Erickson, M. H., and Rossi, E. (1979). *Hypnotherapy: An exploratory casebook.* New York: Irvington.

Erickson, M. H., Rossi, E., and Rossi, S. (1976). *Hypnotic realities.* New York: Irvington.

Feshbach, S. (1956). The catharsis hypothesis and some consequences of interaction with aggression and neutral play objects. *Journal of Personality, 24,* 449-462.

Forrest, G. G. (1984). *Intensive psychotherapy of alcoholism.* Northvale, NJ: Jason Aronson.

Forrest, G. G. (1997). *How to cope with a teenage drinker: Changing adolescent alcohol abuse.* Northvale, NJ: Jason Aronson.

Forward, S. (1989). *Toxic parents: Overcoming their hurtful legacy and reclaiming your life.* New York: Bantam.

Friedman, S. (1997). *Time-effective psychotherapy: Maximizing outcomes in an era of minimized resources.* Needham Heights, MA: Allyn and Bacon.

Gladding, S. T. (1996). *Counseling: A comprehensive profession* (Third edition). Englewood Cliffs, NJ: Prentice-Hall.

Gorski, T. T. and Miller, M. (1982). *Counseling for relapse prevention.* Independence, MO: Herald House/Independence.

Greene, R. R., and Ephross, P. H. (1991). *Human behavior theory and social work practice.* New York: Aldine de Gruyter.

Howard, R. (Executive Producer), and Caron, G. G. (Director) (1988). *Clean and sober* [film]. Warner Bros. Pictures.

Johnson, C. E., and Webster, D. (2002). *Recrafting a life.* New York: Taylor and Francis.

Kaplan, H. I., and Sadock, B. J. (1996). *Pocket handbook of clinical psychiatry* (Second edition). Baltimore, MD: Williams and Wilkins.

Kaye, B., and Jordan-Evans, S. (1999). *Love 'em or lose 'em: Getting good people to stay.* San Francisco, CA: Berrett-Koehler.

Kottler, J. A., and Brown, R. W. (1996). *Introduction to therapeutic counseling* (Third edition). Pacific Grove, CA: Brooks/Cole.

Kreisman, J. J., and Straus, H. (1989). *I hate you—don't leave me.* New York: Avon.

Kubler-Ross, E. (1983). *On children and death.* New York: Collier Books.

Kunzman, K. A. (1990). *The healing way: Adult recovery from childhood sexual abuse.* Minneapolis, MN: Hazelden.

Laban, R. J. (1998). Treatment planning: Room for improvement. *The Counselor, 16*(2), 32-33.

Lindforss, L., and Magnusson, D. (1997). Solution-focused therapy in prison. *Contemporary Family Therapy, 19,* 89-104.

Living sober (1975). New York: Alcoholics Anonymous World Services.

Marlatt, G. A. and Gordon, J. R. (Eds.) (1980). *Relapse prevention: Maintenance strategies in the treatment of addictive behaviors.* New York: Guilford.

Marlatt, G. A. and Gordon, J. R. (Eds.) (1985). *Relapse prevention.* New York: Guilford.

McCollum, E. and Trepper, T. S. (2001). *Family solutions for substance abuse.* Binghamton, NY: The Haworth Press, Inc.

McGregor, D. (1960). *The human side of enterprise.* New York: McGraw-Hill.

McKay, M., Rogers, P. D., and McKay, J. (1989). *When anger hurts: Quieting the storm within.* Oakland, CA: New Harbinger.

Metcalf, L. (1997). *Parenting toward solutions.* Paramus, NJ: Prentice-Hall.

Metcalf, L. (1998). *Solution-focused group therapy.* New York: Free Press.

Miller, G. A. (1985). *The substance abuse subtle screening inventory manual.* Spencer, IN: Spencer Evening World.

Miller, G. (1997). *Becoming miracle workers: Language and meaning in brief therapy.* New York: Aldine de Gruyter.

Miller, G., and de Shazer, S. (1998). Have you heard the latest rumor about . . . ? Solution-focused therapy as a rumor. *Family Process, 37*(3), 363-377.

Miller, S. D., and Berg, I. K. (1995). *The miracle method: A radically new approach to problem drinking.* New York: Norton.

Miller, S. D., Duncan, B. L., and Hubble, M. A. (1997). *Escape from Babel: Toward a unifying language for psychotherapy practice.* New York: Norton.

Miller, W. R., and Rollnick, S. (1991). *Motivational interviewing.* New York: Guilford.

Nelson, B. (1994). *1001 ways to reward employees.* New York: Workman.

Nichols, M. P., and Schwartz, R. C. (1991). *Family therapy: Concepts and methods* (Second edition). Needham Heights, MA: Allyn and Bacon.

O'Hanlon, B., and Weiner-Davis, M. (1989). *In search of solutions.* New York: Norton.

O'Hanlon, B., and Wilk, J. (1987). *Shifting contexts: The generation of effective psychotherapy.* New York: Guilford.

Peca-Baker, T. M., and Friedlander, M. L. (1989). Why are self-disclosing counselors attractive? *Journal of Counseling and Development, 67*(5), 279-282.

Peele, S. (1989). *The diseasing of America: Addiction treatment out of control.* Lexington, MA: Lexington Books.

Pichot, T. (2001). Co-creating solutions for substance abuse. *Journal of Systemic Therapies 20*(2), 1-23.

Pichot, T. (2001). What's the big deal about solution-focused therapy, anyway? *Professional Counselor, 2*(3), 39-41.

Pichot, T. (in press). Discovering the true expert of the therapeutic process. *Professional Counselor.*

Prochaska, J. O., and DiClemente, C. C. (1984). *The transtheoretical approach: Crossing traditional boundaries of therapy.* Malabar, FL: Krieger.

Prochaska, J. O., and Norcross, J. C. (1999). *Systems of psychotherapy: A transtheoretical analysis* (Fourth edition). Pacific Grove, CA: Brooks/Cole.

Prochaska, J. O., Norcross, J. C., and DiClemente, C. C. (1994). *Changing for good.* New York: Morrow.

Rando, T. A. (1984). *Grief, dying, and death.* Champaign, IL: Research.

Rogers, C. R. (1951). *Client-centered therapy.* Boston: Houghton Mifflin.

Rogers, C. R. (1957). The necessary and sufficient conditions of therapeutic personality change. *Journal of Consulting Psychology, 21,* 95-103.

Rosenberg, H. (1993). Prediction of controlled drinking by alcoholics and problem drinkers. *Psychological Bulletin, 113,* 129-139.

Rosenthal, L. (1987). *Resolving resistance in group psychotherapy.* Northvale, NJ: Jason Aronson.

Rossman, M. L. (1987). *Healing Yourself: A step-by-step program for better health through imagery.* New York: Walker.

Roth, A., and Fonagy, P. (1996). *What works for whom? A critical review of psychotherapy research.* New York: Guilford.

Selekman, M. D. (1997). *Solution-focused therapy with children.* New York: Guilford.

Shulman, L. (1992). *The skills of helping: Individuals, families, and groups* (Third edition). Itasca, IL: F. E. Peacock.

Smith, M. J. (1990). *Program evaluation in the human services.* New York: Springer.

Sournia, J. C. (1990). *A history of alcoholism* (N. Hindley and G. Stanton, Trans.). Cambridge, MA: Basil Blackwell.

Straus, M. (1974). Leveling, civility, and violence in the family. *Journal of Marriage and the Family, 36,* 13-29.

Tavris, C. (1982). *Anger—the misunderstood emotion.* New York: Simon and Schuster.

Topping, J. (Producer), and Thomas, B. (Director) (2000). *28 days* [film]. Columbia Pictures.

Wanberg, K. W. (1992). *A guidebook to the use of the adolescent self-assessment profile—ASAP.* Available from the Center for Addiction Research and Evaluation, 5460 Ward Road, Suite 140, Arvada, CO 80002.

Wanberg, K. W. (1997). *A user's guide to the adult substance use survey—ASUS.* Available from the Center for Addiction Research and Evaluation, 5460 Ward Road, Suite 140, Arvada, CO 80002.

Wegscheider, S. (1981). *Another chance: Hope and health for the alcoholic family.* Palo Alto, CA: Science and Behavior Books.

Weinbach, R. W. (1990). *The social worker as manager.* New York: Longman.

Werner-Wilson, R. J. J. (2000). *Developmental systemic family therapy with adolescents.* Binghamton, NY: The Haworth Press, Inc.

Wolpe, J. (1969). *The practice of behavior therapy.* New York: Pergamon.

Wolpe, J. (1973). *The practice of behavior therapy* (Second edition). New York: Pergamon.

Index

Page numbers followed by the letter "b" indicate boxed text; those followed by the letter "f" indicate figures.